GERMANY'S ARMY AND NAVY

Emperor William II. and his Staff.

GERMANY'S ARMY AND NAVY

by Pen and Picture

COMPILED FROM THE LATEST AND BEST AUTHORITIES
BY
GUSTAV A. SIGEL

WITH IMPORTANT ORIGINAL CONTRIBUTIONS ON THE GERMAN ARMY
BY
MAJOR-GENERAL VON SPECHT

Artistically Illustrated

MILITARY PRESS
NEW YORK

German Military Forces of the 19th Century was originally
published under the title *Germany's Army & Navy*
in 1900 by The Werner Company, Chicago.

This edition published by
The Military Press
Distributed by Crown Publishers, Inc.
225 Park Avenue South
New York, New York 10003

Copyright © Bracken Books 1989.

Printed and bound in Italy

Sigel, Gustav A.
    German military forces of the 19th century / Gustav A. Sigel.
        p. cm.
    Includes index.
    ISBN 0-517-68914-6
    1. Germany — Armed Forces — History — 19th century.   2. Germany —
    History, Military — 19th century.   I. Title.
    UA710.S513   1989
    355'.00943'09034—DD20   89-3422
                                                                            CIP

ISBN 0 517 68914 6

h g f e d c b a

INTRODUCTION

The purpose of this book when first published in 1900 was to provide a detailed description of Germany's army and navy at that time. This introduction aims to place that account into a broader historical context.

The German army of 1900 was based upon the modernised Prussian army. There were two key phases in that modernisation. Following the traumatic defeat by France in 1806–7, the army was purged; an integrated command structure set up under a Ministry of War; and a General Staff established. New tactics and promotion by merit was introduced; discipline humanised; mercenary service ended. In 1813–14 conscription was introduced. The success of these reforms contributed to Napoleon's defeat.

A heavily indebted Prussia neglected her army after 1815. More and more men were not conscripted and the nobility reclaimed its domination of the officer corps. By 1848 the army proved ineffective in dealing with civil unrest and Denmark. By the time of the Crimean War and the Franco-Austrian war of 1859, it was clear that a major overhaul was required. The job of extending conscription and the length of regular army service, and improving training and equipment was taken in hand by Wilhelm I. This sparked off a constitutional crisis in Prussia, as a result of which Bismarck was appointed Minister-President in September 1862. Bismarck rode out the crisis and implemented the army reforms. The rewards were soon apparent in the victories over Denmark, Austria and France. The rapid and decisive victories gained in the latter two wars impressed and surprised contemporaries.

Victory meant that the Prussian model was extended to the whole of Germany. The prestige of the army was raised, especially that of the General Staff, now the directing force. The military budget was placed virtually beyond parliamentrary control. Officers had direct access to the Emperor. His own military cabinet controlled key appointements.

So long as Bismarck was Chancellor, political control was retained. His reliance on diplomacy after 1871 meant that the army did not continue to grow. However, with Bismarck's departure in 1890 things changed. Russia entered into an alliance with France. In response, the German army was expanded, increasing from 521,000 men in 1891 to 610,00 in 1900. The Schlieffen plan (named after a Chief of General Staff) was drawn up for the eventuality of a two front war. The civil government was not consulted and the political implications of the plan not considered.

From the mid-1980s until 1913 the army once more was neglected. There was conservative anxiety that expansion might dilute the noble monopoly over officer positions and bring increasing numbers of politically unreliable working men into the ranks. Also a new emphasis was placed upon naval expansion.

Until the mid-1980s the German navy, with a strength of about 17,000 men, had limited functions of coastal defence and protection of merchant shipping. In 1897 Alfred von Tirpitz was appointed Secretary of State for the Navy. In 1898 the first Navy Bill was introduced, to be followed by further bills up to 1914. Von Tirpitz aimed to take advantage of new techniques of steel shipbuilding and gun manufacture to create a force which could pressure Great Britain into making colonial concessions. However, the British responded with their own navy building programme.

By 1900 popular enthusiasm for a powerful navy had been whipped up in Germany. It was difficult for the government to retreat from that policy even as it poisoned relations with Britain and took her into a race she could not win. Meanwhile, by 1910 Germany had to concern herself with the build up of French and Russian armies. Tension mounted in the Balkans where Germany had to support her major ally, Austria. By 1913 the German government was in deep financial and political trouble as it had to expand the army considerably while continuing with high naval expenditure.

Around 1900 the Germany army and navy set the standards for all the major powers. The First World War, in retrospect, places a question mark against those achievements. The navy was barely used during the war. The Schlieffen plan involved a lightning offensive on the western front. It had military flaws, due to lack of resources and deficiencies in execution, and as techniques of defence turned out to be superior to those of attack. The plan also reduced room for political manoeuvre in 1914.

This book concentrates upon the impressive character of the German army and navy in 1900. Measured purely by military criteria and on the basis of what was known at the time, this is understandable. However, with the benefits of hindsight, one can see that the conservative character of the leadership of the armed forces, its political unaccountability, and the diplomatic and political repurcussions of military initiatives were also the source of many problems.

Dr J.J. Breuilly
Dept of History
Manchester University

PREFACE

To praise the German imperial army—bound by the Constitution of the German Empire (1871) to obey unconditionally the orders of the Kaiser—would be a work of supererogation. Its present organization, authorized by military laws enacted between the years 1871 and 1899, is so perfect that it is looked upon as an example of great practical efficiency, and is even taken as a model to be imitated by other nations. The proof of its high efficiency does not lie solely in its great achievements in the field—magnificent as the world admits these to have been—but in the splendid spirit by which it is animated and in the rigid discipline which directs and controls it, in addition to the improving and perfecting processes to which it is constantly and intelligently subjected. The present peace strength, of all ranks, approximates 590,000 men; while it is estimated that on a war-footing the effective strength would not fall short of 3,000,000 trained men. Such an array of fighting men, with its simple but well-planned methods of recruiting, mobilization, and efficiency on taking the field, may well be Germany's pride, as well as the dread model for other nations. To rival it, as far as numbers go, is possible only to one other Continental Power—that of Russia. But in practical efficiency in taking the field, as a body of expert and disciplined soldiery, splendidly organized and scientifically equipped for purposes of offence and defence, and commanded by the most experienced and highly-trained military leaders, the imperial army of Germany may be said emphatically to be unapproached and without a parallel.

While thus formidable in numbers and magnificent in well as the intelligence of its individual members. This, in large measure, is the result of the compulsory preliminary training for the service which every able-bodied man must undergo; and its effect is seen in civil life in the bodily and mental robustness of the Teuton stock and the plodding energy which, whatever be their sphere, carries them successfully through life. The spirit infused into the army also fosters the civic virtues and develops the sentiments of patriotism, race affinity, and kinship, and impresses the nation with a feeling of security engendered by the sense of power. The army is equipment, it is also notable for the physical stamina as thus a splendid training school of the people, for it embraces in its ranks all classes and callings, whose devotion to the Fatherland is undying, even when voluntarily exiled in lands far beyond the sea,

A like nationalizing influence is of late noticeable in the German navy, now making giant strides toward a formidable and imposing strength, and bidding fair to rival the army in efficiency, if not in achievement, to raise the nation to coördinate rank among the Great Powers, and to shed increasing lustre on the German name.

To treat interestingly of both branches of Germany's war service, to outline their methods of organization as well as the history of their respective achievements, is the purpose of the following pages. In undertaking the task the writers have had the assistance of the well-known military author, Major-General von Specht, who not only vouches for the correctness of the information herein, but has personally made certain valuable contributions to the work.

THE PUBLISHERS.

CONTENTS

THE GERMAN ARMY

THE GERMAN NAVY

THE GERMAN ARMY

HISTORICAL SKETCH OF THE ARMY

THE military system of the ancient Germans was based on the then universal military service, nation and army being one, and the claim or duty of military service depending on the possession of landed property. The German youth, when from fourteen to fifteen years of age, was deemed fit to bear arms. He exercised early with bow and arrow, took part in the favorite game of the German lads of the period, to run at or throw themselves against sharp spears held by older men standing in rows, and trained body and eyes in such a manner that the quickness of the onset completely overcame the danger. The happiest day the youth experienced was, when the right to bear arms was granted to him by the National Assembly. He was then solemnly invested by one of the princes or by his father with sword, shield, and spear. This function was deemed the clothing of manhood; henceforth the youth was entitled to go forth to battle, to take part in the doings of the popular assemblies, and take his share in the discussion of all public matters.

All warlike undertakings, especially offensive or aggressive war, had to be sanctioned by the popular assembly. Every one was, however, bound to serve in defensive warfare when the country was invaded by an enemy, and this without summons. Special messengers called the people together for the "Heerbann" (an official summons for general military duty). General military service was, therefore, exacted in the broadest sense of the word.

In pre-feudal times the Germans served as footmen and horsemen and stood together in battle according to their tribes, clans and families. The oldest weapon of offence was the "Frame" or "Framea," a spear with a long shaft and a narrow and short blade. This was so keen and well adapted for hurling and thrusting that it could be employed as necessity called for in both close or distant conflict. The "Ger," a heavy missile, differed apparently from the "Frame." Lances and swords made of iron or bronze, clubs and battle-axes, were used later on during the Migration of the Nations.

Some defensive weapons served as shields; they were formed of wood or of the platted twigs of the willow, painted in bright colors, and protecting the whole body. Later still the shields were mounted with metallic stripes; helmets were also used, together with armor and a coat of mail.

The army was divided into clans (Harste) each of a hundred men. Formed in wedge-shaped columns they went to battle singing the barditus (shield-song). Behind the line of battle was the wagon-train, which was defended by the women.

The strength of the ancient German army lay in the foot-soldiers, though they knew the use of cavalry. Besides the squadrons of cavalry, consisting of mounted men who sat on the naked back of the horses, were added foot-soldiers whose skill was so great, that holding only by the mane of the horse they equalled the swiftest in their onset.

"In their mode of warfare," writes General Peucker, "they followed two simple but sound tactical principles: the first was to take the initiative in the attack, the second to concentrate an overpowering force on the enemy's most vulnerable point. When advancing to the attack, an arrangement of their columns by 'hundreds,' townships, and families, gave them an organization which, skilfully used, was essentially favorable to hand-to-hand encounter which followed the first collision."

Cowardice in deserting the colors, and loss of the shield in battle, were considered a disgrace; to survive the duke or commander of the army, selected for the campaign and killed in the battle, was disgrace for a lifetime.

Such a commander was Ariovistus, the leader of the Suevi, whom Julius Cæsar overcame near Mülhausen in the year 58 B. C. by superior Roman strategy, but only after a terrible struggle in which he himself sustained great loss. Aided by German mercenaries, Cæsar subdued Gaul and furthermore vanquished by his admirable German cavalry his rival Pompey at Pharsalia in 48 B. C. Decisive for Germany's future, also, was the battle in the Teutoburg forest, fought by Hermann (Arminius), prince of the Cherusci, in 9 A. D. An army of 40,000 select Roman soldiers was annihilated, and Germany was saved from imminent danger of being Romanized. Almost equally fatal to the Romans was the battle of 16 A. D. fought by the same chieftain at almost the identical place against Germanicus and Cäcina.

Traitor to the national cause proved Marbod, leader of the Markmen or the Marcomanni. He had the first standing German army of 70,000 infantry and 4,000 cavalry, whom he trained in the Roman fashion. He was not only duke, that is simply commander for the time being of the campaign, but the king or head of the "Southeastern Confederation." Instead of making common cause with Hermann, commander of the Northwestern Confederation, against the Romans, Marbod concluded an infamous treaty with Tiberius, receiving what was then an enormous sum of money from the latter. This event took place in the year 6 A. D.

The West-Roman Empire was dismembered by the migration of the German nations in the course of the next few hundred years. Its provinces were inherited mostly by Germans and by the Frankish Empire of Charles the Great (Charlemagne), who also revived the Roman Empire in form and name. His dominion included all countries from the Schlei to the Garigliano, from the Ebro to the Leitha.

Charles the Great effected a complete revolution in the constitution of the army and an extension of the obligations of military service. Hitherto the bulk of the army had consisted of foot-soldiers. In the previous wars Charles, in his career of conquest, had found it necessary to hasten with his forces from one end of his empire to the other. The success of his attack depended upon the rapidity of his movements, and for such rapid pouncing upon the enemy, the roads were, in their then condition, too indifferent when the bulk of the army was composed of foot-soldiers. He, therefore, proceeded to increase his cavalry, and to such an extent that it speedily formed the main strength of the army. Hitherto the only personally freemen who had landed property were bound to serve in war, but simply as infantry. But now Charles made those freemen who had no landed property subject to the burden of military service, inasmuch as he laid on them a war-tax for the equipment of the smaller freeholders who were bound to military service. The tax amounted to a fifth of their yearly income. The contribution levied on those bound to military service was to be proportioned to the number of hides (hufen), equal to about thirty acres of land, which each man possessed. The owner of twenty hides paid more than the owner of ten or five. The owner of four hides was to serve personally on foot, light-armed. He was required to have a lance and shield, or a double-stringed bow, with twelve arrows. The owner of from five to eleven hides had to serve on horseback, heavily armed. He was required to have lance and shield, sword and dagger, as well as bow and arrows. The owner of twelve hides had to serve with armor-plate, and the owner of more than twelve hides had to take the field with helmet and coat of mail. To the landwehr (militia)—a name even then applied to those bound to serve in defence of the country against attacks of external foes — all who could bear arms belonged, bond as well as free.

This new military organization of Emperor Charles was completed by King Henry I. All his vassals had to perform their military service on horseback, and even the servitors and serfs of the latter had to appear mounted. This was instituted to prepare the indispensable means of freeing Germany forever from the recurring inroads of the Magyars. Nor did he neglect the infantry; he introduced improvements in its organization and gave it a new training. The old style of infantry tactics was to fight in large masses — to break by a phalanx the ranks of the enemy and then to fight hand to hand. The new mode in which Henry I. drilled the infantry was to fight in serried ranks, not in deep columns, but in extended lines. He also trained the foot-soldiers to rapid motions and quick evolutions.

This cavalry service is the beginning of the German knighthood; for a knight originally was nothing more than a horseman or trooper, who entered the military service on his own horse, armed with sword and protected by a habergeon, or short ringed coat of mail, and a shield.

Henry I. was the German king who not only established strongholds like Quedlinburg, Goslar, Meissen, Wittenberg, and Soest, but also fortified open cities with walls, towers, and moats, like Nordhausen, Gronau, and other towns. He furthermore organized military settlements on the eastern frontiers — called frontier-guards (Granitzer) —as in Memleben, Wurzen, Rochlitz, and especially in Merseburg. These military colonies were, in a certain sense, the beginning of a "Standing Army." Previous to this time the main safeguard of the country lay in the castles or burghs. The difference in the construction of the burgh depended on the character and formation of the country. In Middle and Southern Germany, rich in hills and mountains, hill-forts were the common means of defence; in the plains and lowlands of Northern Germany water-forts were the chief reliance. The burgh was either a simple one, consisting of a barbican (watchtower) surrounded with walls; or a larger one, consisting of walls, flanked by two turrets, the outer bailey with courtyard, behind these a moat with drawbridge, and the inner bailey. "Within all these was the keep, on which was placed an embattled parapet and which held the baronial hall (Pallas)."

The chief exercises of chivalry were fought either on horseback, with lance and sword, or on foot, with battle-axe, mace, spear or sword. Fought in columns they were called tournaments; in single conflict, jousts. The tilt was either a running with "points blunted" (rockets) or with "pointed lances."

The most elaborate festival attended by the German chivalry was celebrated by Emperor Frederick Barbarossa at Mayence in 1184, when 70,000 knights witnessed the accolade, or conferring of knighthood on the two oldest sons of the Emperor.

The characteristics of the military system, practiced by the Saxon and Franconian kings, were retained throughout the Middle Ages. The commander-in-chief, in time of war, was the king or emperor. The great suzerains of the crown led their knights, subject to them, and the latter were followed by their men-at-arms and vassals. The chief or standard flag of the army was the "Imperial Banner," with the one-headed black eagle on a yellow field, carried in battle by the Swabians. The defensive weapons were shield, helmet, body-armor, armlets, and greaves; the offensive weapons were the long double-handed swords, battle-axes, maces, and clubs;

Colonel (New Hohenzollern Overcoat). 25th Regiment of Infantry "von Lützow" (Rhenish No. 1).

while the city militia fought with cross-bows, pikes, and halberds. The horses were also armored. In sieges they used battering-towers, battering-rams, catapults, and other engines for throwing projectiles.

The uniforming of the soldiers dates from feudal times, and their origin may be traced back to the colored sashes worn by the different clans over their coats as a rallying sign. Even coats of the same color were in use among the separate clans; in all probability, the city mercenaries were the first to be uniformed.

The mercenary system in Germany appears to have originated in the twelfth century, the feudal system being inadequate and rendering the introduction of a force of regular soldiers a necessity.

By the invention of gunpowder and its application to projectile warfare in the fourteenth century, chivalry lost its prestige, having flourished from the period of the Crusades and the expeditions against Rome. At the close of the fourteenth century the German princes and the cities possessed bombards, carronades, culverins, and muskets. In the year 1388 we find in Germany Tarras muskets, hacquebuts, and arquebuses, and even pistols, hand-guns as they were then termed. The era of the Reformation completed the transformation of the feudal soldiery into that of a mercenary army and replaced the tactics of the Middle Ages by new and more effective measures. Battles were no more decided by foot-soldiers, moving like walls and composed of Hussites and Swiss, but by the premeditated co-operation of the three different branches of the military service — infantry, cavalry, and artillery. Both of the battles at Marignano in 1515 and Pavia in 1525, where for the first time modern trained foot-soldiers fought, illustrate fully the great changes which had taken place in military tactics. The mercenary levies of Germany were termed "Landsknechte." Emperor Maximilian, aided by Count Eitel, Frederick von Zollern, and especially by George von Frundsberg (the father of the "Landsknechte"), gave the levies a thorough organization. The chief of the Landsknechte bore the title of commanding general or commander-in-chief, and as such was responsible only to the sovereign or "pay-lord." The general staff consisted of the war paymaster, the purser-general, the quartermaster-general, the surgeon-general, the army-herald, the provost-marshal, and the functionary who levied the war-tax. The Landsknechte were divided into regiments, brought together by enlistment and commanded by a colonel, who received a monthly pay of 400 guilders. The regimental staff was formed of the lieutenant-colonel, the quartermaster, the regimental chaplain, surgeon, regimental-provost, the sergeant, and a special corporal, who had to tend to the camp-followers and the camp-prostitutes. Each regiment had from ten to sixteen companies (Fähnlein) of 400 men, commanded by a captain. Subordinated to the captain were the lieutenant, the standard-bearer, sergeant-major, chaplain, and corporal. In front of each squadron marched from twelve to fifteen musketeers, armed with a small double arquebus or musket. These

carried on a strap, thrown over the left shoulder, twelve wooden caps, each containing a charge of powder, also a pouch with bullets and a box with priming powder. The musketeers were followed by the arquebusiers. Their chief weapon, the arquebus, was formerly provided with a match-lock, but now carried a wheel-lock, invented at Nuremberg in 1517. The arquebusiers and musketeers wore a short two-edged sword, also a light body-armor, and a morion or head-piece. They were followed by the "pikemen," provided with cuirass, armlets, and greaves, plate-aprons and morions or casques, and armed with a short sword, two wheel-lock pistols, and heavy pike, or a two-handed broad-sword and halberd.

A regiment of cavalry in the sixteenth century mustered 750 men, with 1,000 horse. It was divided into guidons or ensigns; a guidon generally consisted of 180 heavy horsemen (cuirassiers or lancers) and sixty light horsemen or carbineers. The former, like the mediæval knights, rode on heavy stallions and carried a stout lance, together with a long sabre, two pistols and a mace; the latter rode on light horses and carried lighter arms, pistols and sabre, and as chief-weapon, a carbine. The commander of the combined cavalry was called the field-marshal. The Schmalcadic War developed a peculiar species of cavalry, known as the "German Riders." They wore open casques, a light cuirass or a jerkin of leather, with iron habergeon, and were armed with sabre and petronel. They used to ride in deep columns, face the enemy at the distance of a pistol-shot, fire in sections and retreat around the wings of the army proper in such a way that their front rank never ceased firing. The great mobility of those "German Riders" fitted them especially for independent expeditions and exploits, without the support of infantry. The martial spirit of the modern cavalry manifested itself first in those daring riders.

The artillery made great strides at this period. Germany is indebted to the Hussites for the first cast cannon or field-pieces, which had previously been made of wrought-iron staves. The chief places for the manufacture of powder and fire-arms were then Augsburg and Nuremberg. The artillery and the material for projectile warfare was under the direction of the master-general of the ordnance. His subordinates were a lieutenant, a paymaster, a master of the ordnance, and several gunners. The service of the single piece was under a master of the gun and artificers. The guns or carronades were either field-guns or siege-guns. The former were the falconet, falcon, and the culverin, which, served by eighteen men, threw a ball of forty pounds weight. The latter were called the great "quartan-culverin," the songstress, the nightingale, the basilisk, and the "sharfmetze," which threw an iron ball, weighing a hundred pounds. Besides those there were howitzers, which hurled stone balls of two hundred pounds weight.

The use of firearms at a siege necessitated a new mode of fortification, termed "bastion." This changed the former castles or burghs into real fortresses and made the cities also to conform to the new mode of fortification. The typical form of a German city in the Middle

Ages was as follows: The city's precincts were enclosed in a deep moat, defended by outlying towers. Behind the moat were the stone walls, turreted and battlemented. At more or less regular intervals, rampart and walls were strengthened by turrets; there were also at and between these round and square turrets, gates well guarded, battlemented and provided with portcullis and drawbridges, leading over the moat.

All these reforms were introduced during the fifteenth century, but were completed by the Emperor Charles V. at the Diet of Worms (1521). They became essential to the defence of the German Empire during a period of three hundred years, when little change took place in the manner of raising armies.

Since the Diet of Worms, only the immediate knights of the empire were personally bound to serve, in lieu of which they paid a certain sum of money to the Emperor. The provincial estates, however, were obliged to put into service fixed contingents in the case of a general war, which could be declared only by a unanimous decree of the electors, princes, and cities, with the approval of the Emperor. Since the Westphalian Treaty (1648), each provincial estate was entitled to declare and make war independently of the others. The troopers at this time received twelve, the foot-soldiers four, guilders monthly pay. In the year 1681 the entire imperial army was decreed to consist of 40,000 men, and was portioned off to the imperial circles. A standing imperial army never existed, though the larger provincial estates kept a body of regular troops from the period of the Westphalian Treaty, while the southwestern imperial circle had independent troops from the year 1700. The imperial army, after being summoned, was sworn in, received the articles of war, and was made subject to the command of the body of imperial generals. There existed a plan for the organization of the army, which, however, was never completely enacted. The contingents of the smaller provincial estates were quite worthless so far as military use was concerned, a regiment often representing soldiers of fifty different contingents. The officers never had a chance of advancement, having been selected by the sovereign of the territory supplying the contingent, so that, for instance, in a company of troops from an imperial circle, one city would appoint the captain, another the first-lieutenant, an abbess the second-lieutenant, and an abbé the ensign. Even in regard to uniform and arms the regiments differed, and discipline was comparatively unknown. The consequence was that the imperial army was Europe's laughing stock during the entire eighteenth century, in spite of the Prussians, the Hanoverians, the Saxons, and the Austrians exhibiting the well-known prowess of the Germans on the battlefield.

The technical and tactical improvements in military science and warfare made by the Swedish King, Gustavus Adolphus, the most brilliant military leader of the seventeenth century, were soon to be introduced into all European armies. These improvements were the equip-ping of the bulk of the infantry with fire-arms, increasing the usefulness of the cavalry by reducing the weight of the armor and arms, introducing the light or horse-artillery, replacing the heavy culverins by iron four-pounders, which were now loaded with cartridges instead of the old method of loading with loose powder. The new tactics also gave the infantry, protected by cavalry, opportunity for movements and quick evolutions, so that the artillery posted in the rear had more chance to be brought into action.

In Austria we find warriors like Prince Eugene, Ludwig von Baden, Daun, Lichtenstein, and Laudon occupied in introducing improvements in military tactics. In Prussia the Great Elector William was especially instrumental in giving the country high rank as a military power. At his death, in 1688, the Prussian army numbered 26,850 men, with 140 field-pieces. Frederick William I., his successor, steadily enlarged, improved, and disciplined this army. Old Dessauer, the inventor of the metallic ramrod, was its great instructor in tactics and discipline. In his time the army numbered 82,000 men, 26,000 of which were enlisted non-Prussians. Every youth who was of the standard height was obliged to wear "the king's coat"; exempted only were the sons of noblemen and of citizens who were worth from six to ten thousand dollars. The way the King's troops then went through the manual of arms was something wonderful; the handling of the guns, the uniformity of the drill, the firing in files, in battalions, and by regiments, went off like clock-work. At this period the military institutions introduced by Louvois, Louis XIV.'s secretary of war, and the royal marshals came into vogue. The entire infantry were supplied with fire-arms and bayonets; to the cavalry were added uhlans and hussars.

Prior to 1772 enlistment was the principal means of recruiting the military force; from then on conscription supplied the chief material for the standing armies. The splendidly organized force of Frederick William I. was raised to 200,000 men by his successor, Frederick the Great. The latter's military genius inspired this vast machine with proper spirit. Aided by able generals like Prince Henry, Winterfeld, Ferdinand of Brunswick, Seydlitz, Schwerin, Zieten, and others, he succeeded in his battles with almost all Europe by the rapidity of his movements, his iron discipline, and the use of the "oblique order" of battle. He was instrumental in redeeming the German name in Europe and in placing Prussia high in the ranks of European Powers.

The work of Frederick the Great was in part effaced by the great French conqueror, Napoleon, who not only humbled Prussia but the entire German nation by the establishment of the "Rhenish Confederation," in 1806. His power, however, was broken shortly afterwards, especially through the heroic efforts and great sacrifices of Prussia, the military service of which was reorganized by men like Scharnhorst, Stein, and Gneisenau. Jena and Auerstädt were swiftly followed by Leipsic and Waterloo.

In the year 1806 Scharnhorst reduced the number and the extent of exemptions from military service, and abolished the enlistment of foreigners. The compulsory personal service was introduced in Prussia, September 3d, 1814, a memorable expedient of King William III. The military service lasted nineteen years; namely, five in the active army, three in the ranks, two in the reserve, and fourteen in the landwehr.

The Congress of Vienna, in 1816, reunited the German states with the German Confederation or Bund. After preparations lasting for a few years, the organization of the Federal army was effected. A military commission, presided over by an Austrian representative, was subordinated to the Federal diet which controlled the military matters of the Bund.

The Federal army was formed by the contingents of the Federal states and by the reserve. It was divided into ten army-corps, of which Austria and Prussia furnished each three and Bavaria one. The contingents of Würtemberg, Baden and Hesse and of the Rhine, Hohenzollern, Lichtenstein, Hesse-Homburg and Frankfort formed the eighth; those of Saxony, Hesse-Cassel, Nassau, Luxemburg, Saxony-Weimar, the three Saxon duchies of Reuss, Anhalt, and Schwarzburg, the ninth; and the contingents of Hanover, Holstein, and Lauenburg, Brunswick, Mecklenburg, Oldenburg, Lübeck, Bremen, Hamburg, Waldeck, Schaumburg-Lippe, and Lippe formed the tenth. By a Federal decree the main contingent and the reserves were amalgamated and the reserve contingent doubled by one and five-sixth per cent. of the population. From now on to the dissolution of the Bund the strength of the Federal army was 553,028 men, of which 452,474 belonged to the main contingent and 100,554 to the reserve, together with 1,134 field-pieces. The various branches of the service were represented as follows: Sharpshooters, 28,438; infantry, 398,197; cavalry, 69,218; field-artillery, 50,254; pioneers, 6,921.

The German Federal army was called into service twice; namely, during the German-Danish wars of 1848 and 1864. The efforts of Denmark to "danize" the population of Schleswig-Holstein in regard to language, customs, and government, resulted in an open revolt of the people. The Danes overcame the Schleswig-Holsteiners at Bau. The Prussian General, Wrangel, commander-in-chief of the German Federal troops in Holstein, defeated the Danes at Schleswig and conquered all Jütland. The war ended with the armistice of Malmö. The latter having been terminated by Denmark in March, 1849, a Federal army of 35,000 men was then put in the field by the German diet, commanded by the Prussian General, von Prittwitz. It consisted of a Prussian division, a Saxon, and a Hanoverian brigade, and three other mixed Federal contingents, including 15,000 troops of Schleswig-Holstein. Notwithstanding that the Danes were beaten at Eckernförde (where the battleship *Christian VIII* was sunk and the frigate *Gefion* was captured), and also suffered defeat at Düppel, Kolding, and Gudsoe, nothing more was accomplished owing to the shrewd moves of diplomacy. The Danes, furthermore, outnumbering the Germans, inflicted considerable losses on the latter near Fredericia, and the war ended favorably for Denmark.

In spite of the strained relations between Austria and Prussia at a later period, little Denmark provoked the two mighty Federal powers in 1864 to make common cause against her. On February 2nd of the latter year the bombarding of the fortifications at Missunde took place; on February 6th the crossing of the Schlei and the evacuation of the Danewerks by the Danes was effected. The campaign proceeded speedily under command of the Prussian field-marshal, Wrangel, and the Austrian general, Gablenz. The fortifications at Düppel were stormed heroically by Prince Frederick Charles, and on the twenty-ninth of June the glorious capture of Alsen was effected. Schleswig and Jütland were taken by the allies, and King Christian was compelled to conclude an armistice on July 20th, followed by the treaty of Vienna on the thirtieth of October, by which Denmark ceded all her claims to Schleswig-Holstein and Lauenburg, which were given to Prussia and Austria.

The difficulties arising from the possession of the duchies were appeased by the convention at Gastein in 1865. Lauenburg was ceded to Prussia, and a money indemnity was paid to Austria, while Schleswig was to be governed by the former power, and Holstein by the latter. But the old conflict broke out again one year later. The convening of the Holstein House of Deputies by the Austrian governor caused the Prussians to occupy Holstein and to drive the Austrian troops out of the duchy. The Confederation assembled at Vienna, and, on the adoption of a motion, put by Austria (fourteenth of June), for mobilizing the Federal army against Prussia, the ambassador of that country declared the Bund dissolved because of its unconstitutional proceedings. The war began at once and resulted in Prussia and her allies quickly winning the glorious victories of Podol, Münchengrätz, Gitschin, Trautenau, Skalitz, Schweinschädel, Königinhof, and Königgrätz. Austria, Saxony, and the Southern States were defeated in a short time by the finely organized and splendidly led armies of Prussia and her allies. The peace of Prague, concluded August 23d, 1866, closed Austria's hegemony with her predominancy in Germany. Results of the most substantial kind, including annexations and the forming of a new confederation, were secured to Prussia by this treaty. By the treaties of Berlin the Southern States received an independent national existence, and the opportunity of forming a Southern Confederation and of making secret treaties, of offensive and defensive alliance, with the North German Confederation, which latter was about to be founded. The official dissolution of the German Bund with the dissolving of the Federal army took place at Augsburg on the twenty-fourth of August, 1866.

On the fifteenth of December, 1866, Prussia, after having annexed Hanover, Hesse-Cassel, Nassau, Frankfort-on-the-Main, and Schleswig-Holstein, convened at Berlin the deputies of all the States north of the Main and agreed with them as to the new constitution of the

Regiment of Grenadier-Guards "Emperor Alexander."

North German Confederation. This was sanctioned by the Diet April 16th, and legalized July 1st, 1867. Treaties were made with the South German States, securing more uniformity to the army and investing Prussia with absolute control of the military forces in case of war.

The constitution placed all the affairs of the army and navy under the legislative control of the Confederation. The Federal presidency (Prussia) had the exclusive right of delaring war and peace and of concluding alliances. The constitution also made provision for compulsory military service (no substitutes being allowed), and for the disbursement of the army expenditure, service in the ranks, in the reserve, in the landwehr, the landsturm, and for regulating the extent of the army on a peace-footing (one percentage of the population). The military budget was established on the basis of 225 thalers per soldier in time of peace, to be at the disposal of the Federal commander-in-chief. The organization of the army was also regulated and defined. All Federal troops were compelled to obey absolutely the King of Prussia alike in time of war or peace, the oath of fidelity to the colors containing a special provision to this effect.

The army of the North German Confederation consisted, on a peace-footing, of 118 regiments, of 3 battalions each, of infantry (including 4 regiments of the Grand Duke of Hesse of 2 battalions each), 18 battalions of rifles, 76 regiments of cavalry of 5 squadrons each, 13 regiments and 1 (Hessian) division of field-artillery, 9 regiments of siege-artillery, 13 battalions and 1 (Hessian) company of pioneers, 13 battalions and 1 (Hessian) division of military train. Accordingly, the army, divided into 216 landwehr battalion districts, comprised 350 battalions of infantry, 18 battalions of rifles, 380 squadrons of cavalry, 163 batteries of field-artillery, 39 battalions of horse-artillery, 88 companies of pioneers, and 27 companies of the military train. The infantry was armed with the needle-gun, the field-artillery with rifled breech-loading guns of cast steel.

The army was classified into the corps of the Guards, twelve army-corps, and one Hessian division; each army-corps consisting of two divisions of infantry and one brigade of cavalry; while the cavalry of the Guards and the twelfth (Saxon) army-corps were consolidated into one division of cavalry. The peace-footing of the army consisted of 302,633 men (299,704 combatants), 73,212 horse, and 808 guns. On a war-footing it consisted of 12,777 officers, 543,058 men, 155,896 horse, and 1,212 guns. Besides these there were depot and garrison troops, consisting of 6,376 officers, 198,678 men, 15,698 horse, and 234 guns; and reserve troops of 3,280 officers, 182,940 men, 22,545 horse, and 234 guns.

The fortresses of the North German Confederation were Königsberg, Graudenz, Thorn, Posen, Glogau, Kosel, Neisse, Glatz, Königstein, Mayence, Koblenz, Saarlouis, Cologne, Wesel, Wilhelmshaven, Sonderburg-Düppel, Friedrichsort, Stralsund, Swinemünde, Kolberg, Danzig, Pillau, Stettin, Küstrin, Spandau, Torgau, Wittenberg, Magdeburg, Minden, and Erfurt.

The hour when the military organization of the North German Confederation and its Southern allies had to face its fiery ordeal was now approaching.

Napoleon III., alarmed at the sudden rise of the Prussian power, readily found an alleged cause of declaring war against the King of Prussia (July 15, 1870). The result of this was that the Federal diet placed its entire military resources at the disposal of the government. The South German princes, whose neutrality Napoleon had expected, leagued their quickly mobilized forces with the armies of the Confederation, and those of the King of Bavaria, the Grand Duke of Baden, and the King of Würtemberg. This occurred on the sixteenth and seventeenth of July (1870). By this action the whole German army was placed under the command of the King of Prussia, in accordance with the treaties. The German forces numbered 447,000 men as the army for the first offensive operations, while there were ready to follow as first reserve 188,000 men, as second reserve 160,000 men, and 226,000 depot troops,—a grand total of 1,021,-000 men. Led by the old hero-king and directed by General von Moltke the success of the German army was unprecedented in the annals of modern war.

This army of heroes during a period of 180 days not only demolished the throne of Napoleon, but forced the French republic to agree to the terms of the treaty of Frankfort, by which France ceded to the victors Alsace and the German part of Lorraine, and agreed to pay to Germany five billion francs as a war indemnity. A great lustre surrounds this eventful period in the history of the German nation and makes memorable the names of its heroes Emperor William, the Crown Prince Frederick William, Prince Frederick Charles, the Crown Prince Albert of Saxony, Moltke, Blumenthal, Franseky, Werder, Goeben, Alvensleben, and Manteuffel.

The German Grand Army, which had completed its disposition on the French frontier on the third of August, was divided into three parts. The first army, called the Army of the North, had General Steinmetz as its commander; the second army, or the Army of the Centre, was under the command of Prince Frederick Charles of Prussia; the third army, or the Army of the South, was commanded by the Crown Prince of Prussia. The Army of the South had the honor of taking part in the first collision, and it inflicted heavy losses on the French under Douay at Weissenburg on the fourth of August, and under McMahon at Wörth two days afterwards. On the same day the bloody battle of Spichern took place, in which Steinmetz, the commander of the Army of the North, routed and demoralized Frossard's Corps.

These victories of the Germans were followed by three sanguinary battles in front of Metz, which fortress was held by Marshal Bazaine with 130,000 men. Those were the battle of Colombey, fought on the fourteenth of August, that of Mars La Tour on the sixteenth, and the decisive battle of Gravelotte on the eighteenth of August. At the battle of Mars La Tour, in which 67,000 Germans with 222 guns fought against 138,000 French with 476 guns, the German loss was 711 officers, 15,097 men, and

125th Regiment of Infantry (Würtemberg).

2,736 horse. The French loss was 879 officers, 16,128 men (prisoners of war included), and one gun. At Gravelotte, where 178,818 men of the German infantry, 24,584 cavalry, and 726 guns were engaged against 120,000 French troops, besides the garrison of Metz, with its 450 guns and mitrailleuses, the Germans lost 899 officers and 19,260 men; the French lost 595 officers, 12,698 men, and 2,000 prisoners. The result of these three terrible battles before Metz was that Bazaine, with his army shut up behind the fortifications of Metz, was prevented from coöperating with the army of McMahon, which had been gathered at Châlons. On the twenty-fifth of August, McMahon left camp at Châlons and marched to the north with the design of relieving Bazaine at Metz. By the two battles of Beaumont and Musson, August 29th and 30th, McMahon was cut off from the roads eastward to Metz and south and southwestward to Paris, and was compelled to fall back on Sedan. During the thirtieth and thirty-first of August and the first of September, McMahon's army was completely surrounded by the Germans; even the road to the north was barred. Between two and three o'clock on the afternoon of September 1st the army of the Crown Prince of Prussia and that of the Crown Prince of Saxony formed a junction. The fire of five hundred German guns was concentrated on the French, inflicting a terrible punishment. At five o'clock in the evening the heads of all the German columns advanced on Sedan and drove the last combatants up to its walls. Upon this, Napoleon III., who was inside the fortress, ordered the white flag to be displayed on the citadel, and surrendered himself a prisoner of war to the King of Prussia.

By the battle of Sedan the Emperor lost liberty and a throne, while France bewailed the loss of an army of 135,000 men. The battle and the capitulation placed in the hands of the conquerors 83,000 prisoners of war, 419 field-pieces, including 70 mitrailleuses, 459 siege-guns, 66,000 rifles, and other war-material. During the battle 28,000 men had been cut off and made prisoners on the field. The dead included, there was an army, as we have said, of 135,000 men annihilated.

Still more fatal to France was the capitulation of Metz by Bazaine, on the twenty-seventh of October, 1870. His immense army, consisting of 3 marshals, 10 generals, 6,000 officers, and 173,000 men, were made prisoners of war, upon the conditions of Sedan, and the fortress of Metz, the greatest stronghold of France, surrendered with all its war-material, including 53 eagles and other regimental colors, 541 field-pieces, 800 siege-guns, 100 mitrailleuses, and 300,000 rifles.

The armies of the now republican France, created by Gambetta and provided with arms bought from England and the United States of America, could not prevail against the victorious Germans. All efforts to relieve Paris, invested by the latter, failed. The French Army of the North, the Army of the West, the Army of the Loire, of the Westward and Eastward army corps, were defeated in the battles of Beaune-la-Rolande, Beaugency, Les Mans, and St. Quentin; the intended invasion of Southern Germany by Bourbaki's army was frustrated by the heroic efforts of General Werder's troops at the battle of the Lisaine and of General Manteuffel's at Pontarlier, which forced the French to enter neutral Swiss territory. The sorties of the invested Parisians, made at Fontainebleau, Champigny, Le Bourget, Drancy, Meudon, Clamart, and from Mont Valérien failed, with heavy losses to the French.

On the twenty-eighth of January, 1871, the capitulation of the capital of France, with the largest known fortress in the world, took place under the following conditions: All the forts, Vincennes excluded, were surrendered, with all war-material, the regular troops and the marines, also the Garde-Mobile, became prisoners of war, surrendered their arms, field-artillery, and colors, the fortifications of the city were, moreover, dismantled, and the city was to pay an indemnity of two hundred millions of francs.

In 180 days the German armies had fought 156 greater or lesser engagements, 17 pitched battles, had taken 20 fortified places, made 19,316 officers and 613,667 men prisoners (the army of Paris included), and captured 7,441 guns and 107 standards and other French colors.

On the eighteenth of January, 1871, in the palace of the French Kings at Versailles, King William of Prussia was solemnly proclaimed chief regent of the Empire, with the title of "German Emperor," by the desire and consent of all the German states and princes. The legal announcement of the German Empire had taken place on the first of January preceding.

The preliminaries at Versailles, on the twenty-sixth of February, and the definitive peace-treaty of Frankfort, on the tenth of May, 1871, brought the glorious German national war to a close. The immortal fame which Prince Bismarck, the great German statesman, attained by the founding of the new German Empire, and which shall place the German nation under everlasting gratitude to him, is too well known to need repeating here.

German unification, so long desired and sought after, became now a matter of historical fact under an emperor of the House of Hohenzollern. A similar union has been effected, some trivial matters excepted, in the reorganization of the military institutions of the Empire. The illustrations of the present work show that a diversity in the uniforms still exists in the German imperial army; the light-blue color of the uniform having been retained by Bavaria. The Saxons wear a red binding around the bottom of the tunic, while the Würtembergians differ in having their coat of arms on the helmet. The larger Federal states have reserved a somewhat independent administration of their troops, so that four great divisions may be made. The Prussian army comprises the Federal troops of all the states, with the exception of the three kingdoms, Bavaria, Saxony, and Würtemberg. But all those little externals, by which the four contingents differ, disappear before the great achievements of the imperial army, as well as before the enthusiasm common to the German nation, which everywhere welcomes the military forces of Germany and goes out in love and esteem to the entire national soldiery in all parts of the Empire. Faithfully and bravely has this real national army, in whose ranks the nation sees its own sons and brothers, fought and bled on a hundred battlefields, and by its heroism it has won for the German name respect, esteem, and admiration throughout Europe, nay throughout the world.

ORGANIZATION OF THE ARMY

THE fundamental provisions of the military organization of the North German Confederation were almost entirely embodied in the imperial constitution of the sixteenth of April, 1871, repeatedly amended though they were in the course of time. The military institutions of the German Empire are, therefore, founded on the organization of the Prussian army.

Following the example of the Great Elector, Frederick William of Brandenburg, the founder of the Brandenburg-Prussian army, his successors, the kings of Prussia. always took personal interest in the training and equipment of their military forces. Frederick William I., the "Soldier King," had not only trained the functionaries of State and its officials in the ways of the most rigid integrity and honesty, but had drilled his army in the severest discipline and infused into the body of officers, called into existence by himself, the idea of rectitude and honorable dealing in the most exacting form. Frederick the Great, the genial military leader, had raised the tactical efficiency of this little army to the highest standard and had led it to the height of military glory by a successful defense of Prussia against half of Europe in the Seven Years' War. Although the old forms had crumbled away during the Napoleonic wars at the beginning of the century, the same spirit was maintained, and the virtues of piety, honor, fidelity, and obedience continued to be the mainstay of the army, which rose anew upon the foundation of the universal liability to service exacted at the regeneration of Prussia in her long wars for liberty. Reorganized with the utmost care and brought to almost absolute perfection by the first soldier of Europe, King William I., the late German Emperor, the most expert army officer of his time, this army proved its valor in three successful wars,—in 1864 against Denmark, in 1866 against Austria, and, especially, in 1870–'71 against France. Thus the Prussian army, the nation under arms, having for its motto "with God for King and Fatherland," became the type for most of the European armies, and its organization, as we have said, was embodied in the constitution of the German Empire, united under the Emperor's proclamation at Versailles, January 18th, 1871.

Owing to the increase of the French and Russian military forces, the German army was repeatedly subjected to changes; it may be described, in regard to its composition, organization, distribution, armament, and equipment, in time of peace and war, as follows:

I. GENERAL ORGANIZATION, DUTY, AND LIABILITY TO SERVICE

THE German military constitution is based on the imperial military laws enacted during the years 1870–'71, only amended, as we have hinted, in consequence of the continual massing of French and Russian troops on the German frontier.

The Emperor has absolute command of the united German army, alike in time of war and of peace, with this sole restriction, that the kingdom of Bavaria is entitled to minor concessions in time of peace. The navy is exclusively, and without any restriction, under the command of the Emperor.

The land forces of the empire form a union army, each regiment having its own distinctive number and the whole being uniformly armed and equipped. The color and cut of the Prussian army uniform set the standard for all, a cockade with the German colors being worn by officers and men alike, as a sign of the unity of the imperial forces.

The Emperor has the power, and it is his duty, to see to it that every part of the army is complete in numbers and equipment, and that uniformity is established and maintained as to organization, formation, armament, and command. The Emperor also regulates the training of the soldiers and the proper qualification of the officers.

The army is formed on the general and exacting principle of liability to service. Every German is liable to service, and in the performance of this duty no substitute is allowed. Exemption from compulsory service is permitted only in the case of members of the reigning or formerly reigning sovereign houses, who, however, almost without exception, deem it a duty and an honor to enter the army. They serve, as a rule, in the Prussian army, in the 1st Regiment of Foot-Guards stationed at Potsdam.

The general liability to serve in the army commences with the completion of the seventeenth and closes with the forty-fifth year of a man's life. The time is divided be-

Guard Mount at Munich. 2nd Regiment of Infantry—Body-Guards—"Crown Prince." 3rd Regiment of Chevaulegers (vac.) "Duke Maximilian."

After
G. Arnould

tween service in the ranks and in the Landsturm or militia.

The liability to serve in the ranks and in the Land-wehr commences with the completion of the twentieth year of a man's life; it lasts until the thirty-first of March of the year in which a man completes his thirty-ninth year; he therefore serves in all nineteen years.

During the time a man belongs to the army he serves two years in the ranks, five in the reserve (with the cavalry and horse-artillery, three years in the ranks, and four years in the reserve); after which he is attached for five years to the first levy of the Landwehr, seven years to the second levy (with the cavalry and horse-artillery, three years to the first levy, and nine years to the second levy).

The standing army is formed by the ranks and the reserve, the object of which is the replenishing of the army from a peace footing into a war footing.

The Landwehr of the first and second levy serves for strengthening the standing army in time of war, and is formed into regiments, brigades, and divisions.

For the purpose of preserving the fitness for war, every man of the reserve is compelled, in time of peace, to take part in two field manœuvres of eight weeks' duration. Each man in the Landwehr has to turn out from one to two weeks; both are called out by a special imperial order.

The Landsturm (militia), whose duty it is to defend the native soil, as well as to strengthen the army in case of necessity, contains all men who have or have not served from their seventeenth to their forty-fifth year, and who do not belong either to the ranks, the reserve or the Landwehr. They, however, do not have to take part in the field manœuvres in time of peace.

Exemptions from the above-named duties are legally defined. As the military service is deemed one of honor, all criminals and state prisoners are excluded from it as unworthy. The bodily unfit men are rejected. The sole supports of families, and such as cannot leave their homes, may be called upon later or are altogether exempted from service.

Those educated at government expense at military institutes (academies, medical schools, and schools for non-commissioned officers) are compelled to serve longer in the ranks (up to seven years). Those expecting military advancement, or who make a claim for some minor civil office, have also to enlist in the army for seven years under special agreement (Kapitulation).

To prevent an interruption in the studies of those educating themselves for the professions in serving the full term of two or three years, every able-bodied German may serve as a volunteer for one year only, and in any troops. Upon passing an examination, or by producing a certificate from any one of the specially authorized educational institutes, attesting his qualifications in one of the upper classes of a high school (Realschule) or college, the youth need only serve for one year as a volunteer. The one-year service may be rendered in the ranks of any regiment which may be the choice of the volunteer, who, however, has to pay for his board and government equipment. If found proficient he may be transferred after one year's service to the reserve (six

years). Medical students desiring to enter the sanitary corps are allowed to serve a shorter time, namely, six months under arms, and after their graduation six months more with a non-commissioned rank or as under-surgeon. Public school teachers are also required to serve in the ranks for a period of one year only.

II. RECRUITING, ENLISTMENT, DISCHARGE, AND CONTROLLING ORGANIZATION

THE peace footing of the army is, according to imperial law, one percentage of the population. The annual contingent of recruits is fixed by an imperial decree and is determined by the number required to keep up the peace establishment. The number is estimated at from 240,000 to 250,000 men.

The right to locate himself in any part of the Empire gives the recruit the right to enroll himself in any corps of his choice. This privilege is the recruit's, if we except the corps of the Guards, which is recruited throughout the Prussian provinces only, and to which are assigned recruits of superior physique and behavior and of a minimum height of five and one-half feet. Each army-corps, excepting the Guards, has a district within which it is stationed, raised, and recruited. This district is subdivided into brigade and Landwehr battalion districts. The enrollment, examination, and distribution by the higher and lower district commissions takes place according to lists taken from the parish registers. Those found fit to serve in the army are selected for the service with arms, or without arms as hospital attendants and professionals, such as tailors, shoemakers, etc. Men below the regulation standard, but otherwise fit for duty, are passed to the Ersatzreserve, for the purpose of filling up the army in time of war or for the formation of depôt or garrison troops, while those found physically unfit for any service are struck off the list altogether, and those found unworthy are excluded.

Of the supernumerary recruits, those drawing the lucky numbers are temporarily exempt from service in times of peace. The men drawn for the army are then told off to the different branches of service, according to height, physique, and former occupation.

The final decision and allotment to the regiment is usually completed about the beginning of October; the passing into the reserve occurs generally in September, after the Autumn manœuvres. For the keeping of the rosters and a continuous record, and for the passing of those from the reserve into the Landwehr, the larger Landwehr battalion districts are subdivided into company districts. Each man of the reserve and of the Landwehr who changes his domicile has to report the same at the company district, that is, the district officer and district sergeant-major. At the latter place he receives continuously his necessary military papers (passport), also his furlough pass, and permission, if he desires it, to emigrate. The district commands or commissions are charged with keeping the register of the names and addresses of all reserve and Landwehr men in their

34th Regiment of Fusiliers (Pomeranian).

respective districts and with calling them into service for manœuvres or mobilization. The labor of summoning, collecting, and forwarding the men to their destination falls on the district commissions. By semi-annual recruiting commissions, composed also of officers, the military papers are approved and completed, the rosters prepared, and the necessary steps taken to find out who are the missing men.

III. THE ARMY ON A PEACE FOOTING

THE army establishment, defined by the imperial budget, places the peace strength of non-commissioned officers and men (not including the one-year volunteers) at about 479,229 men. The entire peace strength is as follows:

The German army consists on a peace footing of about 23,000 officers and 557,440 non-commissioned officers and men. Including all non-combatants, there are 585,490 soldiers and 97,850 horse, as follows:

215 regiments of infantry and 19 battalions of rifles (Jäger and Schützen),
—a total of 624 battalions of infantry;
93 regiments of cavalry and 4 detachments of mounted rifles (Jäger zu Pferde),
—a total of 469 squadrons of cavalry;
43 regiments of field-artillery of 494 batteries;
17 regiments of foot-artillery and 1 battalion,
—a total of 37 battalions of 149 companies;
23 battalions of pioneers of 96 companies;
7 battalions of railroad troops and 2 detachments of balloon troops,
—a total of 27 companies and 2 detachments of balloon troops;
21 battalions of the military train consisting of 65 companies, shortly to be augmented by 3 battalions of telegraph troops.

The infantry are armed with the breech-loader (rifle model of 1888), allowing the simultaneous loading of five cartridges, united in one frame; the calibre is of 0.31 in. Besides the rifle, the infantry soldier carries a side arm, which can be attached to the rifle as a bayonet.

A uniform arming of the entire cavalry has been perfected by an equipment of lances. The cavalry soldier is armed also with a carbine (model 1888); the cuirassiers carry a straight heavy sabre (Pallasch); the hussars, dragoons, and uhlans have the regular cavalry sabre.

The entire field-artillery is provided with uniform guns of 3.56 in. calibre, made of improved cast steel and mounted on a spring steel plated gun-carriage. The charge is a shrapnell shell and a canister shot (case-shot).

The foot-artillery is equipped with heavy field-guns of from 4.72 to 5.90 in. calibre; howitzers of 5.90 in. calibre; mortars of 8.26 in. calibre; and as siege-guns pieces of 3.64, 4.72, 5.90 and 8.26 in. calibre, mortars of 5.90 in. calibre, turret-howitzers of 8.26 in. calibre; also, revolving and quick-firing guns. The foot-artillery soldier carries a short rifle for personal protection.

The pioneers, who are armed with the Mauser rifle and side-arms, carry the portable materials necessary for fortification and engineering.

The military train, armed with sabre and carbine, attends to the transport of the army.

The entire army consists, the Prussian corps of the Guards included, of twenty army corps. From three to five army corps form an army, named, in time of peace, army-inspections.

Each army corps numbers generally two divisions (infantry and cavalry), besides one battalion of rifles, one battalion of pioneers, one battalion of the military train, one brigade of field-artillery, and one regiment of foot-artillery.

Each division has normally two brigades of infantry and one brigade of cavalry, each brigade consisting of two regiments of infantry or cavalry.

The infantry regiments are composed, as a rule, of three battalions (forty regiments lately organized have only two) of four companies. The battalions have a peace footing of 570 men, and a war footing of 1,000 men.

The cavalry regiments consist of five squadrons (in war time of four, the fifth forming the depôt squadron) with a peace footing of from 130 to 140 horses each, and a war footing in all of 700 horses.

The field-artillery brigade consists of two regiments of generally three mounted divisions (Abteilungen), each usually of three batteries, and one division of horse-artillery of two batteries each. Each battery consists in peace time of from four to six, and in war time of six guns.

A foot-artillery regiment comprises two battalions each, a rifle battalion and a pioneer battalion four companies, with the military train battalion of three companies.

The training and drilling, commencing with the enrollment of the recruits in October, lasts without interruption throughout the year; it embraces all branches of the military service and ends with the September manœuvres of the brigades, divisions, and army corps, after which follow the Emperor's manœuvres, so called from the attendance of the commander-in-chief, and assisted by from one to three army corps (armies) facing and fighting each other in sham-battles.

For the thorough and skilful training of the individual soldier in larger formations in each army-corps district, there are provided large places for the instruction of the troops in shooting, drilling, and in regular evolutions.

In order to secure a uniform technical expertness in the drill of every branch of the military service, there are provided special general-inspections for each branch.

For the warlike training of the army corps the commanding general is responsible; for the perfection and readiness for war of the regiment, and for its complete strength and the requisite qualification of the corps of officers, the commander of the regiment is held responsible.

9th Regiment of Grenadiers (Colberg) "Count Gneisenau" (Pomeranian No. 2).

As a model for the infantry a special battalion of instructors (Lehrbataillon), composed of officers, non-commissioned officers, and privates from the whole army, is formed at Potsdam and drilled under the personal supervision of the Emperor. For the training of the army instructors in general (officers and non-commissioned officers), an infantry school of musketry is provided; for the field-artillery and foot-artillery there is a school of gunnery, while for the cavalry there is a riding academy; and for all there is the military gymnasium. For the education and training of non-commissioned officers, military orphan homes, institutes for the educating of soldier-boys, are provided, also preparatory and normal schools for non-commissioned officers.

After a service lasting for twelve years, the non-commissioned officer receives a bounty of one thousand marks, with the right to claim some minor office in the sphere either of the State or of some civil corporation.

Following the tradition of feudal times and the days of chivalry, the entire nobility serves in the German army and comprises the main body of officers. Since the great increase in the army, within the past forty years, the sources for replenishing the staff of officers have been necessarily extended. Legally the career of an officer is open to every man of respectable parentage, but none,—not even a crown-prince or a prince of a reigning house,—can obtain an officer's commission, save by passing the regular examination. One exception only is possible, namely, for bravery in action—in face of the enemy.

For the training and education of officers there are schools for cadets, preparatory and normal institutes, such as those at Gross-Lichterfelde near Berlin. Besides these there are special military academies. The higher training is provided by the military high schools, by the war academy, and by the artillery and engineering school at Berlin. Bavaria also has similar educational institutes.

The war academy is the principal training school for the higher commanders, especially for the officers of the general staff of the army. The latter, in time of peace, consists of about two hundred and fifty officers, destined to attend to all matters touching the movement, the quartering, and engagement of the troops, also the drawing up of orders governing the strategical and tactical dispositions of the higher commanders and their enforcement.

The greatest attention has, in the German army, also been paid to the thorough scientific and practical training of sanitary officers and surgeons, not only at the universities, but especially at the Kaiser Wilhelm Academy, located at Berlin. This training has been furthermore fostered by appointing surgeons to attendance at garrison hospitals as well as attendance at the lecture courses in operative surgery, delivered by the most eminent professors. The training of nurses and of men to bear off the sick, and in war time the wounded, is carried on in hospitals by annual practical instructions. In the farrier and veterinary establishments horse-smiths and veterinary surgeons receive their training.

The entire war-material is furnished by the gun-factories, manufactories of arms and of projectiles, and by the powder-mills. The bureau of supplies, assigned to each army corps, furnishes all the troops with the necessary clothing. To see to the sustenance of man and horse is the duty of each separate division of troops, providing such is not done by the military bakeries, by the factories of canned-meats, and the bureau of supplies.

A uniform martial law is maintained throughout the entire army, also a uniform military code regulating trials and court-martials.

The chaplains have charge of the spiritual welfare of the army, and are expected to foster and promote religious sentiment.

All affairs regarding the administration, equipment, armament, clothing, and maintenance of the military forces are regulated and conducted by the War Ministry in Berlin. This is the centre from which issue all measures of organization and administration. This ministry, in connection with the lesser ministries of Bavaria, Saxony, and Würtemberg, has to provide for the equipment and maintenance of the entire German army in case of war.

IV. THE ARMY ON A WAR FOOTING

AT the time when armies were raised by enlistment, it was a happy idea of the Great Elector of Brandenburg to assign to each regiment a defined district of the country. As enlistment was changed to conscription, the old practice was retained, though more and more developed in the Prussian army, and still further developed in the German army. The composition of the latter is therefore closely affiliated with the territorial divisions of the country. Each army corps is recruited within its own army corps district and bears its name. The regiments which bear besides the regular number of the military branch to which they belong, the names of princes and prominent generals, are also known by the names of the province and the district from which they are recruited. As an instance, the following are cited as examples: the 38th regiment of Fusiliers, Graf Moltke (Silesian); the 7th regiment of Cuirassiers, von Seydlitz (Magdeburg); the 3rd regiment of Hussars, von Zieten (Brandenburg); the 5th regiment of Hussars, Prince Blücher (Pomeranian); the 114th regiment of infantry, Emperor Frederick III. (Baden No. 6).

By this arrangement the history of each town, of each village, and even of each family, is closely connected with the history of each regiment. Often, not only in the ranks of the nobility, but also in those of the commoners and peasantry, a whole generation may serve in the same regiment. The grandson takes pride to enlist in the company in which his grandfather's name is honorably mentioned in connection with earlier campaigns.

Besides the inestimable moral value of these traditional and historical ties, binding together nation and army, the uniformity of the distribution of the troops, their garrisoning in the recruiting districts, has an enormous advantage, in that the army can be transformed with the utmost speed from a peace organization to a war footing. This is called "mobilization" and is prepared with the utmost care in time of peace, the initiative of war operations, nay, even the success of the war itself, depending on the alertness and promptness with which the mobilization is carried out. The reserve district commanders keep the parish lists of each man of the reserve force and of the Landwehr. When the order to mobilize is issued, the summonses are handed directly to this officer and through him to the soldier, instructing him where and when to go.

The transport of the summoned troops to the frontier or to meet the enemy, with the necessary railway facilities and personnel, are mapped out and arranged in every detail during peace time. The entire railroad system is thus mobilized.

The whole equipment, armament, ammunition supplies, and general fitting out of the forces for war purposes, including both the Landwehr and the depôt troops; all wagons, supplies for the medical department, also the entire rations for the first few days' use of the army in the field,—in short, all that is necessary and expedient for the fighting army, for its subsequent enlargement, and for the defence of the country,—is kept in readiness in a complete and perfect state; it is also replenished and renovated from time to time. By inspections, held only by generals, the whole army is tested in regard to its readiness for war; the entire material down to the small package of bandages carried by every man, to every horse-shoe nail and wagon-lantern, is subject to the most scrutinizing process of inspection.

The necessary completion of the force of officers from the time war breaks out is especially provided for, as all of the officers that are of the age liable still to serve upon leaving the ranks enter the reserve or the Landwehr. The most able and efficient of the one-year volunteers, trained practically and theoretically by officers during their service time, and having passed the necessary examination to become officers of the reserve, are also notified for service. Trained further by repeated exercises, lasting several weeks, of which three have to be made at least in the reserve and later on two in the Landwehr, these reserve and Landwehr officers form in time of peace a standing corps of officers under the direct surveillance of the district commanders. This corps, infused with the proper martial spirit, is amply sufficient to supply the body of officers in the lower ranks in case of war. For the position of the higher ranks of commanders and leaders, the Emperor has officers and generals at his disposal for immediate use and action.

In accordance with the aforesaid, when war is declared the mere telegraphic order of the Emperor is sufficient: "the army is mobilized;" and when a few days have elapsed the entire German army stands ready for action at whatever point the country is menaced. Exempt from immediate mobilization are the troops retained for the

Ersatz, with all the depôt and garrison troops.

In war time the army is divided into: the mobile or active army, and the immobile or garrison troops. The active army is composed of the troops of all ranks, including the reserve and the mobilized forces of the Landwehr. The organization of the army on a war footing is similar to that in time of peace; there are twenty army corps, composed of the same divisions, brigades, regiments, and battalions for both occasions. The additional formations are from two to three independent cavalry divisions, consisting of a number of cavalry regiments, withdrawn from the regular divisions for strategical duties in front of and on the flanks of the army. Added to these are in war time the necessary columns and divisions of the military train, all of which make up the following formation of an army corps on a war footing: two divisions of infantry, one battalion of rifles, the artillery of the corps, the ammunition trains (four for the infantry, six for the artillery), the military train-battalion, three provision and seven transportation trains, the depôt of remounts, the field-bakery, the pontoon train, the sanitary train, the sanitary detachment of twelve field-hospitals. Added to these are the military commissioners (intendantur) and the chaplains, with the military pay chest and the field post-office.

One division of infantry comprises two brigades of infantry, each of two regiments, one regiment of cavalry, one regiment of field-artillery of six batteries, one or two companies of pioneers, one detachment of pontoon train, one sanitary detachment, and one detachment of telegraph troops. Besides those there are the military commissioners, the chaplains, and field-post.

In addition to the above-named columns and trains, each army corps has its own wagons, divided into two columns or echelons; one, called the small baggage train, which carries everything necessary for the troops during a battle or immediately after one, such as the ammunition, provisions, and medicine, while the heavy baggage follows at a greater distance, and carries all supplies required for the sustenance of the army during its operations in the field, with the baggage, sutler, forage, and provision wagons.

An army corps of two divisions comprises: 24 battalions of infantry, 1 battalion of rifles, 8 squadrons of cavalry, from 18 to 20 batteries of artillery, about 25,000 infantry men, 1,400 horse, and from 108 to 120 guns. In war time two of the recently formed forty regiments of infantry remain with their respective army corps. It is intended to bring up the strength of the latter to about 30,000 infantry.

The regiments formed of the surplus reserve are placed in reserve divisions; the Landwehr, made up also into regiments of battalions, squadrons, and batteries, is added, in the form of Landwehr brigades and divisions, to the active army. The war formations prepared and defined in every detail are promulgated only at the outset of the war.

From three to five army corps form an army under a superior army commander. The entire forces under the supreme command of the Emperor are directed from the

Imperial Headquarters. These are composed of the chief of the general staff of the army, the minister of war, the quartermaster-general, and the inspector-general of the troops, with their respective staffs. The garrison forces, composed of the immobile Landwehr of the second levy (from the thirty-second to the thirty-ninth year of a man's life), and the depôt troops remain in the country, commanded by the respective temporary commanding generals; they are completely equipped and clothed, generally formed into battalions, squadrons, and batteries, and may be also called out in case of mobilization and used for the defence of the Etappen (lines of base connecting the field-army with the rear), or to fill up the fighting strength.

The Landsturm (composed of men from the seventeenth to the forty-fifth year) is called out by an imperial order, or, in case of imminent danger, by the commanding generals and commanders of the fortified posts. The Landsturm is also properly prepared in peace time (including the appointment of officers). It is completely equipped and armed, special attention being paid to the fact that the Landsturm of the second levy shall hold all men from their thirty-ninth to their forty-fifth year, that is, all soldiers having passed through the regular service. Thus in from eighteen to twenty days after war is declared, that is, after the order to mobilize has been given, about 1,400,000 men of the standing army are ready to take the field. After about four weeks another body of 960,000 men of the reserves are ready to go into action, being in fighting trim to operate on the threatened frontier. After a further lapse of from four to six weeks the entire Landwehr and the Landsturm, comprising all men that have served, may be summoned, so that four and a half millions of trained men are ready to defend the country. On great emergency this number can be raised to seven millions by calling out the remainder of the Landsturm, including those men who have not served. This may not be called an army merely; it is the nation under arms. Such a campaign would be equal to a Migration of Nations.

This immense military organization of the German empire, made possible by compulsory military service, is the result of the coöperation of all the military authorities with those of the government, the corporations, and the railroad administration bureaus. Without this varied and combined assistance, well defined for all warlike purposes, the complete disposition of the army and its readiness for war would be impossible. For the founding of this great organization, so resolute and so tense, as well as efficient in all its parts, Germany is especially indebted to the ceaseless and untiring efforts of the late Emperor William I and to his trusted and eminent advisers, the two field-marshals, both now deceased — von Moltke, chief of the general staff, and von Roon, the secretary of war.

Emperor William II strenuously endeavors not only to maintain but to raise the standard of the German army. " He keeps the sword in the scabbard, but its edge is sharp," so that in the hour of peril no notch will be found, while the national forces, in full equipment, will be ready to defend German honor, together with the German Fatherland.

On Picket at Night. 89th Regiment of Grenadiers. (Grand-Duchy of Mecklenburg.)

COMPOSITION OF THE ARMY

LIKE all European armies, the German army consists of the following branches of military service: infantry, cavalry, artillery, the engineers, and the military train.

THE GERMAN INFANTRY

THE entire German infantry wears the Prussian helmet, and a dark blue tunic with red facings on collars and cuffs; the shoulder straps bear the color of the army corps and the number of the regiment. The trousers are made of dark gray cloth, the boots have leather tops, the overcoat is of a gray-colored frieze. The Prussian Guards have collars to their tunics with braiding peculiar to their corps, and wear horse-hair plumes on parade. The Jäger are distinguished by wearing a shako, with a green tunic.

The equipment (helmet excluded) of the infantry consists of the belt for the side-arms, two ammunition pouches, the feed-bag, cooking utensils, canteen, entrenching tools, and parts of a tent. In the knapsack and haversack are a pair of shoes, a shirt, a pair of socks, pieces of linen, grease for the rifle, polishing and scouring utensils, a pay-book, and hymn book.

The infantry is provided with arms which enable the troops to fight either at a long or at a short distance. Its ranks hold the largest number of fighting men. They are armed with a rifle, capable of firing at a long range, also with side-arms which can be attached to the rifle as a bayonet. The infantry is the chief stay of the army, and is adaptable for service at any time or in any country. The discipline of the German infantry is known throughout the world and is a model for other nations, excelling all foreign troops in what is called "firing discipline," that is, discipline under fire. In face of the enemy the commands are obeyed as on parade, no firing or change of position being allowed without explicit orders. The unity of the army extends also to the weapon and side-arms of the infantry: all non-commissioned officers and men use a magazine rifle, the quick-loading rifle '88— of 0.310 inch (about one-third of an inch) calibre—the magazine being filled from a metal clip containing five cartridges charged with smokeless powder. The rifle '88 signifies the infantry rifle model of the year 1888. The weight of the weapon is 8.37 pounds, the length 49.01 inches. The rifle has three sights. The fixed sight is adjusted to 273 yards; the drop sight to 386 yards; and the elevating Vernier sight is graduated from 490 to 2,238 yards. The rifle covers a maximum range of from 4,149 to 4,336 yards. The bullet has an initial velocity of 82.02 feet and a muzzle velocity of 2,034 feet.

The infantry side-arm '71, '84 (that is, model of 1871, improved in 1884) has a length of 15.2 inches, and weighs, scabbard included, 17.03 ounces, or 13.29 ounces without the scabbard. It consists of blade, hilt, and scabbard. The blade is made of cast steel, tempered, blued, ground and polished, grooved on each side, flat-backed, and two-edged at the point. The hilt, serving for the handling of the weapon, is made of iron; on the haft are side plates of wood (the sword bayonet of the Jäger has side plates of leather), and has a guard forged of highly carbonized iron, with a round hole for insertion round the muzzle of the gun, and held tight by a steel spring inside the hilt handle. The scabbard is made of black, pliable sole-leather, formed like the blade, and has two mountings of steel-plate; at the lower or pointed end is a frog mounting, and at the upper end the chape with hook to be fastened into the waist belt. The side-arms are adjusted to the rifle as a bayonet at the command before the attack of "fix bayonets!"

The officers, sergeant-majors, sergeants, and ensigns who wear the silver sword-knot and the regular officer's sword, together with the men who have charge of the sick and wounded, are each provided with a revolver (model of 1883). This is made, in its principal parts, of steel, with butt plates of walnut, a barrel with four grooves and of a length of 6.03 inches, a calibre of 0.42 inches, and a cylinder holding six cartridges. The bullet, cylindric in form, with a point pressed out of spun lead, weighs 0.59 ounces; the charge is 23.14 grains of gunpowder. The weight of the weapon is 2.06 pounds, the length is 9.25 inches, and the sight is adjusted to 21.3 yards.

The equipment of the infantry has been materially reduced in weight since 1887, conforming to the changes introduced in modern war tactics. The helmet has been lightened and freed from all superfluous mountings.

Body-Guard of H. M. the Empress. 2nd Platoon.

The haversack is made of waterproof material, instead of linen. The ammunition is entirely separated from the knapsack, being stowed away in two pouches fastened to the belt, each containing forty-five cartridges. To these may be added sixty more cartridges for field operations, which are carried in the knapsack. The entire ammunition for war purpose consists, therefore, of one hundred and fifty cartridges, which may be replenished from the ammunition and company's wagons to two hundred for each man. The weight of the knapsack has been likewise reduced. A separate waterproof bag holds provisions for three days. The cooking utensils are smaller and are made of aluminium and mounted on top of the knapsack, around which, leaving the lower part free, the great coat is rolled. The whole outfit, including the ammunition pouches, is strapped to the belt.

The weight of the knapsack, including the parts of the tent, is 3.45 pounds. The entire load, including clothing carried by a fully equipped soldier of the infantry, amounts to 53.78 pounds, being considerably reduced in comparison with the weight borne in former times. When the knapsack is left off temporarily, the troops can undertake field-operations for three or four days, as is often necessitated during a state of siege; they are then fully provided with pocket provisions and ammunition sufficient for the interval.

The German infantry is essentially a unity—in equipment, armament, and employment. The difference in the uniform and the names of the various regiments are of historic origin, and are retained for convenience or on the ground of expediency. The regiments are hence differently described as Grenadiers, Musketeers, Fusiliers, and Jäger. The different types of the German infantry drawn from the separate contingents are shown in the illustrations.

The élite forces of the army are the Guards, forming in itself a complete army corps, and located at Berlin, Potsdam, and Spandau. While all the other army corps are recruited from their own districts, the corps of the Guards is recruited throughout the Prussian monarchy and of men of superior physique. The Bavarian regiment of body-guard Grenadiers and the Baden regiment of the body-guard is likewise recruited from provincial sources. The élite regiment of the corps of Guards is the 1st regiment of Foot-guards. This regiment was formed in 1807 of the remainder of the original Foot-guards, and these from the regiment known as "Guards No. 15" and the battalion of "Grenadier-Guards No. 6." The battalion dates back to the time of Frederick the Great and derives its title from Frederick William's I. guard of giants, known as the "Tall Fellows."

The first regiment of the Guards is, as has been said, the élite regiment of these élite troops. Apart from the general "facings" of the Guards, the white braiding upon collars and cuffs, the uniform is especially characterized by the white buttons, a reminiscence or relic of the original regiment of the Guards No. 15. Still more deserving of notice is the head-dress worn on parade—the grenadier head-dress. The new model is an exact copy of the original, worn during the era of Frederick the Great; the back is covered with red cloth; that of the Fusiliers with yellow cloth. This distinctive head-dress was conferred upon the regiment by Emperor William II. The head-dress formerly worn by the Grenadiers, made of yellow metal, adorned with crown and star and provided with chin strap, was transferred to the Alexander regiment of the Grenadier-Guards. Besides those two regiments the Prussian Guards have seven more regiments of infantry, one battalion of Jäger, and one battalion of rifles.

The Prussian Guards are trained by the best qualified commanders and constitute a model corps in the strictest sense of the word. During the later great wars the Guards have often been put in the van of battle, and by their valorous deeds have won for themselves unfading laurels, especially at Königgrätz, St. Privat, and Sedan, and before Paris. The brightest jewel in the crown of glory gained by the Guards is the legend "St. Privat," for there they won immortal honor. The northern parts of the French line of battle—Gravelotte and St. Privat-la-Montagne—were occupied by the sixth French army corps and the division Cissey of the fourth corps; St. Privat formed the key of the position. From half-past two until half-past four o'clock in the afternoon a heavy artillery duel was raging, favorable, however, to the Germans. At half-past four o'clock an almost perfect lull set in—the calm before the storm. At a little after five, the battle having been renewed, General von Manstein ordered the third brigade of the Guards to the attack. Advancing in well-formed columns and in the best of order, the battalions were received with a terrible shower of bullets, which thinned their ranks in a frightful manner. The smallest ridges, affording some shelter, were used to good advantage; after every halt there was another advance. Up to seven o'clock in the evening, the brave soldiers had pushed themselves forward to within eight hundred paces of Amanvillers, located to the south of St. Privat, which place they could not take from sheer exhaustion. At half-past five o'clock the commander of the second division of the Guards led the fourth brigade in person in the assault upon the advanced outwork Jerusalem, part of the village St. Privat stretching towards Amanvillers. The enemy was found lying there protected by hedges and rifle-pits, but beyond the reach of the needle-gun. The rapid firing chassepots made big gaps in the columns of the brigade as it advanced in regular fighting order. Without the slightest cover, the brave battalions, having by this time lost almost all their officers, now pushed ahead; but only the edge of the position could be taken by the fourth brigade, which, however, drove the enemy back to Jerusalem.

It was found impossible to reach the first line of the enemy in spite of the fact that the remains of the brigade held the captured territory. Half an hour later, when the fourth brigade had done its task, the first division of the Guards, under General von Kessel, made an attack on St. Privat, that is on Ste. Marie, lying towards the north. The same spectacle seen on the south side was seen also here. The route of the battalions was marked by heaps of dead and wounded, and in a short time all the commanders were *hors-de-combat*. The right wing, nevertheless, advanced up to within nine hundred paces, and the left to within six hundred paces of the enemy. The fighting of the decimated Germans grew less and less. At this moment General von Pape ordered four batteries of artillery to be placed in position at one thousand paces from the village; these were quickly supported by the entire corps-artillery and also by the artillery of the tenth corps. Soon the flames leaped up within the battered walls of St. Privat, and the fire of the chassepots became fainter. Firmly and steadfastly the battalions of the Guards, unwilling to recede, yet impeded in their advance, held their ground amid a storm of bullets, the most trying test of discipline to which troops can ever be put. To fill up the gap, General von Pape placed the second regiment of Grenadier-Guards between the two; and as reserves for the left brigade the fourth regiment of Guards followed. But relief soon came in the now advancing Saxon corps. Seven batteries opened their fire upon the village. Intermingled with parts of the Guards, fifteen battalions of the 45th and 47th brigades now encircled the north and west side of St. Privat. Eighty-four Saxon guns belched out against the town, while the Fusilier-Guards, hitherto held in reserve at Ste. Marie, advanced to the support of their sorely-tried comrades.

At half-past seven in the evening, the general storming of St. Privat took place; the decisive hour of the great battle had come at last. The drums beat the general assault; the troops advanced with flying colors up to the village and scaled the walls that surrounded the town and yards; the houses were then stormed one by one. The third battalion of the Body-guards and the ninth company of the fourth regiment assaulted the church, the third company of the fourth regiment of the Guards bore down on the cemetery, the Fusiliers of the first regiment of the Guards advanced upon the farmsteads lying south of Jerusalem, and the Franz regiment took Jerusalem proper.

In the battle 2,000 French were taken prisoners of war. The sixth French army corps, now conquered, retreated to the valley of the Moselle. The Guards lost almost one-third of their infantry, namely, 307 officers, 7,923 men and 2 surgeons. In these total casualties the battalion of the Guards-Rifles, engaged at Amanvillers, lost the most, namely, 19 officers, 431 men and 1 surgeon; the second Foot-Guards lost 39 officers and 1,076 men; the third regiment of the Guards lost 36 officers and 1,060 men. The first regiment of the Guards lost 36 officers and 1,056 men; the Franz regiment lost 38 officers and 1,020 men; the Augusta regiment lost 27 officers and 902 men; the Alexander regiment lost 27 officers and 820 men; the loss of the fourth regi-

ment was 29 officers and 524 men; of the Elizabeth regiment 21 officers and 433 men.

Just as glorious, though less bloody was the part taken by the corps of the Guards in the battle of Sedan. Ordered by the commander-in-chief to proceed towards Fleigneux and to press the enemy away from the Belgian frontier, the second division of the Guards were sent against the northeastern part of Daigny, where concentrated masses of the enemy fought against the twelfth corps. Only after having repulsed the French upon the opposite bank of the valley, the Guards batteries were able to occupy the heights, east of Givonne, and send from that direction with eighty-four guns the deadly shells against their opponents. In the meantime the sixth company of the Fusilier-Guards had succeeded in taking the village of La Chapelle and in dispersing the franctireurs, which held it. A column of French artillery, riding into Givonne without precautions was held up by the fifth company of Fusilier-Guards, and 11 officers with about 200 men were made prisoners, almost without any resistance; 7 guns, 3 mitrailleuses, many ammunition wagons and 124 horses were also at the same time captured.

From the second position the batteries of the Guards shelled the Bois-de-la-Garenne with a hail of lead and iron up to the hour of half-past two in the afternoon. The fifth light battery, the most exposed at the extreme left wing, suffered heavily; it lost during that time the three officers commanding the platoons by a heavy rifle fire. The hostile masses, suddenly rushing on to effect a breaking through at Carrigan, were driven back by the overwhelmingly rapid fire of the batteries. At nearly three o'clock the infantry finally reached the opposite heights of the valley and the Bois-de-la-Garenne. After a well-nigh instantaneous volley, fired by sixty guns, the first division of the Guards entered the woods, meeting with hardly any resistance, and formed a junction with parts of the fifth, eleventh, and twelfth corps, which from three sides pressed together the enemy at the farmstead of Querimont. More than 5,000 prisoners were here taken by the Guards. About five o'clock the fight ended on this part of the battlefield. The corps of the Guards rallied its scattered troops at Calvary d'Illy. It alone delivered up 111 French officers and 8,500 men, who had been made prisoners, also a French standard, 17 guns, 3 mitrailleuses, and 17 wagons of ammunition.

The deeds of valor performed by the Guards were equaled by those of the infantry regiments of the line in a self-sacrificing and death-defying spirit. We recall the heroism displayed by the 7th regiment of the King's Grenadiers at the assault upon the castle of Geisberg during the engagement at Weissenburg. This regiment is now in garrison at Liegnitz.

On August 4th the first important engagement of the Franco-German War took place at Weissenburg. General Douay, the commander of the second division of the first French corps (McMahon's) had occupied Geisberg, a hill south of Weissenburg, with eight battalions, eight squadrons and eighteen guns; whilst Weissenburg was held only by one battalion. At eight o'clock in the morning of the following day the first shot was fired; at one o'clock in the afternoon, the city was taken by regiments of the fifth and eleventh corps and the second Bavarian corps, and the first battle was won. On the Geisberg, defended at noontime by seven battalions, three batteries and one brigade of cavalry were in position under General Pellé, who was in command, vice General Douay, previously killed in battle. The Geisberg castle, a series of massive buildings, surrounded by a wall fifteen feet high and protected by embrasures, was stormed by the 7th regiment of the King's Grenadiers. The garden surrounding the castle was quickly cleared of the enemy; the rifles while attacking the castle proper were received with a terrific fire. Major von Kaisenberg at the head of the larger part of the Fusilier battalion rushed towards the castle. The color-bearer having fallen, the major grasped the colors himself; three shots however laid him low; again and again the banner changed hands; steadfastly the brave troops follow their commanders who all successively fell, crushed and shattered. The castle which was most obstinately defended could not be taken by storm. At this moment General von Kirchbach ordered the building to be fired upon from three sides. The shells tore the roof off and demolished the apartments, so that the French had to seek shelter in the cellars. At the final assault the Germans succeeded in reaching the castle-yard and in opening the gate with an axe from the inside. The troops then entered the castle and forced the remainder of the defenders to surrender. The regiment of the King's Grenadiers in this affair lost 23 officers and 329 men. On the slope of the hill 10 officers lay dead.

Another act of valor recorded in the annals of German heroism, is the storming of the "Rote Berg" (Red Mountain) at the battle of Spichern, August 6th, 1870. General Frossard, the commander of the second French corps, who had deemed his position at Saarbrücken so perilous that he had notified the imperial headquarters of the fact, had retired with his corps upon the Spichern Heights on the fifth of August. The ninth division of Laveaucoupet threw up entrenchments and constructed rifle-pits on these heights and lined the Rote Berg with soldiers. Shortly after one o'clock, General von François, at the head of only five companies of the 74th regiment began to scale the mountain. As they advanced they were received by the infantry and artillery of the enemy with shot and shell. They reached the base of the mountain and tried to get a footing on the cliffs and crevices of the steep rock, appearing from a distance like hanging swallows.

To support the storming columns, the German batteries on the Galgenberg and the Folster Höhe quickly silenced the French guns on the Rote Berg, and compelled them to be withdrawn, the French leaving five guns between the German and French tirailleur lines.

At three o'clock in the afternoon General von Kamecke ordered a renewed assault of the Rote Berg. Without delay, General von François personally led the ninth, tenth, eleventh and twelfth companies of the 74th regiment up the steep and rocky heights. Climbing from terrace to terrace they gradually reached the summit. In a few minutes the outer entrenchments were gained, from which the French Chasseurs, evidently taken by surprise were driven after a brief resistance. With drawn sword the gallant general led his small body of Fusiliers towards the enemy. Pierced by five bullets he however sank to the ground and died with the words on his lips: "It is glorious to die on the field of battle! I gladly give my life, as I see that the fight is taking a favorable turn." Forward his brave Fusiliers could not go, backward they would not go. The arrival of strong supports of the enemy now became apparent.

General von Alvensleben having assumed the chief command during the progress of the battle could notice, looking upon the Rote Berg, only an extended line of sharpshooters, giving no sign of an advance movement; they were warriors who had already laid down their lives for their country. The third battalion of the 40th regiment now scaled the mountain; masses of the enemy threatened its flanks; the situation of the five companies required immediate action. The ammunition commenced to fall short, and only the exemplary behavior of the troops made it possible to hold the entrenchments on the crest of the hill previously taken. General von Alvensleben now ordered up the regiment of the Brunswick Hussars to take part in the fight. The regiment climbed the mountain, but could not deploy; nor could it effect a change and seemingly must now retire. At this juncture, General von Bülow asked permission to have some guns of the third light battery and the third heavy battery hauled up on the mountain, which was quickly accomplished, though with great loss and the utmost efforts of man and horse. The enemy was at last compelled to withdraw behind the entrenchments. As the division Laveaucoupet made a renewed and final attack on the Germans, it was repulsed by fresh Prussian troops breaking into the flanks of the enemy. The 74th regiment lost 36 officers and 661 men on that day.

At the battle of Vionville, August 16th, one of the bloodiest affairs not only of the late war, but of the century, on the German side five divisions of infantry and two divisions of cavalry, with 222 guns, coped with a superior opposing force of fifteen divisions of infantry and five divisions of cavalry, with 476 guns. To describe the heroic deeds of that memorable day would exceed the scope of this book. Infantry, cavalry, and artillery rivalled each other in acts of gallantry. The battle at first comprised a series of offensive movements by the Germans; afterwards it took the form of a defence of the German positions against a vastly superior enemy, which lasted twelve hours. The third army corps, under the command of General von Alvensleben, fought till noon with its main front against Metz, its rear

THE WERNER COMPANY, AKRON, O.

Kettle Drummer of the Regiment "Gardes du Corps."

against Paris, and gave battle to two French corps. The loss of the corps on that day was 310 officers and 6,641 men. The loss alone of the 52nd regiment attached to this corps was 18 officers and 345 men killed, and 32 officers and 1,202 men wounded. The casualties of the 3rd Westphalian regiment No. 16, also an integral part of the third army corps, was 49 officers and 1,736 men killed and wounded; the loss of the 24th regiment was 47 officers and 1,099 men; the gallant 11th regiment lost 41 officers and 1,119 men.

At four o'clock in the afternoon the brigade Wedell (the 57th and 16th regiments) took part in the battle, 20,000 Frenchmen opposing 4,700 Germans. The brigade advanced steadily, after having passed the burning village of Mars La Tour under a storm of shell and the fire of the mitrailleuses which calamitously reduced its ranks. The rear division thronged between the front one; after a run of from one hundred to one hundred and fifty paces the troops dropped on the ground, jumping up and rushing forward till they reached the edge of a ravine, fifty feet deep and separating them from the enemy. They ran down, traversed the ravine, and scaled the opposite banks, where they were met in mass by Grenier's battalions, and on the left flanks by those of Cissey. The five battalions could not withstand the murderous fire of two divisions. All mounted officers were laid low and the wounded and killed lay in heaps on the ground. The casualties, which included 72 officers killed and 2,542 men killed and wounded, speak well for the bravery of the Westphalians. The commander-in-chief of the German army, King William, passed this encomium upon the third army corps: "At every occasion," said his Majesty, "I shall deem and acknowledge the deeds achieved by the third army corps on the sixteenth of August as part of the most heroic exploits of warfare, General von Alvensleben and his corps having shown a spirit of sacrifice only possible when each individual soldier felt conscious of what was at stake on that day."

The following brief episode in the bloody engagement at Loigny, December 2nd, 1870, in which General Chanzy was defeated by the Duke of Mecklenburg, bears witness to the bravery shown by the Hanseatic regiments. Just as Captain von Marschalk of the third regiment of Uhlans (Brandenburg No. 3) had taken the advanced French batteries, and with them two mitrailleuses, an aide-de-camp of General von der Tann galloped up to General Tresckow asking for immediate support, as the enemy had already advanced six hundred paces toward the outer walls of Château Goury, where the Bavarian corps (von der Tann's) was being pressed very hard. Tresckow sent only three Hanseatic companies after the division Maurandy, which captured a farmstead and two guns, directing the main part of the brigade to support the Bavarians. Major-General von Kottwitz led the 76th Hamburg regiment and the two battalions of the 75th regiment (Lübeck-Bremen) towards Loigny.

As if on parade, with drums beating, colors flying, and the men hurrahing, the four battalions advanced upon Loigny. As they met the left wing of Bourdillon, his right wing at once fell back; some columns then faced the enemy and occupied the gravel-pits, but the first battalion of the Hamburg regiment drove them out at the point of the bayonet. The second battalion of the 76th regiment, and the second of the 75th, now entered Loigny. The other battalions, in conjunction with two Bavarian battalions, coming on a full run from Beauvilliers, took Fougeu at the first onset, where many French were made prisoners, and retained their position in spite of the deadly fire of shells and bullets. A hot fight raged at Loigny, the French offering a stubborn resistance. Only after repeated charges (the military band heading the troops) were the outskirts of the village taken. Soon the buildings caught fire, the spreading flames thus narrowing the scene of action. The troops now struggled, with butt and bayonet, to reach the centre of the enemy's position, and for a time it looked as if the Germans would have to succumb. At this moment, four Mecklenburg and one Bavarian battalions rushed forward from the southeast of Château Goury; and from three sides the Germans forced their way into Loigny. Only the cemetery, surrounded by a high wall, was stubbornly defended by the enemy. At dusk, the French General Sonis advanced with new reserves, among them the Papal Zouaves. At the point of the bayonet they stormed Loigny and carried some parts of the place. The danger for the brave Germans now became imminent. At that moment General von Tresckow made a forward movement with his entire reserves, two battalions of the 75th regiment going round the southern part of the village in the direction of Fougeu. Lieutenant Colonel von Böhn, with eight companies of the 75th, 76th, and 89th regiments, broke in on the left flank of the advancing hostile masses, forcing the French to retreat, with a loss of 1,100 officers and men. Twenty officers and 2,500 men were taken prisoners; the French also lost 1 standard, 8 guns, 1 mitrailleuse, and 7 wagons of ammunition. The cemetery was surrounded and taken by assault.

That the German infantry is not to be daunted by any obstacle, however great, is proved by the midnight assault of the tenth army corps in the battle of Le Mans, January 11th, 1871. Its commander, General Voigts-Rhetz, had received orders to advance on the night of the eleventh on the Mulsanne-Vendôme high road and to effect the junction of his fourteenth brigade of cavalry with the third corps on the highway at Parigné. Since January 6th, the tenth army corps had been continually beset by obstacles; divisions of the enemy, which like themselves were eager to reach Le Mans, threatening its left flanks. The 92nd regiment of Brunswickers, together with the 17th regiment, had dispersed the enemy at Le Tertre and Les Roches and had taken 80 prisoners. This former corps had distinguished itself on the tenth of December while acting as advance guard for the tenth corps at Beaugency. In the fight of Vendôme,

Regiment of Hussars — Body-Guards.

December 14th, the Fusilier battalion of the Brunswickers, aided by two companies of the 17th regiment, took the village of Orgue. On the sixteenth instant the fifth company of the 92nd regiment, by a well-directed fire at La Tuilerie, compelled the enemy to abandon eight of their guns; the tenth battalion of Jäger attacked near Courtriras a wagon-train, driving back the cavalry and a battalion of infantry which protected the column; it captured 63 of the wagons, with one mitrailleuse, and a wagon of ammunition, and took 100 prisoners. The advanced guard (the Brunswick regiment), three squadrons and one battery, repulsed at Rouillé the eighth regiment of the Garde-Mobile, the latter losing 230 prisoners. On January 9th, at L'Homme, the first and second battalions of the 36th regiment succeeded in driving the enemy back over the Brive creek; one battalion of the Brunswickers and the tenth battalion of rifles repulsed the French and drove them into the woods of Bersay, with a loss of 50 prisoners. Five battalions of the 79th and 92nd regiments chased the French out of St. Vincent-de-Lorouer taking 5 officers and 100 men prisoners. On the eleventh, the flanks of the tenth corps were also endangered, Ecommoy not having been taken. The twentieth division advanced on the great highway, protected on the right by the tenth battalion of rifles and the first battalion of the Brunswickers. At Mulsanne the roar of the guns in the direction of Le Mans was distinctly heard, which moved General von Voigts-Rhetz at once to attack the enemy in front with the greatest possible force, and to effect thereby a junction with the third army corps, in action at Le Mans. Like the glacis of a fortification the ground over which the troops had to march rises to the heights of Les Morts-Aures, thus affording no shelter for the advancing force. A French battery, posted across the road, enfiladed the German advance, while masked lines of rifles covered the ridge. The 17th regiment and the Brunswick Fusiliers however scaled the heights, and the first battalion of the 53rd regiment finished the fight at the point of the bayonet. Once more the defenders tried to regain the lost position, but they were received by a terrific rifle-fire, many hundred Frenchmen being made prisoners. The heights of Les Épinettes, thickly lined with riflepits and masked guns, are however not taken yet. Major von Erichsen decided on a surprise of the enemy by a midnight attack. In carrying out his project the troops silently advanced; no rifleman, no sharpshooter, uttered a sound. The long line rolled on at two o'clock in the early morning towards the summit of the hill; a far away sounding hurrah was heard — the signal that the Germans were victorious. The assault made by the tenth corps under the darkness of midnight upon an unusual strong position of the enemy, could only be made by splendidly trained, veteran troops, which were able to find cover at night, barred to them by daylight. The capture of the strong bastion on the right of the position brought about the decisive result of the next day (January 12th).

Just as bravely as the Prussian regiments of the line fought the infantry of the allied troops (those of the Bavarian, Saxon, Würtemberg, and Baden contingents). Already at Weissenburg and Wörth the Bavarians had rivalled their North-German brethren-in-arms by deeds of bravery and had given ample proof of their heroism. Preparatory to the decisive battle at Sedan, General von der Tann, the commander of the first Bavarian army corps, had been ordered to occupy Bazeilles, for the purpose of preventing the departure of the French forces. At four o'clock in the morning the Bavarians with hurrahs entered the village, held by a brigade of marine infantry of the twelfth corps, and were received with a tremendous fire. The street fighting lasted for six hours. By seven o'clock not half of the town was taken, the fighting in some places, for instance around the Villa Beurmann, being especially fierce. The French batteries and mitrailleuses, posted north of Bazeilles, poured a hail of projectiles on the Germans. The gallant Bavarians having been forced to abandon the southern part of Bazeilles, three fresh battalions of the fourth brigade arrived and drove the enemy back upon the heights in the direction of Balan. At last an entrance was gained to the Villa Beurmann by three battalions of the 10th regiment and parts of the 13th and the defenders were captured. A little after ten o'clock Bazeilles fell into the hands of the Bavarian army corps. After its occupation by the first and fourth brigade the fight was continued for a while only by the artillery, till the third division made its appearance under orders to press forward on the bottom lands of the valley towards Balan and the adjoining heights. The Bavarian battalions, supported by the first Bavarian brigade, had to retreat before the renewed efforts of the French to break through. While the French did not succeed in their design to reach beyond Balan, the Bavarians at five o'clock in the afternoon pluckily regained the town. About half-past five, the firing ceased. The Bavarian corps camped on the blood-stained ground, after having been continually under fire for three days, and having lost 121 officers and about 2,000 men. To-day only a simple monument on the road to Villa Beurmann reminds one of the gallantry shown by the Bavarians on the first of September, 1870. The short epitaph reads: "Here rest 500 brave Bavarians." Of the second Bavarian corps, situate south of Sedan, with orders to protect the "Great Bavarian Battery" stationed between Frenois and Vadelincourt, the third division suffered the considerable loss of 87 officers and 1,829 men.

The regiments of the line of the Saxon (twelfth) army corps took a praiseworthy part in the battles of the Franco-German War. The timely action of this corps on August 18th resulted in the capture of St. Privat, as has been mentioned. As a contingent of the Army of the Meuse, commanded by the Crown Prince Albert of Saxony, the twelfth army corps rendered eminent services at the battle of Sedan (September 1st, 1870). At half-past three o'clock in the morning of that day the corps had taken up position at Douzy and at five o'clock an advanced guard of the twenty-fourth division of infantry had been despatched in the direction of La Moncelle, which place was occupied an hour later with the intention of obstructing the enemy in its retreat upon Mézières. The opposing forces were the right wing of the first French corps (Ducrot) and the twelfth corps (Lebrun), which were stationed between La Moncelle and Bazeilles. La Moncelle was taken after a short engagement by the 107th regiment. At 6:30 A. M. the 105th regiment joined in the fray. At this time the two French divisions of Lartigun and Lacratelle pressed against the eastern banks of the Givonne at Daigny. Dense swarms of tirailleurs and a few batteries of mitrailleuses broke through the village and forced the Saxon batteries to make a temporary retreat.

The now advancing battalion of Jäger however drove the enemy back by a well-directed and rapid fire, and the thirteenth battalion of Jäger attacked the left flank of the enemy. The latter captured two mitrailleuses and one gun, whilst the sixth and seventh companies of the 107th regiment took two guns from the enemy. On the right wing of the artillery line, now consisting of thirteen batteries, the 104th regiment arrived about eight o'clock, attacking Daigny, together with parts of the 105th and 107th regiments and the battalion of Jäger. In a hard fight with the Zouaves and Turkos, a Turko standard was captured. On the left wing of the Saxon battle line the forty-sixth brigade of infantry also took part in the battle, arriving at nine o'clock at Bazeilles. The enemy made repeated feints, but were driven back upon the heights of Balan. On the arrival of two additional battalions of sharpshooters the whole lowlands were taken by ten o'clock.

At eight o'clock in the morning the Crown Prince Albert had given orders to the twelfth army corps, after capturing a section of the Givonne, to advance across Illy to the heights near Givonne, to surround, with the corps of the Guards, the enemy, so as to prevent their escape into Belgian territory. This task was assigned to the twenty-third division of the twelfth army corps, the sixth company of which succeeded in capturing two guns. When the division marched up towards Daigny, the battalions and batteries of the enemy moved out and pushed on in solid ranks towards the Givonne Valley. Here a terrible struggle ensued in the narrow space which environs Daigny, Haybes, and Fond-de-Givonne. The Saxon Grenadiers advanced up to Fond-de-Givonne, though they could not hold it permanently.

Previous to this, the first company of the Body-Grenadiers, led by First-Lieutenant Kirchhof, had stormed a small entrenchment west of Haybes, defended by two mitrailleuses and some infantry. The movement toward the North, which had already begun, was abandoned, the French gradually retreating into Sedan. At four o'clock in the afternoon the Saxon corps, together with the forty-fifth infantry brigade and eleven batteries, gained positions to the west of Haybes and Daigny; the forty-sixth pressed forward to Givonne and the twenty-fourth division to Daigny. At half-past four the struggle commenced anew on the Saxon front. The last effort of the French to break through between Balan and Bazeilles was frustrated by the forty-fifth infantry brigade, supported by the Saxon batteries and by some of the Guards.

Only at sunset did the twenty-third division encamp at Givonne and the twenty-fourth at Daigny, forming a junction with the fourth corps. The Saxon corps sustained a loss of 62 officers and 1,365 men, and bore a glorious part in the decisive battle. The French loss included 2,000 men made prisoners of war, besides eleven guns and one standard.

The battle of Villiers-Champigny, fought on the thirtieth of November and the second of December, testifies to the bravery shown by the Würtemberg infantry. According to news received November 29th, a sortie of the Paris army in a southerly or southeasterly direction was contemplated. The commander of the Army of the Meuse had therefore received orders to support with all necessary force the Würtembergers, occupying the line of Villiers-Coeuilly-Champigny. At dawn on the thirtieth of November the Saxons had relieved the pickets of the Würtembergers to the north of Champigny. The main part of the latter rested at Villiers and at Coeuilly. Under a deafening cannonade the divisions of Faron and Malroy of the first French corps, after having crossed the Marne together with the second corps, and having on their left wing the divisions Berthaut and Maussion of the second corps, advanced towards Champigny. The Saxon pickets thereupon fell back upon Villiers, and the French gained at ten o'clock the crest of the plateau of the town. The division Faron having reached Champigny at dawn, the Saxon pickets had to fall back upon the Hunting-Lodge. While the French scaled the slopes of Coeuilly, the Würtembergers moved forward to the Hunting-Lodge with the utmost speed, occupying it and the entrenchments at Coeuilly and also the splendid fortifications of Villiers. Under a destructive fire the French were driven back from this position. General Ducrot, commander-in-chief, now threw his troops upon the park of Villiers. They rushed onward with great gallantry only to be received with a terrific shower of bullets, and to be driven back upon the protecting slopes of the plateau, with a loss of 500 dead and wounded, including two regimental commanders. Simultaneously with this movement, Berthaut's division failed in an attack on the south end of the park and were repulsed by the Würtembergers with a loss of 400 dead and wounded. The Germans at this time received the support of two companies and a battery, sent by General von Obernitz, commander of the Würtemberg division. Further enforced by four companies of Saxon infantry the Würtembergers stormed the heights known as No. 100; but they were compelled to fall back upon Villiers with a heavy loss. The Saxons alone lost all their officers and half of their men. The batteries of the French division Faron had by this time arrived at the heights of the Hunting-Lodge, east of Champigny, when shortly after twelve o'clock the general attack by the Würtembergers was made, under orders from General von Reitzenstein. After having forced the French artillery to retreat, the troops were caught by a terrible fire from the French chassepots. Colonel von Berger here fell, mortally wounded. After having advanced with great bravery up to within one hundred and fifty meters of the enemy, the Würtembergers had themselves to retreat to Coeuilly. Frightfully reduced though they were, they succeeded in reaching the park there which they occupied with the utmost expedition and so prevented the entrance of the French infantry.

The assault of the Hunting-Lodge by three Würtemberg companies met with better success. The assailing troops soon ousted the French, who fled towards Champigny. A staff-officer of the Würtemberg brigade, being present, noticed the perilous position of the troops fighting at Coeuilly; at his request the Würtemberg companies wheeled about to the right and attacked the French at Coeuilly on the flanks. At this moment the Saxon batteries appeared to the south of Villiers. The French, unable to resist the shock, fell to the rear with a loss of more than 2,000 men. At two o'clock a renewed onslaught was made upon Villiers by the French division Maussion and by the division Berthaut on the neighboring quarries, both however being repulsed by the Saxons and the Würtembergers.

The division Bellemare of the third French corps, after having effected a passage over the Marne, advanced to Brie. The Saxons, threatened in their rear, at three o'clock withdrew from their positions on the heights of Brie-Villiers, and retreated towards the cemetery, north of Villiers. To hinder the French from breaking through, the Saxon artillery moved at four o'clock on the plateau between Noisy and Villiers. At dusk the division Bellemare scaled the slopes of Brie, designing to attack Villiers. A heavy fire by the Saxon and Würtemberg artillery, however, frustrated the last French effort. All attempts to storm Villiers finally came to naught, with a loss of over 600 men. The infantry of the enemy advancing at four o'clock upon the railroad embankment, was also repulsed by the artillery and by the Saxon and Würtemberg companies engaged there. The loss was very heavy, that of the Germans being 66 officers and 1,627 men; the loss of the French exceeded 4,000 men. The day was, nevertheless, a glorious one for the Würtembergers, 10,000 Germans having coped with 70,000 French.

The contests of the second day of December were of a like character with those of the thirtieth of November. The Würtemberg brigade, occupying Villiers and the Hunting-Lodge, entered Champigny at seven o'clock in the morning, taking many prisoners. The rout of the French toward Joinville occasioned great disorder and almost a panic; it was stopped only by the resolute action of General Ducrot, who finally succeeded in infusing into the masses of his retreating soldiery some sign of order and arousing the division Faron to a more successful resistance at a ravine close to Champigny.

With like success some Würtemberg companies reached the neighborhood of Bois-de-la-Lande, but were repulsed by superior forces of the enemy. In the further course of the fray the Saxons, fighting with great gallantry at Brie, suffered such heavy losses that General von Franseky was induced to draw nearer the three divisions and the artillery of the second corps. The Würtembergers, having fought since dawn at Champigny, marched to Coeuilly, where they were relieved by the infantry of the second corps. The second Würtemberg brigade arrived at Chennevriers in the afternoon.

Three companies of the fifth Würtemberg regiment and the third Würtemberg battalion of Jäger, frustrated the same afternoon the efforts of the French to scale the walls of the park at Villiers. The 1st Würtemberg regiment lost in two days 23 officers and 580 men; the second Würtemberg battalion of Jäger lost 17 officers and 253 men; the 7th Würtemberg regiment lost 19 officers and 413 men. The Germans won the second fight, with a sacrifice of 156 officers and 3,373 men, dead and wounded. The French loss was 426 officers and 9,053 men. On the second of December 30,000 Germans repulsed 90,000 French.

On December 18th (1870) the Baden regiments of infantry fought with a death-defying gallantry in the engagement at Nuits. On the sixteenth of the month, General von Werder had been ordered to protect the railroad lines in the rear by occupying the region of Nuits-sur-Armançon and Sémur. As the enemy once more showed activity south of Dijon, General Werder directed General von Glümer again to take the field. The latter had been recently wounded but was now restored. He took command of the Baden division and proceeded with it in the direction of Dijon, while Werder transferred his depôt or base lines to the right bank of the Saône. Glümer left Dijon on the eighteenth with the first and second Baden brigades, seven squadrons, and six batteries, and moved southward upon different roads. Werder himself kept with the principal column, marching through Saulon-La-Rue and Epernay. Already at the Vouge creek small detachments of the enemy appeared, which, however, were quickly dispersed by the regiment of Body-Grenadiers forming the advanced guard. In front of Boncourt, east of Nuits, more stubborn resistance was encountered. The French General, Crémer, had occupied Nuits and Boncourt, and his batteries were posted on the steep heights west of Nuits. During the engagement the remainder of his division arrived by rail, aggregating about 10,000 men. Shortly after noon on the same day Colonel Baron von Wechmar stormed Boncourt with a battalion of Fusiliers. The French who defended the place escaped towards the farmstead of La Berchère; this, later on, was also taken by the second battalion and two companies of Fusiliers. The six batteries of the Baden artillery were fully occupied in driving the dense masses of hostile sharpshooters from the vicinity of the railroad embankment. After a while, the bulk of the troops having arrived, Glümer ordered the

Cavalry Patrol. 16th Regiment of Dragoons (Hanoverian No. 2).

first and second battalions of the 2nd regiment to advance in line of battle on the right, the battalion of Fusiliers being posted on the left. Glümer then extended the right wing by sending out two companies of the 3rd regiment, while five squadrons of dragoons meanwhile flanked the left wing of the enemy near Quincey. A general assault was now ordered by General Glümer, in which the General and Prince William of Baden were wounded. Werder now assumed the command, Colonel von Renz taking the place of Prince William. Von Renz, himself however fell pierced by three bullets, while his aide-de-camp also was killed. Baron von Gemmingen, the commander of the 3rd regiment of dragoons, also received a mortal wound.

The infantry advanced 1,500 paces down the sloping banks of the Meuzin creek, each soldier leaping his way down the descent, some 50 paces at a time, and after a momentary halt pushing on again. The last 400 paces were covered at a run. The cut itself, and, later on, the defence behind the long wall on the east side of the depôt were taken after a terrible hand-to-hand fight. At four o'clock the enemy retreated in disorder to Nuits. The Fusiliers of the 2nd regiment then advanced against the southern part of the town, but only with the supporting fire of two batteries could they enter the place, which was finally given up by the defenders at five o'clock. Another column of Baden troops having arrived on the highway, it dashed into the town at the same moment; a third column took Vosne, to the north of Nuits; a fourth tried in vain to storm the heights of Chaux, to the west of Nuits, which were occupied by Crémer's batteries. The Badeners rested at Nuits, encamping in the public square. Several hundred rifles and much ammunition were found in the town. The French suffered the loss of 16 officers and 1,700 men, among whom were 650 prisoners not wounded. The loss of the Germans amounted to 18 officers, 211 men killed, and 37 officers and 656 men wounded; 18 men were missing. The total German casualties were 55 officers and 885 men.

The history of the late war abounds in like heroic deeds, for almost every regiment had the opportunity by honorable distinction to gain the gratitude and love of the entire German nation.

Our illustrations represent Prussian regiments of infantry in parade uniform as well as in full marching order. The Würtembergers who formerly differed in their dress by the double-breasted tunic, are now known only by slight differences in the helmet. Another picture represents the Bavarian infantry, distinguished by the light-blue color of their uniform and by some characteristics of the helmet. The Saxon infantry is known by the red-striped binding round the tunic and by the coat of arms on the helmet. Since 1860, the first twelve infantry regiments of the line bear the designation of Grenadiers. As a characteristic mark, they bear on the breast of the eagle affixed to the helmet a small oval shield with the entwined initials F. W. R. and wear on parade black horse-hair plumes in the helmet. This mark of distinction can be traced far back in history

to these regiments, since they are the oldest troops of the line, and were created at the reorganization, in 1808, out of the old regiments which then in part went out of existence.

Besides these regiments four other regiments of the Prussian Guards (Emperor Alexander, Emperor Franz, Queen Elisabeth, and Queen Augusta) bear the name of Grenadier regiments. The first and second battalions of the Foot-Guards and of the just named regiments of infantry Nos. 1 to 12 are designated battalions of Grenadiers and wear white leather belts and straps. The remaining infantry wear black leather belts and straps. The name Grenadier regiments is also common to the two Saxon regiments, Nos. 100 and 101; to two Würtemberg regiments, Nos. 119 and 123; to two Baden regiments Nos. 109 and 110; and to one Mecklenburg regiment, No. 89.

There are in the German army thirteen regiments of Fusiliers and one of equal rank (Royal Saxon), the regiment of Schützen (sharpshooters). In Prussia Frederick I formerly had a guard of Fusiliers; Frederick the Great created, in 1773, five regiments of Fusiliers; in 1808 every Prussian regiment received a battalion of Fusiliers, each of which was especially trained to fight in skirmishing lines. This special service however fell into disuse, but the name "Fusiliers" was retained for the third battalion, these wearing black leather belts and straps. By an imperial decree, of January, 1889, the white leather belts and straps of the infantry were abolished, except in the case of the aforenamed battalions of the four regiments of Foot-Guards and the twelve regiments of Grenadiers. Since then only the third battalion of the aforenamed regiments are called "Fusiliers."

The above mentioned Saxon regiment of Schützen (sharpshooters), which bears the regular number of 108, is the only infantry regiment wearing a green uniform and a shako. An identical uniform, but with white buttons, is common to the Saxon battalion of Jäger (rifles). In the German army the word "Schützen" is synonymous with "Jäger." The formation of special regiments, battalions, and companies of Schützen—in existence at the first half of the century—is not any longer customary in the Prussian army, only the battalion of the Guards-Schützen (rifles) retaining the above name. The Saxon regiment of Schützen is an élite body, recruited from superior social material. The horse-hair plume, fastened to the left side of the shako, is not a parade ornament, but a part of the regular uniform. The shako is usually provided with a black cover. The Jäger can trace back the history of their organization to the year 1740. At that time Frederick the Great established a detachment of 60 men, consisting of trained foresters; in 1795 a regiment of Jäger was formed, of which a part was taken prisoners of war at Lübeck in 1806. At present the Prussian foresters serve with the battalions of Jäger, the latter receiving by the above regulation splendid recruiting material and a good corps of noncommissioned officers. The Prussian battalions

Saxon Horse-Guards.

of Jäger, together with the battalion of Guards-Jäger and Guards-Schützen are fourteen in number, and are distributed unequally among the different army corps. Like the infantry they are equipped and trained under the same rules of drill and exercise with the gun. In regard to marksmanship more is required of these troops. Bavaria has two battalions of Jäger, Saxony has three, and Mecklenburg one battalion; but all of them contain fewer foresters in their ranks than do the Prussian battalions.

THE GERMAN CAVALRY

IN THE infantry the armed foot-soldier represents the combatant; the cavalryman is only equal to his task when he is in the saddle. The great expense incurred in supplying and maintaining the mounts, necessarily limits the cavalry of any army to a fraction of the whole. The tasks of the cavalry in war time are various and manifold; among these are the reconnoitring of the enemy's position, guarding against surprise by the enemy, establishing and maintaining all army communications, and, finally, entering the battlefield in solid array with the purpose of crushing the hostile forces. A matter of the utmost importance is the reconnoissance, which falls to the duty of the cavalry. This branch of the service is rightly called "the eyes of the army." Its mission is to veil the army's movements from the enemy, while at the same time reporting those of the latter, and this with the utmost speed and certainty. Special attention is paid to the training of the German cavalryman in such a manner that he learns to observe and report his observations quickly and accurately. The responsibility of larger reconnoitring parties will, in almost every instance, be borne by an officer; but cavalry patrols, consisting of only one noncommissioned officer and a few privates, have proven equal to the most difficult tasks. The late war demonstrated that the German cavalryman not only knows how to ride, but that he possesses the qualities of resoluteness, coolness, courage bordering on rashness, adroitness, cleverness, and the proper spirit of self-denial.

As an instance of this, reference may be made to the bold reconnoitring expedition made by Count Zeppelin, an officer of the Württemberg general staff, in company with three Baden officers of the 2nd regiment of Dragoons, Winsloe, Baron von Wechmar, Baron von Villiers, and three privates. It was undertaken from the advance guard near Hagenbach, in Alsace, in the direction of Hagenau and Niederbronn. On July 24th the little band galloped, swinging their sabres with hurrahs, first through Lauterburg, the border-town of Alsace, situated near the Rhine. At Neuweiler, half a mile southeast of the former place, they encountered a French patrol, consisting of a gendarme and a lancer, who at once opened fire. The gendarme, missing his aim, was taken prisoner but was

afterwards released; the lancer, after having wounded Zeppelin's horse, was put *hors de combat*. They found the Selzbach, about three-quarters of a mile to the south, thinly lined with cavalry. Turning, therefore, to the westward, and approaching the town of Hundsbach, one and a quarter miles south of Weissenburg, they cut the telegraph wires connecting Hagenau with Strasburg. The riders then reached the watering-place of Niederbronn, north of Reichshofen, occupied by Chasseurs of the 12th regiment. Sabre in hand they galloped at full speed through the place and passed the night at the Scheuerlenhof, a farmstead south of Reichshofen. The clergyman of Niederbronn having informed General Bernis, commander of a brigade belonging to Failly's corps and consisting of the 5th regiment of Hussars and the 12th regiment of Chasseurs, of the raid, the French surrounded the farmstead while the German riders were at breakfast. Wechmar, looking after the horses, was the first to espy the enemy; the others rushed into the yard, where a short but fierce fray ensued. Wechmar dropped a French noncommissioned officer, and another French lieutenant received two revolver bullets. Winsloe, however, was laid low, while Wechmar was wounded in the side; Villiers was injured in the nose, and he and Wechmar were taken prisoners, together with the dragoons. Zeppelin alone, dragging a horse along which he had captured from an officer, cut his way through the enemy. Followed by the French chasseurs, he galloped at a furious pace towards the frontier, where he was welcomed with cheers by the exultant Germans. The pluck of the little band impressed Marshal Leboef so forcibly that he invited the two captive officers to dine with him and treated them with the utmost courtesy. Winsloe, unfortunately, died of the wounds received during the fight.

To discover the strength of the troops garrisoned at Bitsch, Lieutenant von Münchhausen, of the 13th regiment of Schleswig-Holstein Dragoons, crossed the frontier at night with a platoon of horse and posted them in the adjoining woods. At the same time he stationed a private on the top of a hill overlooking the surrounding country, from which he was enabled to observe the French camp and the principal gateway of the fortress. Wearing a waterproof cloak and cap, he himself stole through the not overwatchful French pickets. Penetrating the camp, he put on his helmet and called out at the top of his voice: "Long live his Majesty, the king of Prussia!" Wheeling about, he saluted in a scornful way and rode off mocking the amazed crowd, but unharmed by the numerous chassepot bullets that came whistling after him. By the discharge of the rifles the whole camp became alarmed; at the same time a number of troops and a battery marched out of the fortress. In this way the private was enabled to give a fair estimate of the garrison's strength. He informed his daring lieutenant of having seen more troops gathered there than at any autumn manœuvre. Hence they must have numbered about 20,000 men, the corps being that of General Failly.

On August 7th, 1870, the third squadron of the second Body-Hussars No. 2, under Captain von Zastrow, advanced along the highway of Nancy-Strasburg in pursuit of the French army, defeated at Wörth. At this moment a small cavalry patrol was ordered to reconnoitre the country on the right side of the highway. The little troop trotted gaily along, between hills clad with wood and vine, and reached the village of Buchsweiler. The place seemed to be occupied by large detachments of the enemy; nevertheless, the patrol made their exit from the town at a point guarded by two sentinels, whom they made prisoners. The leader of the patrol sent the captives under escort of a hussar back to the squadron riding in the rear. Not being satisfied with this *coup de main*, the leader dashed, with his hussars brandishing their sabres, back into the town, which was now densely filled with soldiers. Reaching the public square, our daring riders rushed upon some infantry, gathered in panic-stricken groups, which sought shelter in the houses. A speedy retreat became a matter of necessity, the enemy rallying upon their front and also firing from the houses. But as quickly as the troopers had arrived, as quickly they disappeared before the eyes of the dumbfounded French, having secured valuable information for their captain.

On December 11th, 1870, the 1st Hanoverian regiment of Uhlans sent from Courville a patrol, consisting of an officer, a noncommissioned officer, and four uhlans, with the purpose of reconnoitring Le Mans and its suburbs. The patrol rode through Champront, leaving the highway to the right. Having been fired upon by franctireurs in the woods, they turned about and reached Nogent-le-Rotron, La Ferté-Bernard, and arrived at Conneray, close to Le Mans. Coming in contact with the enemy's pickets, they ascertained that about 15,000 soldiers of the Garde-Mobile were in position before Le Mans. The patrol, after having rested for a time at Le Ferté-Bernard to feed their horses, returned by a circuitous road in order to evade the enemy, and safely reached its regiment. They had been in the saddle from half-past six in the morning till three o'clock on the following morning, and had covered during these nineteen hours twenty-three German or ninety-three English miles.

On the morning of November 24th, 1870, the 6th regiment of Cuirassiers despatched from Neuville-aux-Bois, near Orleans, a patrol of ten horse on a reconnoitring expedition towards Châteaudun. They were ordered to draw close to the latter town and, if possible, to enter it. The patrol, though fired upon at every village which it passed, rode along without taking any notice, according to their instructions. The bridge over the Loire, situated on the highway, they discovered was held by a strong detachment of the enemy. The patrol therefore forded the stream south of Châteaudun and reached the town proper. It was crowded with regular troops, besides some of the Garde-Mobile and franctireurs, also with some artillery and cavalry. Returning, the patrol found the passage over the Loire again blocked, compelling them once more to cross the stream. The next village to be passed was held by many franctireurs, whose fire inflicted on the patrol a loss of four men and five horses. To rest the fagged animals and exhausted men, the night of the 24th–25th of November was passed in the adjacent woods. At dawn of the next day the remnant of the patrol once more rode close up to the outskirts of Châteaudun, again gathering valuable information about the enemy, and returned to their regiment at noon of the following day.

These examples, selected from a number of similar exploits performed by German troopers, illustrate the great difficulty and risk of reconnoitring, the duty of which, as we have said, falls upon the cavalry. For this particular service special formations of " Meldereiter " (troopers carrying information) also named " Mounted Jäger " are employed, according to a recent imperial decree. They are independent mounted detachments, composed of specially trained men of superior physique and intelligence. Such detachments of " Meldereiter," comprising four officers, twelve noncommissioned officers and ninety-six men, are, as yet, to be found with only a few army corps; though they are henceforth to be established in all imperial army corps and developed into a special branch of service. They are to be recruited independently, the troopers being liable to a service of three years. Each detachment is to consist of 800 horse.

In open battle, either in an engagement with infantry and artillery or with horse, the cavalry is employed in larger or smaller force, according to circumstances. As a general thing, it may be asserted that a charge of cavalry against well-disciplined intact infantry has little or no chance. The chances of success would be better in an attack made on artillery or on infantry having fallen into disorder. In the late war the French cavalry met with only very slight success, in spite of its most heroic efforts.

At the battle of Wörth, August 6th, 1870, McMahon ordered the cuirassier regiments of the brigade Michel and Nansouty's regiment of Lancers to attack the advancing infantry of the eleventh army corps (Hessian-Nassau-Thuringian). With a death-defying spirit the regiments led the charge: in the first line of the attacking columns were the cuirassiers, in rear of whom were the lancers. The tremendous shock was directed against parts of the 32nd and 80th regiments of the eleventh corps, and the pioneers of the same corps. Without forming any squares the infantry received the assailing French cavalry indiscriminately. The effect of the steady well-directed, and rapid fire was terrific. The three French regiments were annihilated in short order, without having reached the infantry line at all.

In much the same way, on the 1st of September, 1870, at the battle of Sedan, the stupendous cavalry charges, thrice made by the divisions of Gallifet and Margueritte at Floing, were foiled by the steadfastness of the opposing German troops. When the division Liébert commenced to waver, Ducrot summoned General Margueritte to make an assault with his cavalry division in the direction of Floing. Margueritte having been mortally wounded while reconnoitring in the neighborhood, General Gallifet took command of the horse, the troopers calling out at the top of their voices: "Go ahead! revenge the General!" The 1st regiment of Chasseurs d'Afrique, without waiting for further orders, dashed madly upon the German lines. Gallifet, with a farewell to his officers, put himself at the head of the 3rd and 4th regiments of Chasseurs d'Afrique, followed by the brigade Tilliard (the 1st regiment of Hussars and the 6th of Chasseurs d'Afrique), the brigade Lavaresse (the 1st and 7th regiments of Lancers), and also by several other squadrons of cavalry. A hurricane of riders, 4,000 in number, swept down the slope towards Floing, only to sacrifice themselves as they did at Wörth. Before they reached the German lines, they fell into disorder; rifle bullets and shell crashed into their ranks, throwing the riders into confusion; but they wildly dashed upon a battery of eight guns. The men who served the pieces defended themselves with their side-arms and sponges. The fifth company of the Weimar regiment, under Captain von Schellenbühel, repulsed the riders by its rapid fire. Attacked in the rear by the cuirassiers, the company faced about and drove them back. The skirmishing lines of the Hessians and Nassauers were broken through at some points, but the companies in the rear dispersed the bulk of the French horse with well-directed volleys, many falling down the steep heights to destruction in the stone-quarries. Two squadrons of cuirassiers broke through the Prussian infantry lines and charged two squadrons of the 18th Hussars. Major von Griesheim faced them with two platoons and attacked them with the other platoons on their right flank; they then fled towards Floing, where the remainder were either captured or killed. As badly fared the lancers in their attack on the 83rd regiment; they overran the skirmishing lines, but succumbed to the rapid fire of the infantry at a distance of thirty paces. Other squadrons were annihilated by the fire of the 46th regiment and the fifth battalion of Jäger.

The second cavalry charge was directed against the same troops as those attacked by the first. Three companies of Jäger, having just scaled the heights near Floing, a squadron of cuirassiers dashed upon their left wing and also on the 46th regiment, and were followed by several squadrons of chasseurs. The cuirassiers were almost swept off the field, while the chasseurs fled to the left. A troop of French hussars found themselves opposed in their advance by some German infantry; they then wheeled round the left wing, but the German rifles, turning about checked their further progress; and in a moment most of the hussars succumbed, the remainder escaping towards the lowlands.

Before the third attack, Gallifet remonstrating with Ducrot against the unavailing sacrifice of the riders, the latter replied: "Sacrifice the horse by all means for the honor of our arms!" "Well then," answered Gallifet, "we shall charge as long as a rider is left," and off he dashed with his men. But before they could reach the front, their ranks were broken by the fire of two German batteries, which, reaching the summit of the hill, poured their shells into the flanks of the advancing French riders. In the ensuing turmoil man and horse fell in a blood-weltering mass; the remainder escaped into the Garenne woods and on towards Cazal. In the three charges the French lost 83 officers and 709 men; the generals Girard and Tilliars were also killed. King William, who closely watched the fight, exclaimed: "Alas, the brave men!" as he observed the repeated, but fruitless, attacks of the French troopers.

The feat, however, in which the French cavalry had failed, both at Wörth and at Sedan, was accomplished at Vionville, on August 16th, 1870, by the death-defying valor and self-sacrificing spirit of the German cavalry. The German infantry, the strength of which had been reduced to a minimum by incessant assaults made by vastly superior French forces, and lasting for hours, was at Vionville at the point of succumbing. The cavalry, under General von Bredow, at this juncture received orders to ride down the French. "You must break through at the woods, General!" were the instructions delivered by Colonel von Voigts-Rhetz. General von Bredow replied: "I shall break through the infantry at the woods?" "Certainly," was the reply: "We have already taken the village and cannot draw close to the woods; the fate of the battle depends on your cleaning up everything that yet stands along the road. You must attack, and that most energetically!" General von Bredow looked at his riders and at the route to be taken; he knew that only a few of his brave men would return. Into two orders of battle his columns were formed: in the first were three squadrons of the Magdeburg regiment of Cuirassiers, led by Count von Schmettow, on the left wing along the border of the woods; and in the second were three squadrons of the Altmärkische regiment of Uhlans No. 16, led by Major von Dollen, on the right wing, one hundred paces to the rear; the gallant Bredow with his staff keeping about in line with the cuirassiers.

24th Regiment of Dragoons — Body-Guards (Hessian No. 2).

With loud hurrahs the six squadrons started on a trot, wheeling about to the left in the valley. Traversing the slope they deployed to the right. After having reached the plateau, they rode at breakneck speed against the batteries of Tixier and those of the sixth corps, and against the division of Lafont de Villiers. They received on the left the chassepot fire of Tixier's infantry and that of the 9th regiment; in front they had to face shell and shrapnel. Of the first battery only two pieces had time to limber up, but before this happened the cuirassiers fell upon them like a hurricane. Ahead of all was Schmettow, with Lieutenant Craignish of Campbell at his side, and a noncommissioned officer. Schmettow unhorsed the French major, while Campbell and the sergeant put another officer *hors de combat*. In the battery everything was laid low; the "wild hunt" dashed against the infantry of Lonnay's brigade, formed in two columns, on the side of which was a battery. The cuirassiers rode down the front column, breaking through their fire; the uhlans closing up, the battery was captured and everything that did not take to flight was cut to pieces. The second line of the French was now attacked. Here, after an advance of three thousand paces, the small body of horse was surrounded on all sides, first by the division Forton and the division Valabrêgue breaking forth from an opening in the woods. Two squadrons of the French cuirassiers (the 10th) fell upon the rear of Schmettow's riders, the 7th Cuirassiers fell on their flanks, the brigade Murat of the Dragoons threw themselves in front, followed by Valabrêgue's Chasseurs and Hussars, 3,100 horse against 800 of the six squadrons.

The exhausted riders had now to cut their way back. After rally had been sounded, General von Bredow retreated a short distance to the valley of Rezonville, then wheeled about to the right. Schmettow's aide-de-camp fell from his horse wounded, one trumpeter was shot down, Captain von Heister was unhorsed after receiving thirteen wounds. Campbell tried to wrest a standard from the French cuirassiers and was rescued only by the most heroic efforts of his men. Count von Kalckreuth received fifteen wounds, Major von Dollen was unhorsed and taken prisoner, while Captain Mayer of the cuirassiers was killed. The brigade, however, forced its way back through the batteries previously ridden down, and through the columns of infantry which followed them up and fired several volleys into them. Unpursued by the enemy, however, they arrived beyond Vionville. The wounded and unhorsed riders, and those detained by the exhaustion of their horses, had to surrender. Schmettow ordered the first trumpeter whom he met to sound the regimental signal. The trumpet was found to be pierced by a bullet, and its sound was like that of a dirge, penetrating to the very marrow of the bones. Of eleven platoons of cuirassiers only three could be mustered, consisting of seven officers

and seventy men, and six officers and eighty men of the uhlans. Later on it was ascertained that the Cuirassiers had lost 7 officers, 189 men and 209 horses, the Uhlans lost 9 officers, 174 men and 200 horses; of the total force of 800 men, 363 were left dead or wounded, officers included. The sacrifice of the gallant band of heroes had, however, not been made in vain, a breathing spell having been accorded to the almost exhausted Brandenburg infantry.

Another successful charge of the German cavalry on the French infantry was effected in the afternoon of the same day. Again the situation of the German army had become a critical one after the onset of the brigade Wedell, and again it fell to the lot of the cavalry to bring relief. At six o'clock General von Brandenburg and General von Rheinbaben received orders to make a reckless charge. Colonel von Auerswald, accompanied by Count von Brandenburg, led forth three squadrons of the first Dragoon-Guards, going at a trot to attack the right flank of the French. In the face of the enemy's galling fire, Auerswald rushed upon the 13th regiment of Grenier's brigade Bellecourt, the Dragoons breaking through and riding down a part of the French infantry. A terrible pell-mell ensued around the eagles, and from all sides the projectiles crashed into the dragoons; but the 57th regiment (brigade Wedell) effected its retreat over the highway, the enemy's infantry being compelled to countermarch through the ravine. Of the Dragoon-Guards, who rallied in the rear of the batteries, five out of thirteen officers were killed, the remainder being wounded, while 125 men and 220 horses were disabled. Here many of the Prussian nobility, worthy of their ancestors, laid down their lives: Colonel von Auerswald, who, though mortally wounded and compelled to surrender his command to Captain the Prince Hohenzollern, cheered the King. Major von Kleist, Captain the Count Westarp, Prince Henry XVII of Reuss, Count von Wesdehlen, one Schwerin, one Flemming, and the two brothers von Tresckow, were among the slain.

In the meantime, the second regiment of Chasseurs d'Afrique attacked, from the north, the left flank of mounted Guards' battery, protected in front by the fourth squadron of the Dragoon-Guards. Captain von Hindenburg of the Guards faced the four squadrons of the enemy; of his 140 men 67 were laid low, Hindenburg being one of them; but the battery was saved, and could proceed to Mars-la-Tour. The Dragoon-Guards were relieved by the 13th (Schleswig-Holstein) regiment of Dragoons, commanded by Colonel Count Finkenstein. The Chasseurs d'Afrique were repulsed and pursued to the heights of Ville sur Yron.

There now appeared on the open ridge of Ville sur Yron a large force of French cavalry. Ladmirault led forth the Chasseurs d'Afrique of Du Bareil's division, the cavalry division Legrand and the brigade Garde de

At the Riding Hall. Flying Jump. 13th Regiment of Uhlans (1st Royal Hanoverian Uhlans).

France upon the plateau stretching towards the Yron creek. He wheeled about to the left and then advanced to the right in four compact masses overlapping each other, the brigade of Montagu's Hussars forming the van. On the German side the cavalry forces drawn up between Trouville and Puxieux started to give battle: in front were the 13th (Schleswig-Holstein) Dragoons under Major von Trotha, followed by the fourth squadron of the second Dragoon-Guards. They drew somewhat to the right and wheeled about half to the left towards Montagu's brigade of Hussars. In the rear Barby's brigade appeared, wheeling to the left around Mars-la-Tour, followed by the 4th Westphalian Cuirassiers, the 13th Hanoverian Uhlans, and the 19th Oldenburg Dragoons; in the second rear column were the 16th Hanoverian Dragoons and the 10th Magdeburg Hussars.

As the 3,000 German horsemen, after having reached the heights north of Mars-la-Tour, sighted the enemy, they broke forth in triumphal cheers: "There they are, there they are!" they cried. The Schleswig-Holstein Dragoons, waiting majestically for the charge of Montagu's brigade of Hussars, delivered fire and dashed upon the enemy, sabre in hand and with deafening cheers. A terrible conflict ensued, the small horses of the French being run over by the heavy German steeds. The French succeeded in breaking through, only to be received and cut to pieces by the Magdeburg Hussars. General von Montagu was taken prisoner. The squadrons separated; wheeling about, the Dragoons also took part in the attack. General Legrand now rushed forward with the French Dragoons; the first squadron of the Oldenburg Dragoons fell upon them, most of them being unhorsed, as only sixty riders kept their saddles. But the French shock was checked; a furious hand-to-hand encounter took place. General Legrand's riders were cut to pieces by the Oldenburgers; the Hanoverian Dragoons also closing up, the Germans were victorious. On from the extreme left swept the 13th Uhlans and fell on the flank of the Empress' Dragoons, the fifth squadron of the second Dragoon-Guards moving against them from another quarter. Colonel von Schack, the leader of the Hanoverian Uhlans, rode deep into the ranks of the enemy, where he fell. The bulk of the Chasseurs d'Afrique rushed upon the Hanoverian Uhlans, but at this moment the Westphalian Cuirassiers broke into the Chasseurs in a wedge-shaped mass, the Hanoverian Dragoons also attacked them on flank and rear. The earth trembled under the stamping of the 6,000 horse, man fought against man with long sword, sabre, carbine, and revolver. Not long did the furious mêlée last; the enemy's horsemen extricating themselves, first one by one, then in squads, and soon the whole mass escaped, disappearing like a huge cloud of dust in a northerly direction, pursued by the German riders to the woods of Bruville. The trumpets sounded the rally, the

field was cleared of the enemy. The regiments drew up and returned to Mars-la-Tour, later on to Puxieux. The Schleswig-Holstein Dragoons covered the retreat, followed at a considerable distance by Clérembault's French troopers. Of the second Dragoon-Guards, Count Finkenstein had fallen; Colonel von Schack of the Hanoverian Uhlans was killed in the battle, and his body was not recovered for some time. The Oldenburgers lost 13 officers and 104 men.

The German cavalryman, being armed with a carbine, and trained to its use, is at the same time qualified for the duties of a foot-soldier. He is thoroughly drilled in the use of firearms and well versed in the duties of the tirailleur and picket service. The cavalry carbine, model '88, now also known as rifle '91, is somewhat shorter and lighter than the infantry rifle of '88, with a sight adjusted to 1,317 yards; otherwise it has the construction and calibre of the infantry rifle, and uses the same ammunition. In light warfare it is the duty of the German cavalry to seize and carry off outposts of the enemy by surprise; to destroy telegraph lines in the enemy's country; to blow up viaducts and bridges; and to do the foraging. For the purpose of destroying telegraph and railroad connections the German cavalry is provided with the necessary tools and explosives. But not alone is it their duty to wreck the means of intercourse in a hostile country, but it is also their duty to reconstruct, where necessary, telegraph lines and erect new and temporary bridges. Of much moment is the laying of telegraph lines, performed by detachments of cavalry in the open field. Several riders provided with coils of wire gallop ahead, followed by others carrying the necessary material, including insulators. Stopping every hundred yards, a lance is thrust in the ground and the wire is fastened thereon. As a matter of course, trees, stakes, and the like, if near by, serve the same purpose. This is continued till the whole work is done, and that within a very short time. The construction of a temporary bridge also takes surprisingly little time; it is accomplished by laying across the stream a sawn wood trestle, or in an emergency by the throwing across of two lances, or by the laying down of hollow cylinders of tin or aluminium. The cavalry does not need these bridges, as, under favorable circumstances, it merely crosses the streams by swimming the horses, even in the case of large detachments. Drills on an extensive scale for training man and horse for this feat take place annually at all the depots of cavalry regiments.

The German cavalry is distinguished as Cuirassiers, Uhlans, Hussars, and Dragoons. While the existence of these various classes of the fighting service cannot be called an absolute necessity, especially since the drill, tactics, and employment of the different regiments in war have become uniform, historical tradition and difference in the uniforms favor and justify the retention of this classification. The principle of unity in the cavalry is absolutely followed in the German army and is exemplified by their arms, of a uniform pattern, consisting of the lance, with a small flag showing the provincial colors, the carbine, sabre, and long sword—the heavy straight sabre of the cuirassiers. The lance having been introduced as the uniform thrusting-weapon in the entire German cavalry, Major-General von Specht, a prominent military author, comments upon it as follows:

"With the lance of the Roman legionary the side of the crucified Christ was pierced. In commemoration of this the Holy Lance of Longinus was incorporated with the consecrated arms, and the Roman Catholic Church celebrates the festival of the arms of Christ—*festum armorum Christi*.

"This weapon is a primeval one. Armed with the spear of pointed wood, provided by progressive skillfulness with a point of sharpened horn, bone, or flint, the man of the stone-age went forth to kill the game for his sustenance, or to ward off animals of prey. With the bronze-headed spear the Persians and Greeks fought at Marathon, and provided with an iron point was the *hasta* and the later *lancea*, besides the sword, the main weapon of the Roman armies. Under the clash of the lances the Visigoths chose their king on the battlefield; while to the Franks the 'King's Lance' was the symbol of sovereignty; the Holy Lance with the imperial sword being the coronation insignia of Charles the Great.

"Since the time of Alexander the Great's lancers 'Sarisophores,' the lance was pre-eminently the weapon of the cavalry; it was used by the knights at the tournaments, those warlike games of times of peace, and on the battlefield; especially was it used by the knightly crusaders, the retinue of each being termed so many 'lances.' It remained the chief weapon throughout the Middle Ages in the pike of the foot-soldier (Pikeniers) and in the spear of the Spear-riders (Spiessers) and Kyrissers (Cuirassiers).

"With the decay of chivalry and the introduction of firearms, the lance disappeared from the army. Gustavus Adolphus banished it from the Swedish cavalry, his example being followed by most of the European Powers. With the Slavs, however, as with the Cossacks, it continued to be the national weapon, the Polish cavalry showing great prowess and skill in its use. After their model, Frederick the Great created his 'Bosniaks,' Napoleon I his Lancers; in Austria the Uhlans were instituted and their numbers gradually increased. But by the continual improvement of firearms, by the steady increase of infantry, and their efficiency and usefulness in battle, the employment of cavalry in actual fighting and its power of attack seemed greatly reduced. The necessity of the cavalry being provided with an accurate-firing weapon was so fully demonstrated that the value of the side-arm relatively dwindled into insignificance, though the Uhlan had gained fame by his menacing lance during the Franco-German war of 1870-71.

"But, on Emperor William II ascending the throne, a thorough innovation took place. Being himself a splendid cavalryman, he recognized the importance of the lance as the 'queen' of weapons, and in 1889 the equipment of the entire cavalry with the lance, previously used only by the Uhlans, was ordered. Unchanged in its measurement,—the wooden shaft buried a thousand years in the remains of the pile-workers was about ten feet long,—the German lance now weighs three pounds nine ounces, with a length of ten feet five inches. Originally made of wood,—the Austrian weapon was of ash, and the French of kings' bamboo from Tonkin,—the German lance is now a tube, made of rolled steel-plate. The weapon carries below its head a small flag, showing the provincial colors, and is adorned with an eagle, as the distinction of the noncommissioned officers. Thus the lance represents the uniform weapon of the German cavalry, its superiority over other weapons being acknowledged by some and disputed by others.

"The advantage of the lance in single combat and in the pursuit of an enemy, either on foot or on horseback, is undoubtedly great, and the shock of a forest of lances, striking in appearance, seems to be irresistible. It is, however, claimed that the excitement of man and horse completely excludes in the rider a correct judgment and proper command of the situation; that the man riding at full speed is liable to miss his aim, and, fearing to be unhorsed, is unable to thrust with the necessary force. Furthermore, it is asserted that the rider thrusts less, but awaits the onset,—the wounds to be inflicted proving less serious,—and thus the importance and effectiveness of the lance is greatly overestimated. For close combat, following the inroad of the enemy, the lance is deemed to be too long and cumbersome. Too much is required of the muscles; too much is expected of the agility and training of man and horse, which are absolutely necessary for a successful handling of the weapon; finally, it is claimed that the load which the horse has to carry—the man being armed with carbine, sabre, and lance—is excessive. The question of lightening the horse's load is now in a fair way to be solved, improvements having been made from time to time to effect a lightening. On the other side of the argument, it is insisted that the tax put upon rider and horse has proven a blessing. The high value bestowed upon the exercise with the lance and expressed by presenting those men who excel in the drill with special marks of distinction, has brought the training of the horseman in power, agility, and control of the horse to the goal of perfection, assuring the German cavalry a future of glorious results. This efficiency is the consequence of a training at once thorough, unceasing, and practical.

"The lance-shaft, which has at the upper end a four-edged point 12.9 inches long and made of well-tempered steel, is also pointed at the butt-end, so that, at close combat, thrusts can be made to the rear as well as to the front, without the necessity of reversing the lance. When the rider is mounting or dismounting during a halt, the butt-end of the lance is thrust in the ground. Mounted, the lance rests in the socket, fastened to the stirrup. On parade, at reviews, and at the command 'attention!' the lance is held with the right hand in a vertical position; on the march it hangs in the lance-knot on the right arm at the command 'lances on arms!' During drill and in active service the lance is seized by the middle of the shaft, and carried by the hand held upon the right thigh in such a manner that the head-end, slightly slanting, rests near the horse's ear, while the butt-end points downward to the rear. This is the mode in which the weapon is held at the command 'lances on thigh!' From this position, at the command 'lower the lance to the charge!' the head is brought to a level, the butt-end is adjusted to the arm and pressed upon the body, while the right hand grasps the lance by the centre of the shaft back of the ring. The lance retains this position when the horseman rides at a rapid gait towards a stationary or an advancing object,—when he thrusts at a full run. In the thrust to front, rear, and side, and towards the ground, the hand pushes forward the lance, which hangs on the arm, strongly and with a burrowing motion.

"After thorough preparatory exercises on foot, calculated to strengthen the muscles of the arm, and daily repeated during the entire service of the cavalryman, the training on horseback commences. This is so systematically increased, that the horseman, riding at full gallop, can strike any stationary or advancing object with never-failing skill, and is able, at the same time, to cope successfully with two or more adversaries, either on horse or on foot, and armed with lance, sword, and bayonet. Thus the lance, handled every day easily and playfully, becomes a terrible weapon, giving the rider such self-confidence that nothing appears to him unattainable or irresistible. This was the main point considered at the introduction of the lance as the weapon of the entire German cavalry. The chief functions of the cavalry in time of war, besides the protection of its own army and the reconnoissance of the enemy, also include the task of clearing the field of the enemy's cavalry. The fight with the hostile cavalry is the first duty of this arm of the service; the superior leading of the army, due to an effective reconnoissance, is the final result. 'Without such first duty there can be no after-result.' Bereft of the cavalry, the hostile army is a 'blind lion,' unfit for any offensive movements.

"In the encounter of cavalry with cavalry the weight of the clash is, however, the main issue. For the shock, the lance is without doubt the superior weapon. Convinced of the superior power of thrusting, and morally raised to the point of invincibility, the wall of riders, bristling with lances and rushing on like a torrent, will be indeed irresistible. The after-thrusts made in pursuit of the enemy, will be felt by their deadly effects. The cavalry, thus having fulfilled its strategical task, will also, when tactically employed in the battle, and possessing the maximum of physical and moral power, achieve the highest points. The lance will prove to be the real weapon of the battlefield, whose thrusts a prostrate enemy, though out of reach of the sabre, cannot escape.

"In view of these facts, the importance of the lance begins to dawn upon European armies, and the apprehension of the superiority of the German cavalry has risen to such a degree, that the reinstatement of the lance and the increase of lancer regiments are now actually in progress. But the weapon alone is not the deciding point. Its effectiveness depends on the hand which wields it and the spirit which controls the arm. Emperor William has been instrumental in reviving and fostering the old martial spirit of the cavalry. To put it on its own feet, fit for all strategical tasks, and render it independent of the infantry, it has been provided with a good firearm—an excellent carbine. To equip it for the highest deeds of valor on the battlefield, the Emperor has supplied the cavalry with the best thrusting-weapon

—the lance; at the same time infusing into this branch of the service a confidence and enthusiasm for the weapon that in the future will insure the best results. This enthusiasm the German cavalry will retain as long as it preserves the energetic equestrian spirit and adheres to the saying of the old field-marshal, Wrangel: 'Every day is lost to a cavalryman, on which he does not drill or exercise with horse and weapon.'"

According to the lighter and heavier material of horse and men, and for the purpose of easier training and greater efficiency of the different regiments in war time, they are distinguished as *heavy* and *light* cavalry. Out of the typical mediæval knight, heavily armed with a coat of mail, armlets, and greaves, the cuirassier of to-day has developed. Of the former iron-armor only a comparatively light cuirass is left, useless against modern weapons, the penetrating force of which has been brought to such a high state of perfection; the modern cuirass serves only for parade purposes. In the Seven Years' War the Seydlitz regiment of Cuirassiers, at the head of which was General von Seydlitz, won special distinction for their brilliant charges against the French and Russians at the battles of Rossbach and Zorndorf. The German army has ten regiments of Prussian Cuirassiers, including the regiment Gardes du Corps, and the regiment of Cuirassier-Guards. To the same class belong the two regiments of Bavarian "Heavy Riders," the Saxon Horse-Guards, and the Saxon Carabiniers; making a total of fourteen heavy regiments.

Apart from the Saxon and Bavarian regiments, the white or blue jerkins of leather with colored collars, the white leather trousers, high riding-boots, and heavy steel cuirassier helmet are common to the cuirassiers. The regiment Gardes du Corps deserves special notice. A Garde du Corps was in existence under the first Prussian king, Frederick I, but it was disbanded by his economical successor. Frederick the Great revived the corps in 1740, making it one squadron strong. To-day the regiment has five squadrons, like the rest. It is stationed at Potsdam, and is recruited from choice material of both men and horses, the latter being chestnut in color. It has the proud distinction of having the King of Prussia for its honorary colonel, who is also honorary captain of the first squadron, hence called the body-squadron.

Another picture shows the Cuirassier of the 7th (Magdeburg) regiment of Seydlitz, which, together with the 16th (Altmärkische) Uhlans, at the battle of Vionville–Mars-la-Tour lost more than half of its men while riding into the very jaws of death on that ever memorable day. The late imperial chancellor, Prince Bismarck, was the honorary colonel of the regiment since the twenty-seventh of January, 1894, the twenty-fifth military jubilee of the present Emperor, William II, and it was the uniform of this regiment that he always preferred. Still another picture represents a soldier of the Saxon Horse-Guards. Especially striking is the well-fitting light-blue tunic

After G. Arnould

THE WERNER COMPANY, AKRON, O.

COPYRIGHT 1899 BY THE WERNER COMPANY.

Exercise with the Lance.   7th Regiment of Cuirassiers "von Seydlitz" (Magdeburg).

with broad white braiding.

The Horse-Guards belong to the oldest troops, their history reaching back to the year 1680. The present name "Gardereiter" was conferred upon them in the year 1822. The other Saxon heavy cavalry regiment, previously mentioned, is called "Carabiniers." The uniform has the color of the cornflower; while the facings of the Horse-Guards are white, those of the Carabiniers are black.

Though the cuirassiers originated in the heavily armed riders of the Middle Ages, the uhlans and hussars are to be traced back to the national light troopers of Poland and Hungary. Until recently, the uhlans alone carried the lance as a characteristic weapon, now common to all mounted troops. Besides the lance, the uhlans wear the traditional uniform, reminding one of the Polish national dress and consisting of the "ulanka," "chapka," and the overcoat, and, in place of the shoulder-straps, epaulets. In Prussia, Frederick the Great first instituted a regiment of uhlans in the year 1741; which, however, not having proved itself worthy in the face of the enemy, was transformed into a regiment of hussars in 1742. In the year of 1808 two Prussian regiments of uhlans were formed. At present the German army has twenty-five regiments of uhlans. Prussia has three regiments of Uhlan-Guards and of the line the regiments 1st to 16th (see picture), Bavaria owns two regiments, Saxony the 17th and 18th regiments, and Württemberg the 19th and 20th regiments.

In the late war, the French soldiers and country people stood aghast at the uhlans. With surprising quickness their patrols appeared here and there, always unexpectedly; the cry "les ulans, les ulans," was sufficient to strike terror everywhere.

Poland being the abode of the uhlans, Hungary may rightly be called the native seat of the hussars. We find the first Prussian hussars during Frederick William's time, in the year 1721. At that period a troop of thirty hussars was attached to a regiment of uhlans. Frederick the Great raised the hussars to high rank as riders and organized nine regiments. Well known in folklore are the heroic exploits of the Zietenhussars, which regiment shared in nearly all the pitched battles of the Silesian and Seven Years' wars. The third Prussian Hussars of to-day bear the name "Zietenhussars." At present, the German army has twenty regiments of hussars; the Prussian contingent has a regiment of Body-Hussars, also the regiments 1st to 16th, and the 17th regiment of Brunswick Hussars. Saxony owns the 18th and 19th regiments of Hussars, the other contingents having none. The traditional uniform and equipment of the hussars include the braided tunic and busby or fur cap, tightly-fitting trousers, and a sabretasche. On the front of the cap is a ribbon on which is the star of the guards or a monogram. The first and second Body-Hussars and the 17th regiment of Brunswick Hussars wear, as a special distinction, a skull as a traditional sign of this regiment giving no quarter. On the picture we see a soldier of the first Body-Hussars with the skull. The black hussars were called by the French, who dreaded them on account of their great boldness, "*Hussards de la mort.*"

The dragoons are descendants of the arkebusiers, who often fought on foot, and on some occasions acted as mounted infantry. These troops existed as early as the time of the Great Elector, the name of "Old Derflinger" being closely associated with the history of that branch; but not until the time of Frederick the Great were the dragoons considered cavalrymen in the proper sense of the word. The German army has in all twenty-eight regiments of dragoons, of which the following belong to the Prussian contingent: two bodies of Dragoon-Guards and the regiments 1st to 16th; the 17th and 18th (Mecklenburg) regiments; the 19th (Oldenburg) regiment; the 20th, 21st, and 22nd (Baden) regiments; and the 23rd and 24th (Hessian) regiments. Württemberg has the 25th and 26th regiments; Saxony has no dragoons; Bavaria has six regiments of Chevaulegers, perfectly conforming to the above regiments of dragoons. The name "Chevaulegers" is derived from the French of the time of Henry IV, designating light cavalry equipped with firearms. During Napoleon's time the higher princes of the Rhenish Confederation conferred the French name upon their light cavalry regiments, which has been retained and officially used by Bavaria. Characteristic of the dragoons are the helmet and blue tunic of the infantry. The different regiments are distinguished by the color upon their collars and cuffs. An illustration in the book depicts the Hessian dragoons, another depicts the Hanoverian dragoons, distinguished by the small flag on the lance, showing the provincial colors.

THE GERMAN ARTILLERY

The third of the chief branches of the army's service is the artillery. Equipped with cannon, it forms, with the other two branches, the infantry and cavalry, the main combatant force of the army. The artillery is clothed similarly with the infantry, with this distinction, however, that the helmet is surmounted by a ball instead of a spike. The collar and cuffs of the tunic are black, the shoulder-straps are red and bear the number of the regiment. The artillery is classified into manœuvring and garrison corps, according to its employment, either to fight closely associated with other troops and in positions subject to change, or independently in positions of a stable or stationary character. The manœuvring-artillery is employed chiefly in field operations, and is, for this reason, called field-artillery. As stated under the organization of the army, it is armed with a field-gun of a uniform pattern, made of improved cast steel, with steel-plate caissons. The gun is of 3.56 in. calibre and

Captain. 1st Regiment of Hussars — Body-Guards.

fires a shrapnel shell and canister shot (case shot). The field-artillery brigades consist each of two regiments; the eleventh, twelfth, and second Bavarian brigades, however, consist each of three regiments. The regiments comprise from three to four mounted divisions (Abteilungen), each of two to three batteries; while twenty-two regiments have each one division of horse-artillery. The total strength of the field-artillery is 173 divisions, formed into 43 regiments, with 447 mounted batteries and 47 horse-batteries. The single batteries vary on a peace-footing. Some are drawn by four, others by six horses; a certain number have two ammunition wagons. There are in time of peace 2,542 guns and 97 ammunition wagons. Prussia furnishes 346 mounted batteries and 38 horse-batteries, formed into 2 regiments of the Guards and 31 regiments of the line. The Guards artillery is distinguished by its yellow braiding and by the eagle peculiar to the Guards affixed to the helmet. The horse-hair plumes worn by these troops on parade are white, while those of the horse-artillery are black. Bavaria has 48 mounted batteries, and 6 horse-batteries; the horse-hair plumes of the latter are red. The Saxon artillery consists of 30 mounted batteries and 3 horse-batteries, forming 3 regiments. As may be seen in the illustrations, the Saxon artillery wear a green uniform with red facings. This equipment, only to be found in the Saxon contingent, was introduced in the year 1714, and is retained up to the present time, regardless of changes made in the cut of the uniform and in the style of the head-dress. Würtemberg furnishes 2 regiments of mounted field-artillery, divided into 23 batteries. The changes made in the organization and composition of the field-artillery, and going into effect on October 1st, 1899, are treated upon in the supplementary article by Major-General von Specht.

In the late war the German field-artillery decided many of the pitched battles, not only by its superior material, but by its great accuracy of aim, efficient service, and masterly handling. Of this, the battle of Gravelotte furnishes a vivid and convincing illustration.

The ninth German corps, which ushered in the battle, occupied Verneville on the forenoon of the eighteenth of August. This corps, consisting of twenty-three battalions, with about 21,000 men, was opposed by at least 50,000 French, with 162 guns. The French troops occupied strong positions, and were supported by Canrobert's batteries posted at St. Privat. The Germans deployed east of Verneville and opened the battle with a heavy artillery fire. The first shells fell short, the following, however, found their range in the midst of the enemy's camp. The latter, visibly surprised, hurried to the fortified positions and rifle-pits, all the heights being lined with batteries in a short time. As, by this manœuvre, the distance became too great for the German gunners, General von Puttkammer ordered ten batteries

to draw up closer to the enemy. The latter replied furiously, the French riflemen at the same time inflicting a heavy loss on the Prussian artillery. At one o'clock two Hessian batteries of the advance-guard, stationed south of Habonville, took part against Canrobert's guns, which were posted south of St. Privat. After the arrival of three additional foot-batteries, the Hessian artillery moved towards a ridge east of Habonville, while eight batteries of the Guards, 48 pieces strong, took position north of Habonville. Repeatedly the French battalions of Grennier and Cissey sallied forth against the Hessian division commanded by Prince Louis of Hesse, and were repulsed only with the greatest difficulty. The situation of the Hessian troops, who suffered terribly and were almost unable to replenish their ammunition, became more and more critical. Their left wing, especially, was exposed to a galling fire from some French mitrailleuses. The four Hessian foot-batteries which were in action at this period of the engagement sustained the loss of several officers, and 5 chief gunners and 40 men were put *hors de combat*. At this moment, the French infantry rushed upon the Hessian artillery. The captain of one of the batteries, though badly wounded, succeeded in bringing two of his pieces to the border of the woods, where they were saved only by the heroic efforts of some Hessian troops which had just arrived. Four guns, however, were lost, two of which were subsequently taken to Metz by the French. Although the chief danger to the batteries was averted by the brilliant charge of the fusilier battalion of the 85th regiment, which lost 12 officers and 400 men in the action, Lieutenant-Colonel Darapsky ordered the artillery, which by this time had suffered increased losses, to withdraw to the rear of La Cusse woods. The order was executed with the utmost coolness. One of the batteries, while limbering up, was riddled with case shot, killing the captain and wounding many men, but it continued firing on the enemy while it withdrew. The artillery lost, in about three hours, 17 officers, 2 surgeons, 187 men, and 370 horses. Three batteries of the Hessian division did not leave the scene of action, but stood their ground, the French making no further sally in this direction.

While the action described was going on, a heavy artillery fight was raging on the right wing of the first army. At noon, General von Steinmetz ordered all the guns to enter the duel with the seventh French corps. Four batteries of the fourteenth division, under General von Zastrow, drew up between the woods of Ogeon and Gravelotte, and opened fire on the French positions at Point du Jour. From two o'clock onward the artillery, coming from the direction of Ars, fell into line of battle. General von Steinmetz and his staff kept near these batteries in the heaviest fire of the enemy, who poured a hail of shell and mitrailleuse bullets upon the Prussian guns, inflicting a heavy loss, especially on their left wing.

But the French also suffered heavily; caissons were demolished and ammunition wagons were blown up. The Germans soon received support from three batteries of the third division, while four batteries of the fifteenth division also drew nearer the scene of action by order of General von Goeben. They took position between Malmaison and Gravelotte and were followed by the remainder of the corps artillery. The battle now took such a grave turn that some higher commanders, among them General von Hindersin, the inspecting General of artillery, directed the operations personally. The French commenced to lose ground. Some of their mitrailleuses became so disabled that they had to be removed to the rear. At the same time the enemy by mistake fired upon its own hospital, which lay between Malmaison and Gravelotte, where several hundred French and German soldiers, who had been wounded at the battle of Vionville, met a horrible death by the French fire.

In the storming of St. Hubert, which followed shortly afterwards, the field-artillery and horse-artillery took a praiseworthy part. The batteries of the eighth corps advanced over the road of Jarny; five of them drew up on a hill-top near Mogadore. The horse-battery of the first cavalry division took the lead, joined on its right wing by two foot-batteries. Three additional horse-batteries rode through Gravelotte and took up favorable positions south of the highway. Soon it became evident that the concerted fire of the Germans silenced some of the French guns, and prevented others from getting into position. All efforts were now concentrated against the enemy's position at St. Hubert. Though the advanced German horse-battery fared badly from the fire of some mitrailleuses, the artillery of the seventh corps pressed through the ravine of Ars, and formed a junction with the eighth corps. The effect of the combined German fire now commenced to tell. French batteries were forced to retreat and their fire gradually became fainter. The German shells burst into the reserves standing back of Point du Jour, which soon had to be given up by the defending troops. St. Hubert was gradually reached by the guns of the eighth corps. The well-defended place was stormed by detachments of the 33rd, 60th, and 67th regiments, and the Rhenish rifles, in face of a tremendous fire and with a terrible loss.

While these events were happening, a success was gained by the artillery on the left wing of the second army which opposed St. Privat. General von Pape ordered the artillery of the first division of the Guards to take position south of Habonville with its front toward St. Privat. Supported by some artillery which had just arrived, sixty guns were trained upon the French artillery, which by this time had made a forward movement, compelling the latter to fall back upon its former position. After the arrival of the twenty-fourth division, a general assault was made upon Ste. Marie, which contained many massive buildings surrounded by high walls. Three batteries of the twenty-fourth division took position northwest of the Guards, while the bulk of the artillery wheeled round west of the ravine leading to Auboué. Three batteries of the twenty-third division deployed to the left of the twenty-fourth division's firing line. By this manœuvre 180 guns formed one solid line firing from the woods of La Cusse upon Canrobert's and Cissey's batteries at Ste. Marie. The German fire was so effective that the latter places soon were able to be stormed by nine battalions of the Guards, of the forty-seventh brigade and of the 108th regiment. During this assault the Guards artillery moved to the southeast of Ste. Marie, while shortly afterwards the Saxon batteries advanced on the west side of Ste. Marie, and formed a long line, with its front facing the east. Their united fire was far superior to that of the opposing sixth corps and told on the enemy in a destructive manner. The right wing of the German artillery, however, suffered greatly by the fire of the enemy holding the farmstead of Champenois, and General von Manstein ordered an attack to be made on the latter. To accomplish this, a Hessian horse-battery took position to the south of the farmstead, and was shortly afterwards supported by some guns of the third and ninth army corps. The Guards also closing up with the Hessian battery, a fire of fifty-nine guns was directed against Champenois, which was in a short time in flames. The German batteries lost heavily as they advanced, and the infantry was at this juncture ordered into action. The first battalion of the 2nd regiment rushed forward, while a Brandenburg battery pressed on in the tirailleur fire of the enemy. With hurrahs the infantry attacked the burning farmstead and routed the enemy, who offered a stubborn resistance. By this brilliant charge the artillery line was made secure. Seventy-eight guns covered with their fire the territory stretching from the Genivaux woods to the Bois de la Cusse, and silenced the enemy's fire on this part of the battle line. The energetic co-operation of the artillery at the capture of St. Privat has been mentioned under the chapter on "The Storming of the Prussian Guards upon St. Privat."

The surrounding and capture of the army of Châlons, which was achieved by the German third army, in connection with the army of the Meuse, at Sedan on September 1st, 1870, was chiefly due to the efficient service of the German field-artillery. Lebrun's batteries, numbering some 160 guns and mitrailleuses, had taken position on the heights of La Moncelles rising to the north of Bazeilles. Their right wing directed a heavy fire on the Bavarian troops, which advanced under great difficulty (see under Infantry "The Bavarians at Bazeilles"). Whilst a hot fight was raging, a Saxon battery arrived and took position to the northeast of Moncelles. The

Bavarian batteries, thus supported, engaged a vastly superior force of French artillery. Somewhat later, Prince George of Saxony ordered the entire artillery of the twelfth corps to advance beyond Douzy. By this manœuvre twelve batteries were brought into action east of Moncelles, thus securing a good foothold to the Bavarian infantry which took Bazeilles after a stubborn resistance. At noon the last two batteries of the twelfth corps passed through Moncelles and drove back some French guns posted before Balan. It happened about this time that some shells had burst close to where the Emperor Napoleon and his staff had taken their positions, near Balan. Seeing a brigade suffering terribly from the fire of the Germans, Napoleon asked: "From what place do these shells come?" An artillery officer replied that they came from a battery posted at a distance of 4,900 metres. The Emperor, unwilling to believe in so terrible an effect at that distance, immediately ordered a strong fire to be directed against the batteries at Wadelincourt. The shots, however, fell short at a distance of 1,500 metres, dropping in the river Meuse.

General von Wimpffen, after having taken the chief command of the French army, in place of the wounded General McMahon, endeavored in vain to break through the German lines, first to the east and afterwards to the north at Givonne. At nine o'clock in the morning, three batteries of the first division of the Guards took up position at the woods of Villers-Cernay and were joined by a fourth deploying at the Chevalier woods. These batteries were augmented by some artillery of the first corps, which fired with great havoc at a distance of 4,000 paces upon the French infantry, cavalry, and artillery stationed in the woods of Givonne. The German firing line was also reënforced by four foot-batteries of the second division and some horse-artillery of the first corps, which took position to the north of the Chevalier woods. Ninety guns threw their shells upon the batteries, earthworks, and troops of the enemy, while on the left twelve Bavarian and ninety Saxon guns came into action. By noon all passages over the Givonne river were in the hands of the Germans, who prevented Wimpffen's escape here as well as at Mézières. To the southwest, at Bazeilles, the German guns also covered by their fire the fortress of Sedan. Two batteries were posted near the railroad south of Vilette; one was trained upon Torcy, five lined the heights of Frenois, while two commanded the territory south of Wadelincourt.

At this juncture it fell to the lot of the German artillery to cut off the enemy's retreat towards the north at St. Menges, Fleigneux, and Illy. This task was assigned to the fifth and eleventh corps, which crossed the river Meuse at Donchery and marched towards Menges by order of the Crown Prince. Three batteries of the fifth corps took position on the slope to the northwest of the Hattois woods, where they engaged a superior force of French artillery posted on the slope, stretching from Illy towards Floing. After several guns had been disabled, General von Gersdorf ordered the entire corps artillery into action. In a short time eighty-three guns crowned the long plateau opposite the Hattois woods. One of the German batteries suffered such a loss that a reserve of men and horses had to be brought up. But soon the German artillery received support from the fire of two horse-batteries stationed on the left bank of the river Meuse. The artillery of the fifth corps and of the tenth division also took part in the battle, deploying on the heights between Illy and Fleigneux, and forming a junction with the left wing of the eleventh corps. One hundred and thirty-two guns crowned the heights stretching from Illy to the Ardennes woods. The noise of this great outstretched line of artillery rumbled like that of a heavy thunderstorm, sending forth flash upon flash, while the German shells prevented all means of escape to the enemy. Meantime the havoc was appalling, the enemy's artillery being almost annihilated. The only chance of escape for the French army was towards Mézières, but this was barred by the Würtemberg division, which covered the rear of the third army at Mézières.

The iron circle around the French army was thus closed successfully, and became tighter as the day passed. On the heights to the right of Moncelles-Balan, the artillery of the eighth division took up position and trained its guns on the French massed in front of Fonde-de-Givonne. Six Bavarian batteries here united their fire with the Prussians against the heights of Balan. The fire of the fifth corps was directed against Calvary hill, which lay towards Fleigneux and was held by Ducrot with a strong force of artillery. The French guns were, in consequence, dismounted and deprived of their men and horses, ammunition wagons exploded, and even the reserve batteries were compelled to retreat. Of the artillery of the Guards, ten batteries deployed on the left bank of the Givonne, joined by five additional batteries on the left wing, also by seven Saxon and two Bavarian batteries, so that from that direction 144 German guns hurled their shell into the Garenne woods, which was defended by 120 guns of the first French corps. The artillery of the second Bavarian corps and that of the fourth corps joined in this operation against the Garenne woods. From all sides death and destruction faced the enemy, which was now being pressed together closer and closer, with no chance of escape. To make the situation more intolerable for the French, some of the German artillery crossed the Givonne river and moved upon the heights to the west of the valley. Sixty guns formed here the right wing of the Prussian and Bavarian artillery line. These guns covered with their fire every

1st Regiment of Uhlans "Emperor Alexander III. of Russia" (West-Prussian).

section of the Garenne woods so effectually that not the smallest patch of the wooded plateau could escape the effect of the German shells. The French, retreating at Daigny, were horrified at seeing themselves confronted by the iron jaws of the guns posted at Floing, and those fleeing from Illy in the direction of Sedan were received by a hail of shot fired from Wadelincourt. While the destruction of five divisions and two brigades was being effected on the plateau of Illy and in the Garenne woods, the fight at Balan, where General von Wimpffen made his last effort to break through the German lines, took once more a critical turn. Here, too, the artillery had to speak the last and deciding word. The Bavarians holding the town of Bazeilles, situated to the southeast of Balan, were compelled to retreat in the face of superior French forces, which sallied forth and pressed the Bavarians so hard that for a time only the outskirts of Bazeilles could be held by the Bavarian Jäger. At this critical moment three Bavarian batteries arrived and took up position near Balan. They were soon supported by five other batteries, which deployed in the valley, and also by thirty-six guns of the fourth corps, which poured a hail of shells into Balan from the heights of Ailicourt, to the west of the river Meuse. General von Wimpffen, seeing his troops thus reduced by the murderous fire of nineteen batteries, ordered a general retreat, though he and his staff remained in the thickest of the German fire at Balan.

Every French soldier now thronged into the fortified town of Sedan. To effect a speedier surrender of the fortress, King William ordered the Würtemberg artillery to draw nearer and direct its fire upon Sedan. The shells fell on the masses sheltering themselves in the crowded streets, throwing them into dire confusion. On the right bank of the Meuse, by order of the Crown Prince of Saxony, all the artillery of the Guards and of the twelfth corps moved close up to the fortress. The fate of the French army was now sealed, its unconditional surrender, including the French Emperor himself, to the victorious Germans became a certainty. In the battle 683 German guns had opposed 419 French guns and mitrailleuses, and 139 siege-guns, all of which fell into the hands of the victors.

The garrison-artillery is employed in engagements of a less varying character, such as occur in offensive and defensive operations of fortified towns or of the sea-coast, where the positions, both of points of attack and the weapons used, are subject to little material change. The garrison-artillery is classified, according to its employment, into siege-artillery, garrison-artillery proper, and artillery for coast-defence. Siege and garrison-artillery are almost identical in material and employment, while artillery for coast-defence may also rightly be considered a branch of the garrison-artillery. Siege and garrison-artillery are served by troops similar to the

infantry, which are called foot-artillery in the German army. The foot-artillery is provided with ordnance of from 4.72 to 5.90 in. calibre, with howitzers of 5.90 in. calibre, with mortars of 8.26 in. calibre, with siege-guns of 3.64, 4.72, and 8.26 in. calibre, with mortars of 5.90 in. calibre, with turret-howitzers of 8.26 in. calibre, and, in addition, revolving and quick-firing guns. The foot-artillery soldier carries a short rifle for personal protection. Our illustrations represent the Rhenish foot-artillery. There are seventeen foot-artillery regiments, of two battalions, each of four companies, while the 2nd regiment and the 2nd Bavarian regiment have three companies. The second battalion of the 12th regiment has five companies. The 13th (Royal Würtemberg) was transferred to the Prussian organization in 1893. The foot-artillery is uniformed similar to the infantry, and is characteristically distinguished by white shoulder-straps. White horse-hair plumes are worn on parade only by the foot-artillery of the Guards. The uniform of the Saxon contingent is of the same color as that of the Saxon field-artillery. The Bavarian uniform differs from the Prussian in the mountings on the helmet, which has a spike in place of the ball; it has black instead of dark-blue facings, and dark-blue trousers.

The bombardment of Strasburg, which resulted in its surrender, was a splendid example of the efficiency of the German siege-artillery. Prior to the late war with France, Strasburg had been considered a fortress of the first rank, and was France's sally-port against southern Germany. The town was fortified on Vauban's system. It was provided with deep moats, but not with advanced works which could make the city secure in case of a bombardment. The area in the vicinity of the town was more accessible on the north and west than on the south, where a great sheet of water could be created by artificial damming. Perilous to the fortress itself were the suburbs, adjacent to the *glacis*, and favoring an assault in close quarters. The defence of this important frontier-fortress, badly neglected by the French government in time of peace, devolved upon General Uhrich, an energetic, yet cautious, soldier. The garrison numbered about 20,000 men, including 450 officers. Their usefulness in defending the town was questioned, as a sufficiently strong corps of engineers was lacking. This explains how the Baden contingent, detailed to observe Strasburg and consisting of but one division, twelve squadrons, and nine batteries, advanced almost unchecked upon those points which facilitated a successful assault upon the plains known as Robertsau, Schiltigheim, and Königshofen. The armament of the fortress was ample. Twelve hundred mortars and guns of the heaviest calibre and of the latest construction were in position, though these were no match for the German artillery. On August 13th, 1870, a besieging army arrived, consisting of 46 battalions, 24 squadrons, and

After R. Knötel

Railway Troops.

18 field-batteries. They were soon followed by a siege-train of 200 field-pieces and 88 mortars, with 30 companies of foot-artillery, 1 siege-train of engineers, and 10 companies of sappers and miners,—40,000 men in all. On August 15th the commander of the besieging army, General von Werder, arrived at Mundolsheim, near Strasburg. He was attended by the chief of his general staff, Lieutenant-Colonel von Leszczynski. The next day the enemy made the first important sortie towards the south against Illkirch, losing three guns in this enterprise. On August 18th, the siege-train was put in position, after General von Werder had determined to force the town to surrender by bombarding it. The heavy siege-guns, posted near Kehl, on the right bank of the Rhine, and the field-guns on the left bank of the river now engaged the fortress; while these operations were going on, the erection of thirteen batteries for the bombardment of the northwestern front of the city was begun. On the evening of the twenty-fourth, the Germans were able to open fire upon the town, a part of which was soon in flames. At this crisis, the Bishop of Strasburg craved quarter for the citizens, but was unsuccessful in his mission, inasmuch as the Governor was not yet ready for terms of surrender. The fire was continued through the night of the twenty-fifth, ending at two o'clock, when it was at its hottest. The effect was terrific. The depot, the new church, and the valuable library had been destroyed; the roof of the Cathedral had also caught fire. But, in spite of these disasters, General Uhrich refused to surrender. After this, the fire of the siege-guns was directed upon the fortifications proper, and the more deliberate methods of a regular siege commenced, according to the plans of Captain Wagner of the corps of engineers. The assault was at this time directed against the northwest corner of the fortress.

During the night of August 29th–30th, the first parallel was opened, and the number of siege-batteries was increased by eleven others. Soon the German artillery proved its superior qualities, as regards both its material and its advantageous employment. On the night of the thirty-first of August, the second parallel was opened. At dawn a strong sortie made by the garrison failed, the Germans losing 7 officers and 149 men. On the ninth of September, the second parallel, with all its rearward connections, was completed. The Germans had now ninety-six mounted field-pieces and thirty-eight mortars in full fire, doing apparently effective work. The guns of lunette No. 44 were soon silenced, the large Finkmatt barracks was destroyed by fire, and the Steinthor gate was so much injured that it had to be buttressed with sand bags. The part of the town subjected to the German fire was now in ruins. The garrison thereupon withdrew their guns behind the parapet, and fired only their mortars. During the night of the 11th–12th, the opening of the third parallel was begun at the foot of

the *glacis* between lunettes Nos. 53 and 55. By the fourteenth of the month this work was finished and more batteries were put in position, so that the crest of the *glacis* could now be reached and occupied by infantry. The assault, henceforth, was exclusively directed against bastion No. 11, beyond lunettes 52 and 53, leaving the work of reducing the flank defences on the east to the siege-artillery. After the fourteenth, a breaching shot fire was opened against the escarpment of lunette 53. The indirect breach shot against the hidden walls stood the first severe test. The taking of lunettes 52 and 53 marked a decided feature in the progress of the attack. Both lunettes were now equipped by the Germans with batteries of mortars and guns, in the hope of silencing the fire from the redoubts and counter-guards of the attack in front, against which dismounted guns and counter-batteries were also directed. At the same time a breach shot was opened against the eastern flank of bastion No. 11 and the western side of bastion No. 12. The walls of bastion No. 11 fell in on the twenty-fourth of the month, after a shelling of 500 rounds. The destruction of the earthworks at the angle which remained standing was postponed till the storming of the place. The assault upon the inner wall and the fortress proper was now imminent, as there was but a short distance to the breach of bastion No. 11, which intervened between the besieging army and the town.

On the twenty-seventh of September, at five in the afternoon, a white flag was seen flying from the tower of the Cathedral. By the capitulation, which was signed the same night at Königshofen, 1,200 guns, 200,000 small arms, and 2,000,000 francs in the bank passed into the hands of the victors. The garrison also became prisoners of war. The walls lying in the line of attack were so battered that they were now useless for defence. Under the wreck of the front face of the fortification lay scattered guns and gun-carriages. The garrison had lost 2,500 men, among whom were 661 dead. The loss of the besiegers was 39 officers and 894 men dead and wounded.

The most memorable feat, however, achieved by the German artillery, was the successful investment and bombardment of Paris, the largest fortress of the world. All efforts on the part of the Paris garrison to break through the lines of the besieging Germans failed. Sorties took place at Châtillon on September 19th, at Chevilly on September 30th, at Bagneux on October 13th, at Malmaison on October 21st, at Le Bourget on October 30th, at Villiers on November 30th and December 2nd, and at Le Bourget again on December 21st. A bombardment of Paris was now agreed upon by the Germans, all necessary material for the batteries was brought up during the month of December and put in readiness by the twenty-sixth of the month. On the following day seventy-six guns opened fire on Mount Avron and the neighboring forts. These replied promptly and rapidly, the former with seventy-four guns. But soon it became apparent that Mount Avron, in spite of the numerically greater strength of the French artillery, could not for any length of time withstand the concentrated fire of the German guns. At noon on the twenty-seventh the firing became faint; towards evening, and during the night following, only irregular shots were heard, whilst the Germans kept up a steady fire. On the twenty-eighth Mount Avron was almost silenced, the forts only replying to the German fire. The moral effect of the bombardment, by which the French suffered only a nominal loss of 160 dead and wounded, was so great that Mount Avron, together with the other forts, was evacuated on the night of the twenty-eighth. The artillery attack on the southern forts, Issy, Vanves, and Mount Rouge, was next begun. On January 4th, 98 guns were ready to open fire upon 350 heavy French siege-guns, the efficiency of which was much impeded by the great distance. Notwithstanding the greater numerical strength of the French guns, the German artillery had the advantage of position, of a splendid observation, and of superior material. On the morning of January 5th, the German batteries stationed on the plateau of Châtillon opened fire, followed by the remainder of the batteries posted in the neighborhood. The French replied at once and directed a terrible counter-fire, especially against the batteries at Châtillon, inflicting heavy losses. At noon, however, the situation gradually improved, for the greater accuracy of the German aim began to tell. Fort Issy was silenced by two o'clock, the fire of Vanves lost force gradually, while only Mount Rouge replied with vigor. On the right, the Germans succeeded in silencing the French artillery situated at Les Hautes-Bruyères. The German battery No. 1, isolated in the park of St. Cloud, suffered most in this engagement, being shelled in front from the city's parapet and on the left flank by the fire from Mount Valérien. After the forts had been reduced, the German fire was chiefly directed against the outer batteries and the city ramparts; this necessitated, however, an advance of the German artillery. The bombardment of the city proper was ushered in by from forty to fifty rounds of exploding shells fired against the nearest parts of the city. The last sortie, which was made by the invested French army from Mount Valérien, utterly failed. The siege-guns, no longer needed on the northern side of Paris after the evacuation of Mount Avron, became now available on the southern investing line. From forty to fifty guns, which had been used against the recently surrendered town of Mézières, were also brought up and utilized against the forts of St. Denis. Fire was also at once opened upon the latter, and was likewise directed against the old castle of Villetaneuse, and against Aubervillers and other exposed parts of the northern side of Paris. The siege-park was established at Villiers-le-

Bel. It required 700 farmers' wagons to bring up the necessary material. On January 21st, at nine in the morning, all the batteries opened fire upon the forts, which replied only for a short time. After a successful attack on Villetaneuse castle, the entire French artillery was silenced by the Germans in a few days, the latter showing their superiority over the enemy in every respect. A more energetic bombardment of Paris which had been agreed upon at this juncture by the Germans, and which was to be ushered in by the capture of St. Denis, did not take place. By order of the commander-in-chief of the German forces, all hostilities were suspended on the night of the twenty-seventh of January. The defences of the enemy had suffered greatly. The city walls were destroyed, the casemates demolished, the garrison buildings ruined and burned,—a great feat accomplished by the German artillery. The loss of the Germans in the assault included 30 officers, and 350 dead and wounded, while the French loss amounted to about 800 men. The loss of the city's population was given at 97 dead and 278 wounded. On the twenty-third, Jules Favre had made his appearance at Versailles for the purpose of negotiating the capitulation of Paris. With the stroke of the midnight hour on the twenty-seventh, the fire of the German batteries was suspended. On the following day a general armistice commenced, after Paris had surrendered with 602 field-guns, 177,000 rifles, 1,200 ammunition wagons, and 1,362 siege-guns. The garrison, which consisted of 7,456 officers and 241,686 men, were declared prisoners of war. The troops of the line were to lay down their arms, only 12,000 men and the National Guard were to retain them for the preservation of order.

THE GERMAN ENGINEERS

ALL technical military work to be performed by the troops in the field falls to the lot of the pioneers. Each battalion of pioneers includes in its equipment, sappers, miners, and a pontoon train. The engineer troops are charged with the building and maintenance of fortified places, with the erection of field redoubts, with the construction of bridges and railroads, with the repair of railway and telegraph lines destroyed by the enemy, and with the demolition of others, when this becomes a necessity. These troops are also engaged in time of war in all kinds of siege-work, such as digging trenches, the construction of batteries, and the laying down of mines. Of the twenty-three battalions of pioneers, Prussia has nineteen, Bavaria two, Saxony one, and Würtemberg one. To the engineer troops also belongs the Prussian railway brigade of three regiments, one company of which is furnished by Saxony and one by Würtemberg. Besides these, there are a Bavarian railway battalion, and a Prussian and a Bavarian detachment of balloon troops. The uniform of the pioneers is similar to that of the field-artillery, characteristically distinguished, however, by the white buttons and white mountings attached to the helmet, which has a spike instead of a ball on top, and by black leather belts and straps. The railway troops are clothed similarly to the pioneers of the Guards, the shoulder-straps showing an "E" and the number of the regiment in Roman letters. The balloon troops wear the same uniform as the railroad troops do, with an "L" on the shoulder-straps. Their head-dress is the shako of the Guards rifles. The Bavarian pioneers are distinguished both by the form of the mountings upon the helmet and by their dark-blue trousers. The Saxon pioneers are clothed like the Saxon field-artillery, which wear a green uniform with red facings, distinguished, however, by white buttons, and by white mountings on the helmet.

The successful investment of Paris testifies to the efficiency of the German engineer corps. The German investing line extended for thirty-four miles; the telegraph lines connecting the headquarters of the three armies had a length of nearly sixty miles. The army which surrounded Paris numbered, on October 21st, 1870, 202,030 foot-soldiers, 33,734 horses, and 898 cannon. As soon as the German troops had taken up their position, they constructed a double tier of fortification works, which was declared by General Trochu, the defender of Paris, to be a masterpiece of military engineering. The villages, castles, and public parks, situate within reach of the guns of the Paris forts, were put in a condition that they could be defended by infantry troops. All the streets were provided with *abattis* by felling trees and placing them in a line with their branches pointed against the enemy. Redoubt after redoubt were built and equipped both with heavy and with light batteries. On the north side of Paris the Morée creek was dammed, and the mass of the stream thus gained was further increased by conducting the water of the Orqu canal into the creek. By this operation the land lying between Sevran and Dugny was inundated, so that the roadbed of the highway leading towards Le Bourget was visible only at Pont Iblon, the water at that place barring the entrance to a defile. At the outlet, on the other side of Le Bourget, some earthworks were thrown up. The banks of the Mulette creek, flowing through Le Bourget, were lined with fortifications, which were occupied by the infantry. South of Paris, the Bavarians prepared three investing lines. The batteries posted on the south side of Paris were 2,500 paces off from the city's fortifications, while those on the north side were stationed at a distance of 4,000 paces. All the positions were equipped with telegraphic communication. Outposts, provided with telescopes, were placed at advantageous places; a light-signal service was likewise established. A trestle-bridge was constructed over the river Marne, six pontoon bridges were constructed over the river Seine, while the service of three ferries was also organized.

The investment of the fortress of Strasburg also fully demonstrates that the German engineer corps was equal to the task falling to its lot in the late war. On September 9th, the work of the second parallel, somewhat hindered by rainy weather, was completed. Ninety-six rifled cannon and thirty-eight mortars were ready for action. Without delay, the preliminary work of the third parallel was then begun. In order to lower the water of the inundation and the water in the ditches, the Rhine-Rhone canal near Erstein and the "crooked" Rhine, together with the upper waters of the Ill and the Schwarz, were dammed and led off. In the second parallel, trenches were dug for the men and suitable wooden quarters were erected for the officers. The zigzags leading to the third parallel were constructed and occupied on the night of the tenth of September, the parallel proper was occupied between the twelfth and fourteenth of September, without any loss. During the night of the ninth, Captain Ledebur had discovered a mined gallery near lunette No. 53, which had been deserted by the enemy. The captain was let down by ropes into the trenches, and, with the aid of some sappers, removed the charges of powder. Communication from this gallery to the third parallel was effected by driving a shaft through the stone work. A secondary parallel, 212 paces long and four and one-half feet wide, was dug, beginning at the centre of the third parallel and reaching to the *glacis* of lunette No. 53. The crowning of the covered way of this lunette was begun by means of double traverse-saps, and finished in four days. During the night of the nineteenth, two mines were fired, which blew up part of the counterscarp opposite lunette No. 53 and laid it level with the water line. On the twentieth of the month, the Germans began laying an earth and fascine dam across the moat, during which operation the captain of the engineers was killed. A party sent across in boats closed the breach by throwing down some earth and stone work. The breach was scaled and occupied by a company of the 34th regiment. The pioneers closed the gorge and dug underground passages in the direction of the counterscarp. On the same day a battery was constructed immediately in front of the *glacis* of lunette No. 52. A battery of mortars moved upon the crest of the *glacis* on the next day. At this juncture it was decided to construct a bridge of barrels, of which a large number was on hand. This work was begun at dusk, under no better protection than a screen of boards to prevent observation, and it was finished on the same night by Pomeranian pioneers. Lunette No. 52 was found deserted by the enemy and occupied by some troops of the 34th regiment, and by pioneers and artillerymen. The seven guns in the lunette were spiked and the gorge was closed. The bridge of casks was now replaced by a dam. Based upon a report by Captain Ledebur, who made a reconnoitring tour, swimming through the sheet of water back of the lunettes, it was decided to direct operations against the crest of the *glacis* in front of lunette No. 51. From the twenty-second to the twenty-fifth of September the Germans advanced by means of "flying saps" and "sap rollers" against lunette No. 51, and succeeded in gaining the *glacis*, in which operation the gallant Captain Ledebur was killed. The lunettes Nos. 52 and 53 were now equipped with batteries and mortars, and new batteries were constructed in front of lunette No. 54. The

"Battery Halt."   7th Regiment of Field Artillery (Westphalian).

effect of their fire on the fortress has been described minutely under the section on "The German Artillery."

In the late war with France, the engineer troops displayed great proficiency in constructing railroads, which is the first and most important object of the general inspection of the lines of base. At the period of the third army's advance over the Vosges, several railroad lines were built in the northern part of Alsace by the first and second division of railway troops. After the tunnel at Zabern was cleared of all obstructions, the railroad track between Bruchsal and Germersheim, and from there to Nancy, was completed by the eighteenth of August. A new line of base was likewise established, beginning at Colomby and passing through Void to Bar le Duc, rounding the fortress of Toul, which barred communication. This new line was later on extended to Nogent l'Artaud. In order to finish the road, two viaducts 120 feet long had to be built near Vitry. As a passage could not be effected through the tunnel at Nanteuil, thus preventing a continuous route, it was found necessary to build a new road by going around the tunnel. This was done to prevent the reloading of the transports for the army of the Meuse at Château-Thierry and of the third army at Nanteuil, from which places all material had to be carried on wagons. This work was finished by the twenty-third of November. On August 25th the railroad between Nancy and Ars, which was of importance in establishing communication between the second and third armies, was ready for operations. In order to avoid the fortress of Metz, the general inspection of lines of base caused the building of a new railroad from Remilly to Pont-à-Musson. The first and second divisions of railway troops completed the road, which was sixteen miles long, in forty days. A viaduct 50 feet long and 12 feet high had to be built over the ravine near Remilly; another one, 500 feet long and 23 feet high, was built over a valley. Two trestles had also to be erected, one 50 feet and the other 280 feet long. A forest three miles wide and dense with beech wood and heavy underbrush had to be cleared. To procure better railroad facilities for the army of the Meuse, a railroad from Chalous, through Reims and Soissons, to Mitry, near Paris, and another line from Reims, through Laon and La Fère, to Gonesse, near Paris, were built. The German railway troops also finished the line from Blesmes to Chaumont and extended it further southwest to Châtillon. From the latter place the road branched off in a northwesterly direction to Troyes and Paris, and southwest to Joigny and Monterau. Particular attention was also paid to the construction of a southern road from Châtillon, via Montargis on the Loing, to Orleans. The line Blesmes-Chaumont-Châtillon was opened on December 2nd, the section from Chaumont to Troyes on December 25th, while the rest of the line was finished by the middle of January. The line Reims-Soissons-Mitry was ready for operation on November 21st; the line from Reims to Gonesse, touching Laon and La Fère, at the end of December. All these railroad connections had the one great drawback, that not more than sixteen trains

could be despatched daily because the direct line was still occupied by the French and the trains were compelled to run over the section from Frouard to Blesmes. This inconvenience, which delayed the siege and bombardment of Paris for three months, was not removed until all the northern French fortresses had fallen into the hands of the Germans.

An interesting feature of the engineer corps is the balloon troops. In a recent issue of the "Illustrated Zeitung," of Berlin, that journal comments upon these troops and their doings as follows:

"Very seldom the public at large hears of the manœuvres of these troops, although they are constantly engaged in working and experimenting along their lines in the Tempelhof drilling-grounds. This much may be asserted, that in the event of war the achievements of the German balloon troops will not be outrivalled by those of other nations. A uniform system of balloon-filling and manœuvring has been effected throughout the armies of the Triple Alliance. The system is that known as the 'Majert-Richter,' while the other European armies use the 'Young' system. The balloon is filled with hydrogen gas, which is prepared by the troops of the balloon detachment in a small factory situated on their own grounds. In time of war, and during the manœuvres, the necessary gas has to be transported to the place on wagons. This is done by means of steel cylinders, similar to those by which fluid carbonic acid is transported. The steel cylinders are about 8 feet long, with a diameter of 5.1 in. and a strength of the outer bands of 0.12 in. The gas is condensed from 100 to 150 atmospheres. The wagons carrying the steel cylinders surround the balloon in a circle while the contents of one cylinder after the other is transferred to the balloon, which is able to make an ascent in about one hour's time. At the manœuvres and in war time only captive balloons are used, while at fortified places and at camps enclosed by the enemy the unfettered balloon is to be employed. During fair weather the captive balloon may rise to a height of 1,800 feet, thus allowing a splendid observation. By means of a good telescope the uniforms of an advancing enemy can be distinguished from the balloon at a distance of nine miles. The reports from the captive balloon are transmitted to headquarters on the ground by a telephone, the wires of which are inclosed in the guy-rope. The captive balloon can rise by the aid of a single wire-rope, which ought to be strong, but not very thick. The manipulation of the rope requires, however, a wagon especially constructed and provided with a windlass, which brings the balloon back at a uniform rate by winding the rope on a drum. If the balloon rises only to the height of from 300 to 450 feet, the wagon with the windlass is not needed, as the balloon is then held by soldiers with four ropes. By the aid of these ropes the balloon may be moved in any direction, the troops keeping pace with the movement of the balloon. These movements are important in time of war, as the balloon can be reached by infantry fire at a height of 6,000 feet, and by artillery fire at a height of about three miles. In order to keep the balloon out of range of fire, its position has to be constantly changed. Should the balloon be hit by a

Heavy Artillery at the Gun.   8th Regiment of Heavy Artillery (Rhenish).

bullet it descends slowly, unless the rent made in it is large.

"Experiments of a decidedly novel character have recently been made with a balloon which differs in form from all balloons hitherto used. The new model is a large balloon, cylindric in form, at the end of which two small balloons are attached and suspended in a horizontal position. Connected with the main balloon by several ropes, hangs the gondola, which can be shifted to the opposite side by a simple contrivance. The swinging motion of the balloon and the gondola, common to balloons of the older type, is avoided by the peculiar construction of this novel invention. The shifting of the two small balloons, which are manipulated from the basket by means of ropes, gets rid of all former inconvenience. Both observation and survey were made difficult, nay, often impossible, by the balloons of the older construction, which changed their position continually. The balloon of the new pattern is comparatively steady, even during high winds. When experimented with, the new model rose and was lowered many times, enabling every officer present to test his instruments while seated in the basket. For this purpose the ring on the top of the gondola was attached to the wagon of the balloon troops by a rope. This rope, about 3,000 feet long, was manipulated by the aid of a roller-drum placed in the wagon. In order to lower the balloon, a pulley was attached to the rope. From the pulley about thirty smaller ropes were suspended, each being held by a soldier. The men marched with the pulley towards the captive balloon, lowering it by this mode of procedure. When the balloon was thus brought to the ground and a change of occupants was made, the soldiers ran back and the balloon rose again."

THE GERMAN MILITARY TRAIN

EVERY army needs, in time of war, a large amount of powder and shot, of provisions for men and horses, and of other equipments, which have necessarily to be transported on wagons. This task falls to the lot of the military train, a branch of the army's service which has but recently received a better and more ample organization. Every German army corps has, in time of peace, one train battalion of three companies, while in the Bavarian battalions the third company belongs to the sanitary service. The troops of the military train wear a black shako, made of leather, and a blue tunic. The shoulder-straps, which are of a light-blue color, show the number of the battalion. For the personal protection of the train-soldier, he is equipped with sabre and carbine. The organization of the military train, when mobilized, comprises the staff of the battalion, three sanitary detachments, one depot of remounts, and one column consisting of the field-bakeries. When the battalion goes into action there are added a pontoon train, a detachment of field-telegraph troops, and twelve field-hospitals attached to the sanitary service. These organizations are further augmented by the commissariat, the war-chest, the provision bureaus, and the field post offices. The provision trains consist of thirty-six provision wagons, one reserve

wagon, and one portable forge. The provision wagons are laden with bread, crackers, canned goods, and victuals of every description. These moving trains supply the troops with the necessary provisions, while at the same time they replenish their stock of goods from the depots situated on the lines of base. The wagon trains comprise eighty-two vehicles and serve especially for the transport of oats, which is not carried by the provision columns. The field-bakery columns number twenty portable bakeries with a *personnel* of two hundred bakers and other professionals and train-soldiers. At the mobilization of the army, the trains of the army corps are divided into two echelons. One, called the small baggage, follows the troops at a distance of seven to ten miles. It carries everything necessary for the troops during, or immediately after, a battle, while the heavy baggage follows at a greater distance and carries all supplies required for the sustenance of the army during its operations in the field.

The German army has twenty-one train battalions, of which seventeen are furnished by Prussia, namely, sixteen battalions of the line and one battalion of the Guards. The battalion of the Guards is distinguished from those of the line by its white braiding on the tunic and the star of the Guards, instead of the eagle, affixed to the shako. The troops of this battalion wear white horse-hair plumes on parade, while the battalions of the line wear black plumes. The officers are equipped with helmets. Bavaria furnishes two battalions, both of which are equipped with helmets. Würtemberg has one battalion, uniformed similarly to the Prussian battalions of the line. The battalion of the Saxon contingent wears a tunic of a light-blue color, with black facings and red cuffs, though with a shako of a different form.

As the maintenance of the army while in an enemy's country depends almost entirely on the military train, the responsibility which fell to this branch of the army's service during the late war can hardly be fully realized. All communication with the German army in France was effected over the lines of base. The proper administration of the parts of the enemy's country which were held by the troops formed the solid basis of the inspection departments of the lines of base. At the head of this entire organization was the quartermaster-general of the army, Lieutenant-General von Podbielski. It was a gigantic task which had to be shouldered by this official of the Royal headquarters during the late war. Besides a faithful supervision of the lines of base, he had likewise to provide for the speedy transportation of the reserve troops, for the proper sustenance of the army, for the safe conveyance of the hospital-trains, and for the prompt communication through the agency of the post and telegraph service. Von Podbielski, however, proved equal to the task, overcoming all obstacles by his great preciseness, vigilance, and foresight. At the beginning of the war the organization of the field-post, of the field-telegraph, and of the field-railway displayed great proficiency. On July 31st, 1870, 170,000 maps, showing the different sections of France, were distributed to the officers of the army by the general staff at Berlin and the telegraph bureau at Munich. The provisioning of the troops massed near the Rhine was beset by many obstacles, which, however, were promptly overcome by the efficiency of the commissary-general of the army, Lieutenant-General von Stosch. In the corps districts a supply of victuals, oats, and hay sufficient for six weeks was secured. During the first days of the campaign the troops supplied themselves with provisions, while later on they drew their rations from the depots established at the different Rhenish towns, which had been provided with provisions for six weeks. Each army corps was supplied with four hundred wagons; the general inspection of the lines of base had three thousand wagons at its disposal.

Each of the great German armies had a general department which supervised the lines of base; it consisted of a company of pioneers and a detachment of railway and telegraph troops. This department of inspection moved along with the advance-guard of the army. The department of inspection connected with the third army, which had its headquarters at Nancy on August 18th, was transferred to Bar-le-Duc on the twenty-sixth of the month. The second army's department, which arrived at Saargemünd on August 11th, moved to Pont-à-Musson on the 16th, and later on to Remilly. The department of the army of the Meuse followed the army's headquarters to Clermont and Beaumont. It arrived at Sedan on September 4th for the purpose of clearing the battlefield, and was eventually transferred to Dammartin, near Paris. At the larger towns, situated on the lines of base, depots, hospitals, and bakeries were established, and a telegraph service was instituted. This service was alloted to the field-telegraph troops, to troops assigned for the maintenance of the lines of base, and to government operators. The field-telegraph service was performed by five Prussian, two Bavarian, and one Würtemberg detachments, which followed the army's operations in the field. These troops sometimes did their work ahead of the advance-guards, under the fire of the enemy. The telegraph service of the lines of base was performed by troops which belonged to three Prussian and one Bavarian detachments. The troops followed in the path of the field-telegraph detachments and established regular lines, with cross-lines, while the government telegraph officials finished the temporary work previously done by the troops. Central field-telegraph bureaus were established at Nancy, Epernay, and Lagny, in order to facilitate the communication of the army with Germany. Later on, Versailles became the centre of the telegraph service with two main lines, one going over Sedan and the other over Saarbrücken. The service of the field-telegraph, together with that of the lines of base, covered 6,730 miles, with 407 stations; while the government telegraph service operated over 7,770 miles, with 118 stations.

A postal service was likewise established in the field. The North German Confederation furnished a general post office for the chief headquarters, a post office for each army, and thirteen field post offices, with three field-deliveries for each army corps. Later on, the Confederation supplied the eight cavalry divisions, the five divisions of reserve troops, the chief commands of the army of the Meuse and the army of the South, and the thirteenth and fourteenth corps, each with a branch office. Each bureau of inspection of the lines of base received three post offices, and the government of Alsace and Lorraine a field post office. In the course of time a courier postal service was established, with fixed stations, as well as regular mail-coaches for the forwarding of packages. At Nancy a general post-office department was organized on August 24th, embracing forty post offices over the newly-occupied territory. At the beginning of October a second post office was established at Strasburg, both controlling at that time 158 postal stations.

The sanitary affairs of the army were well looked after during the late war. Field-hospitals were erected at five hundred different places. Two commissions were appointed, whose duty was to attend and care for the hospital-trains arriving at Weissenburg and Saarbrücken. Nancy and Lagny were the stations from which the hospital-trains left for Germany. At Lagny between 1,400 and 1,700 sick and wounded arrived daily from the different French battlefields, and were here put on the hospital-trains. Over 45,000 people, including 8,398 train-soldiers, were employed in the different sanitary departments of the army. The total sick and wounded of German soldiers in France was 295,634. Of this number 240,426 were transported to Germany. Eleven millions of dollars in cash and five millions in presents were sent to the German troops during their stay on French soil; while foreign countries contributed at the same time gratuities amounting to two and one-half millions of dollars. For the forwarding of all this material three principal depots, one reserve depot, and twenty-six branch depots had to be established. Sixty thousand men of the North-German and South-German landwehr, the troops of the general government of Alsace and Lorraine included, were needed to protect the German lines of base. These troops had to undergo a great deal of hardship and were often in much peril. They were especially exposed to the attacks of the hostile country people and franctireurs, who often tore up railroad tracks, destroyed telegraph wires, and "held up" army wagons and stages.*

*The war episodes introduced into this narrative, being descriptions, not of battles but of heroic achievements by larger and smaller bodies of troops, are taken from the following works: " War and Victory, 1870-71," a memorial by Dr. J. v. Pflugk-Harttung, and "The Franco-German War of 1870-71," by Dr. Hermann Fechner.

THE GERMAN COLONIAL TROOPS

Though the troops employed for the defence of the Imperial Colonies are not a part of the German army and navy, their organization is here briefly treated. The Colonial troops of East-Africa, the Kameruns and Togo of West-Africa are recruited from natives. Their forces, numbering 2,422 men, are trained and commanded by German officers and noncommissioned officers. The troops of East-Africa consist of Sudanese, Zulus, and Askaris, and are employed for preserving public order and safety in the Colonies, chiefly, however, for suppressing the slave trade. The organization of the troops includes, with the German Emperor as commander-in-chief, one commander, one sub-commander, seven lieutenants, one surgeon, one commissary, and ten companies, each of 150 men. The Colonial troops of southwestern Africa, which number 558 men, mostly mounted, consist of volunteer officers, noncommissioned officers, and privates of the German army. The privates bind themselves to a longer active service, lasting from four to five years longer than the usual contract stipulates. All German officers, surgeons, and paymasters, who enter the Colonial service, withdraw by this step from the regular organization of the army, which they may, however, reënter if they wish to do so. The time of service in Africa, if it extends over a period of six months, counts double in the pension. Imperial subjects, who are liable for military service and reside in the Colonies, may fulfill their liability to serve by entering the ranks of the Colonial forces. Those German soldiers and sailors who live in the Colonies on furlough may be called to service in case of emergency, according to the law of September 7th, 1896.

12th Regiment of Field Artillery (Royal Saxon).

CLASSIFICATION AND DISTRIBUTION OF THE ARMY

COMMANDER-IN-CHIEF of the German Imperial army in time of war, His Majesty, the German Emperor and King of Prussia, William II.

THE IMPERIAL HEADQUARTERS

Reporting Adjutant-General of the Emperor; the Adjutant-General in attendance and in command of the headquarters; the General of the suite, also in attendance.

THE MILITARY CABINET

Departmental chief and the chiefs of the different divisions, including the ministers of war of Prussia, Bavaria, Saxony, Würtemberg.

THE GENERAL STAFF OF THE ARMY

PRUSSIA: Chief; quartermaster-general; quartermaster-in-chief; chiefs of divisions of the great general staff; chiefs of the army corps.

Subject to the chief of the general staff are: War Academy at Berlin; the bureau of national survey, Berlin; the railway brigade, Berlin, consisting of 1st and 2nd regiments of railway troops, Berlin, and 3rd regiment, Jüterbog; experimental division of the railway brigade, bureau of the military railroad, Berlin; detachment of balloon troops, Berlin.

BAVARIA: Chief; topographical bureau.

SAXONY: Chief; topographical bureau.

WÜRTEMBERG: Chief.

Commission of national defences: Berlin.

Commission of the imperial districts: Berlin.

Military plenipotentiaries of the German Federal States: Bavaria, Saxony, Würtemberg.

National Gendarmerie: Prussia, Bavaria.

THE ARMY INSPECTIONS

Chief-command in the Marks: Berlin.

1st army inspection, Berlin: First, Second, Ninth, Tenth, and Seventeenth army corps.

2nd army inspection, Dresden: Fifth, Sixth, Twelfth, and Nineteenth army corps.

3rd army inspection, Hanover: Seventh, Eighth, Eleventh, Thirteenth, and Eighteenth army corps.

4th army inspection, Munich: Third and Fourth Prussian, and First and Second Bavarian army corps.

5th army inspection, Carlsruhe: Fourteenth, Fifteenth, and Sixteenth army corps.

The corps of the Guards is not subject to inspection.

GENERAL INSPECTION OF THE CAVALRY, BERLIN

1st cavalry inspection at Königsberg; 2nd at Stettin; 3rd at Münster; 4th at Saarbrücken.

Royal Bavarian inspection of the cavalry, Munich; departments: Riding Academy and Institute of Horse-shoeing.

ARTILLERY INSPECTIONS

Inspection of field-artillery, Berlin; departments: School of Gunnery for Field-Artillery, Jüterbog; 1st and 2nd instruction divisions, Jüterbog.

General inspection of the foot-artillery, Berlin.

1st foot-art. inspection, Berlin.

    1st foot-art. brig. Berlin: Regt. of Foot-Guards art., 4th, 5th, and 6th regts. of foot-art.

    2nd foot-art. brig., Thorn: 1st, 2nd, 11th, and 15th regts. of foot-art.

    Inspection of the 1st and 2nd artillery depot; school of gunnery for the foot-artillery, Jüterbog; school for artillery sergeants, Berlin.

2nd foot-art. inspection, Cologne.

    3rd foot-art. brig., Metz: 7th, 8th, and 9th regt. of foot-art.; 12th Royal Saxon regt.; 1st and 3rd Royal Bavarian bats. of 2nd regt. of foot-art.

    4th foot-art. brig., Strasburg; 3rd and 10th regts. of foot-art.; 13th bat. of foot-art.; 14th regt. of foot-art.

    3rd and 4th inspection of artillery depots.

GENERAL COMMISSION FOR ARTILLERY TESTS, BERLIN

1st commission for artillery tests: 1st division of field-art.; 2nd division of foot-art.

2nd experimental division of the commission for artillery tests. Experimental company (practice-ground, Cummersdorf). Depot-bureau of the commission for artillery tests. Ordnance bureau, Berlin.

Royal Bavarian inspection of the foot-artillery, Munich; school of artillery sergeants, Munich.

GENERAL INSPECTION OF THE ENGINEER AND PIONEER CORPS AND OF THE FORTRESSES, BERLIN

1st inspection of engineers, Berlin:

    1st inspection of fortresses, Königsberg: Königsberg, Dantzic, Pillau, Boyen, Memel.

    2nd inspection of fortresses, Kiel: Friedrichsort, Cuxhaven with Heligoland, Geestemünde, Wilhelmshaven, Swinemünde.

Piece Drill.   21st Regiment of Field Artillery "von Clausewitz" (Upper-Silesian).

2nd inspection of engineers, Berlin:

3rd inspection of fortresses, Posen: Posen, Glogau, Neisse, Glatz ; depot-building bureau, Breslau.

4th inspection of fortresses, Thorn: Thorn, Graudenz, Küstrin, Spandau, Magdeburg.

3rd inspection of engineers, Strasburg:

5th inspection of fortresses, Strasburg: Strasburg, Neubreisach, Bitsch, Ulm.

6th inspection of fortresses, Metz: Metz, Diedenhofen.

7th inspection of fortresses, Cologne: Cologne, Coblenz, Mayence, Wesel.

Board of engineers, Berlin. School of fortification, Charlottenburg. Inspection of the military telegraph service, Berlin. Military telegraph school, Berlin.

1st inspection of pioneers, Berlin: Bat. of Guards pioneers; 2nd, 5th, 6th, and 17th bats. of pioneers; 1st and 18th bats. of pioneers (First army corps, Königsberg).

2nd inspection of pioneers, Mayence: 11th, 14th, and Royal Würtemberg; 13th, 15th, and 19th bats. (Fifteenth army corps, Strasburg); 16th and 20th (Sixteenth army corps, Metz).

3rd inspection of pioneers, Magdeburg: 3rd, 4th, 7th, 8th, 9th, and 10th bats. of pioneers.

Royal Bavarian inspection of the engineer corps and of the fortresses, Munich. Detachment of balloon troops, Munich. Military telegraph school, Munich.

Inspection of jäger and schützen, Berlin.

Inspection of the troops which maintain the communication of the army, Berlin.

Railway-brigade, Berlin: 1st, 2nd, and 3rd regts. of railway troops; experimental division of the railway-brigade, Berlin; bureau of the military road, Berlin. Detachment of balloon troops, Berlin; inspection of the telegraph troops, Berlin; operating bureau of the railway brigade, Berlin; cavalry telegraph school.

INSPECTION OF THE TECHNICAL INSTITUTES OF THE INFANTRY AND ARTILLERY

Small arm factories at Spandau, Dantzic, Erfurt, Amberg; ammmunition factory at Spandau; bureau of artillery construction at Spandau; artillery workshops at Spandau, Deutz, Strasburg, Dantzic, Munich, Dresden; gun foundries at Spandau, Ingolstadt; projectile factories at Siegburg, Ingolstadt; pyrotechnical laboratory at Spandau; powder factories at Spandau, Hanau, Ingolstadt, Gnaschwitz; experimental bureau at Spandau; ordnance bureau at Berlin.

Inspection of the artillery depots, Berlin: 1st subinspection of the artillery depot at Posen; 2nd at Stettin; 3rd at Cologne; 4th at Strasburg.

Inspection of the train depot, Berlin: 1st subinspection of the train depot at Dantzic; 2nd at Berlin; 3rd at Cassel; 4th at Strasburg.

United Artillery and Engineering School, Berlin.

GENERAL INSPECTION OF THE TECHNICAL AND EDUCATIONAL INSTITUTES OF THE ARMY

Supreme Board of Military Examiners, Berlin.

Inspection of the military schools, Berlin: Military schools at Potsdam, Glogau, Neisse, Engers, Kassel,

Hanover, Anclam, Metz, Dantzic, Hersfeld.

Corps of Cadets, Berlin: Normal school of military cadets at Gross-Lichterfelde; schools of cadets at Köslin, Potsdam, Wahlstadt, Bensberg, Plön, Oranienstein, Carlsruhe, and Dresden.

Inspection of infantry schools, Berlin: School of musketry, Spandau; military gymnasium, Berlin; schools for noncommissioned officers at Potsdam, Jülich, Biebrich, Weissensfels, Ettlingen, Marienwerder; preparatory schools at Weilburg, Neu-Breisach, Jülich, Wohlau, Annaburg, Bartenstein, Greifenberg; military institute for soldier's sons, Annaburg.

Commission for rifle tests, Spandau.

Inspection of the Royal Saxon schools for noncommissioned officers at Dresden; normal and preparatory school at Marienberg.

Royal Bavarian inspection of the military educational institutes, Munich: War academy, Munich; artillery and engineering school, Munich; military academy, Munich; corps of cadets, Munich; normal and preparatory school for noncommissioned officers, Fürstenfeldbruck; school of musketry, Augsburg.

Riding academy, Hanover.

Royal Bavarian riding academy, Munich.

Royal Saxon inspection of the riding academy, Dresden. Riding academy, Dresden.

Veterinary inspection, Berlin: Veterinary school, Berlin; horse-shoeing institutes at Berlin, Breslau, Königsberg, Gottesaue, Hanover, Frankfurt, Munich, Dresden.

Inspection of the military penitentiaries, Berlin.

Inspection of the military penitentiaries, Munich.

THE ARMY CORPS

CORPS OF THE GUARDS, BERLIN

1st division of Guards infantry, Berlin.

1st brig. of Guards inf., Potsdam: 1st. regt. of Foot-Guards, Potsdam; 3rd regt. of Foot-Guards, Berlin; bat. of Guards rifles, Potsdam; bat. of inf. instructors, Potsdam.

2nd brig. of Guards inf., Berlin: 2nd regt. of Foot-Guards, Berlin; regt. of Fusilier-Guards, Berlin; 4th regt. of Foot-Guards, Berlin.

2nd division of Guards infantry, Berlin.

3rd brig. of Guards inf., Berlin: 1st regt. of Grenadier-Guards "Emperor Alexander of Russia," Berlin; 3rd regt. of Grenadier-Guards "Queen Elizabeth," Charlottenburg; bat. of Guards rifles, Gross-Lichterfelde.

4th brig. of Guards inf., Berlin: 2nd regt. of Grenadier-Guards "Emperor Franz," Berlin; 4th regt. of Grenadier-Guards "Queen Augusta," Berlin.

5th brig. of Guards inf., Spandau: 5th regt. of Foot-Guards, Spandau; 5th regt. of Grenadier-Guards, Spandau.

Division of Guards cavalry, Berlin.

1st brig. of Guards cav., Berlin: Regt. of Gardes du Corps, Potsdam; regt. of Cuirassier-Guards,

Berlin.

2nd brig. of Guards cav., Potsdam: 1st regt. of Uhlan-Guards, Potsdam; 3rd regt. of Uhlan-Guards, Potsdam.

3rd brig. of Guards cav., Berlin: 1st regt. of Dragoon-Guards "Queen of Great Britain and Ireland," Berlin; 2nd regt. of Dragoon-Guards "Empress Alexandra of Russia," Berlin.

4th brig. of Guards cav., Potsdam: Regt. of Hussars, Body-Guards, Potsdam; detachment of mounted Guards rifles; 2nd regt. of Uhlan-Guards, Berlin.

Brig. of Guards field-art., Berlin: 1st regt. of Guards field-art., Berlin; 2nd regt. of Guards field-art., Potsdam; Guards bat. of the train, Berlin.

Attached to the corps are: Regt. of Guards foot-art., Spandau; bat. of the Guards pioneers, Berlin.

FIRST ARMY CORPS, KÖNIGSBERG

1st division, Königsberg.

1st brig. of inf., Königsberg: 1st regt. of Grenadiers "King Frederick III." (East-Pruss. No. 1), Königsberg; 41st regt. of inf. "von Boyen" (East-Pruss. No. 5), Tilsit.

4th brig. of inf., Königsberg: 3rd regt. of Grenadiers "King Frederick William" (East-Pruss. No. 2), Königsberg; 43rd regt. of inf. "Duke Carl of Mecklenburg-Strelitz" (East-Pruss. No. 6), Königsberg.

1st brig. of cav., Königsberg: 3rd regt. of Cuirassiers "Count Wrangel" (East-Pruss.), Königsberg; squadron of mounted rifles of the First army corps; 1st regt. of Dragoons "Prince Albrecht of Prussia" (Lith.), Tilsit.

2nd division, Insterburg.

2nd brig. of inf., Gumbinnen: 33rd regt. of Fusiliers "Count Roon" (East-Pruss.), Gumbinnen; 147th regt. of inf., Insterburg.

73rd brig. of inf., Rastenburg: 4th regt. of Grenadiers "King Frederick II." (East-Pruss. No. 4), Rastenburg; 59th regt. of inf. "Count Hiller von Gärtringen" (Posen No. 4), Goldap.

2nd brig. of cav., Insterburg: 11th regt. of Dragoons "von Wedel" (Pom.), Gumbinnen; 12th regt. of Uhlans (Lith.), Insterburg.

37th division, Allenstein.

3rd brig. of inf., Lyck: 45th regt. of inf. (East-Pruss. No. 8); 146th regt. of inf., Sensburg.

75th brig. of inf., Allenstein: 150th regt. of inf., Allenstein; 151st regt. of inf., Allenstein.

37th brig. of cav., Allenstein: 10th regt. of Dragoons "King Albert of Saxony" (East-Pruss.), Allenstein; 8th regt. of Uhlans "Count zu Dohna" (East-Pruss.), Lyck.

1st brig. of field-art., Königsberg: 1st regt. of field-art. "Prince August of Prussia" (East-Pruss.), Insterburg; 16th regt. of field-art. (West-Pruss.), Königsberg; 1st bat. of the train (East-Pruss.), Königsberg.

Attached to the corps are: 1st bat. of rifles "Count York von Wartenburg" (East-Pruss.), Ortelsburg; 1st regt. of foot-art. "von Linger," Königsberg; 1st bat. of pioneers "Prince Radziwill" (East-Pruss.), Königsberg; 18th bat. of pioneers, Königsberg.

SECOND ARMY CORPS, STETTIN

3rd division, Stettin.

5th brig. of inf., Stettin: 2nd regt. of Grenadiers "King Frederick William IV." (Pom. No. 1), Stettin; 42nd regt. of inf. "Prince Moritz of Anhalt-Dessau" (Pom. No. 5), Stralsund.

6th brig. of inf., Stettin: 9th regt. of Colberg Grenadiers "Count Gneisenau" (Pom. No. 2), Stargard; 54th regt. of inf. "von der Goltz" (Pom. No. 7), Kolberg.

3rd brig. of cav., Stettin: 2nd regt. of Cuirassiers "The Queen's Own" (Pom.), Pasewalk; 9th regt. of Uhlans (Pom.), Demmin.

4th division, Bromberg.

7th brig. of inf., Bromberg: 34th regt. of Fusiliers (Pom.), Bromberg; 129th regt. of inf., Bromberg.

8th brig. of inf., Gnesen: 49th regt. of inf. (Pom. No. 6), Gnesen; 140th regt. of inf., Inowrazlaw.

74th brig. of inf., Stettin: 148th regt. of inf., Stettin; 149th regt. of inf., Schneidemühl.

4th brig. of cav., Bromberg: 3rd regt. of mounted Grenadiers "Baron von Derfflinger" (Neumärk), Bromberg; 12th regt. of Dragoons "von Arnim" (Brandenb. No. 2), Gnesen.

2nd brig. of field-art., Stettin: 2nd regt. of field-art. (Pom. No. 1), Stettin; 17th regt. of field-art. (Pom. No. 2), Bromberg; 2nd bat. of the train (Pom.), Alt-Damm.

Attached to the corps are: 2nd regt. of foot-art. "von Hindersin" (Pom.), Dantzic; 17th bat. of pioneers, Stettin.

THIRD ARMY CORPS, BERLIN

5th division, Frankfurt-on-the-Oder.

9th brig. of inf., Frankfurt: 8th regt. of Grenadiers—Body-Guards—"King Frederick William III." (Brandenb. No. 1), Frankfurt; 48th regt. of inf. "von Stülpnagel" (Brandenb. No. 5), Küstrin.

10th brig. of inf., Frankfurt: 12th regt. of Grenadiers "Prince Karl of Prussia" (Brandenb. No. 2), Frankfurt; 52nd regt. of inf. "von Alvensleben" (Brandenb. No. 6), Kottbus.

5th brig. of cav. Frankfurt: 2nd regt. of Dragoons (Brandenb. No. 1), Schwedt; 3rd regt. of Uhlans "Emperor Alexander II. of Russia" (Brandenb. No. 1), Fürstenwalde.

6th division, Brandenburg.

11th brig. of inf., Brandenburg: 20th regt. of inf. "Count Tauentzien von Wittenberg" (Brandenb. No. 3), Wittenberg; 35th regt. of Fusiliers "Prince Henry of Prussia" (Brandenb. No. 3), Brandenburg.

12th brig. of inf., Brandenburg: 24th regt. of inf. "Grand Duke Frederick Franz II. of Mecklenburg-Schwerin" (Brandenb. No. 4), Neu-Ruppin; 64th regt. of inf. "Fieldmarshal Prince Frederick Charles of Prussia" (Brandenb. No. 8), Prenzlau.

6th brig. of cav., Brandenburg: 6th regt. of Cuirassiers "Emperor Nicholas I. of Russia" (Brandenb.), Brandenburg; 3rd regt. of Hussars "von Zieten" (Brandenb.), Rathenow.

3rd brig., of field-art. Berlin: 3rd regt. of field-art. "Great Master of the Ordnance" (Brandenb. No. 1), Brandenburg; 18th regt. of field-art. "Great Master of the Ordnance" (Brandenb. No. 2), Frankfurt; 3rd bat. of the train (Brandenb.), Spandau.

Attached to the corps are: 3rd bat. of rifles (Brandenb.), Lübben; 3rd bat. of pioneers "von Rauch" (Brandenb.), Spandau; Landwehr inspection, Berlin.

FOURTH ARMY CORPS, MAGDEBURG

7th division, Magdeburg.

13th brig. of inf., Magdeburg: 26th regt. of inf. "Prince Leopold of Anhalt-Dessau (Magdeb. No. 1), Magdeburg; 66th regt. of inf. (Magdeb. No. 3), Magdeburg.

14th brig. of inf., Halberstadt: 27th regt. of inf "Prince Louis Ferdinand of Prussia" (Magdeb. No. 2), Halberstadt; 165th regt. of inf. (Hanov. No. 5), Goslar.

7th brig. of cav., Magdeburg: 10th regt. of Hussars (Magdeb.), Stendal; 16th regt. of Uhlans "Hennings von Treffenfeld" (Altmärk.), Salzwedel.

8th division, Halle.

15th brig. of inf., Halle: 36th regt. of Fusiliers (Magdeb.), Anhalt; 93rd regt. of inf., Dessau.

16th brig. of inf., Torgau: 72nd regt. of inf. (Thür. No. 4), Torgau; 153rd regt. of inf. (Thür. No. 8), Altenburg.

8th brig. of cav., Halle: 7th regt. of Cuirassiers "von Seydlitz" (Magdeb.), Halberstadt; 12th regt. of Hussars (Thür.), Merseburg.

4th brig. of field-art., Magdeburg: 4th regt. of field-art. "Prince Regent Luitpold of Bavaria" (Magdeb.), Magdeburg; 19th regt. of field-art. (Thür.), Erfurt; 4th bat. of the train (Magdeb.), Magdeburg.

Attached to the corps are: 4th regt. of foot-art. "Encke" (Magdeb.), Magdeburg; 4th bat. of pioneers (Magdeb.), Magdeburg.

FIFTH ARMY CORPS, POSEN

9th division, Glogau.

17th brig. of inf., Glogau: 50th regt. of inf. (Lower-Siles. No. 3), Rawitsch; 58th regt. of inf. (Posen No. 3), Glogau.

18th brig. of inf., Liegnitz: 7th regt. of Grenadiers "King William I." (West-Pruss. No. 2), Liegnitz; 19th regt. of inf. "von Courbière" (Posen No. 2), Görlitz.

9th brig. of cav., Glogau: 4th regt. of Dragoons "von Bredow" (Siles. No. 1), Lüben; 10th regt. of Uhlans "Prince August of Würtemberg" (Posen), Züllichau.

10th division, Posen.

19th brig. of inf., Posen: 6th regt. of Grenadiers "Count Kleist von Nollendorf" (West-Pruss.

No. 1), Posen; 46th regt. of inf. "Count Kirchbach" (Lower-Siles. No. 1), Posen.

20th brig. of inf., Posen: 37th regt. of Fusiliers "von Steinmetz" (Westphal.), Krotoschin; 47th regt. of inf. (Lower-Siles. No. 2), Posen.

77th brig. of inf., Ostrowo: 154th regt. of inf., Jauer; 155th regt. of inf., Ostrowo.

10th brig. of cav., Posen: 2nd regt. of Hussars "The Empress's Own" (Body-Guards No. 2), Posen; 1st regt. of Uhlans "Emperor Alexander III. of Russia" (West-Pruss.), Militsch.

5th brig. of field-art., Posen: 5th regt. of field-art. "von Podbielski" (Lower-Siles.), Glogau; 20th regt. of field-art. (Posen), Posen; 5th bat. of the train (Lower-Siles.), Posen.

Attached to the corps are: 5th regt. of foot-art. (Lower-Siles.), Posen; 5th bat. of rifles "von Neumann" (Siles. No. 1), Hirschberg; 5th bat. of pioneers (Lower-Siles.), Glogau.

SIXTH ARMY CORPS, BRESLAU

11th division, Breslau.

21st brig. of inf., Schweidnitz: 10th regt. of Grenadiers "King Frederick William II." (Siles. No. 1), Schweidnitz; 38th regt. of Fusiliers "Fieldmarshal Count Moltke" (Siles.), Glatz.

22nd brig. of inf., Breslau: 11th regt. of Grenadiers "Crown Prince Frederick William" (Siles. No. 2), Breslau; 51st regt. of inf. (Lower-Siles. No. 4), Breslau.

78th brig. of inf., Brieg: 156th regt. of inf., Brieg; 157th regt. of inf., Brieg.

11th brig. of cav., Breslau: 1st regt. of Cuirassiers—Body-Guards—"Great Elector" (Siles.), Breslau; 8th regt. of Dragoons "King Frederick III." (Siles. No. 2), Oels; 4th regt. of Hussars "von Schill" (Siles. No. 1), Ohlau.

12th division, Neisse.

23rd brig. of inf., Neisse: 22nd regt. of inf. "Keith" (Upper-Siles. No. 1), Gleiwitz; 62nd regt. of inf. (Upper-Siles. No. 3), Cosel.

24th brig. of inf., Neisse: 23rd regt. of inf. "von Winterfeldt" (Upper-Siles. No. 2), Neisse; 63rd regt. of inf. (Upper-Siles. No. 4), Oppeln.

12th brig. of cav., Neisse: 6th regt. of Hussars "Count Goetzen" (Siles. No. 2), Leobschütz; 2nd regt. of Uhlans "von Katzler" (Siles.), Gleiwitz.

6th brig. of field-art., Breslau: 6th regt. of field-art. "von Peucker" (Siles.), Breslau; 21st regt. of field-art. "von Clausewitz" (Upper-Siles.), Neisse; 6th bat. of the train (Siles.), Breslau.

Attached to the corps are: 6th regt. of foot-art. "von Dieskau" (Siles.), Neisse; 6th bat. of rifles (Siles.), Oels; 6th bat. of pioneers (Siles.), Neisse.

SEVENTH ARMY CORPS, MÜNSTER

13th division, Münster.

On the March.   2nd Regiment of Field Artillery "Horn" (Royal Bavarian).

25th brig. of inf., Münster: 13th regt. of inf. "Herwarth von Bittenfeld" (Westph. No. 1), Münster; 56th regt. of inf. "Vogel von Falkenstein" (Westph. No. 7), Wesel.

26th brig. of inf., Minden: 15th regt. of inf. "Prince Frederick of the Netherlands" (Westph. No. 2), Minden; 55th regt. of inf. "Count Bülow von Dennewitz" (Westph. No. 6), Detmold.

79th brig. of inf., Paderborn: 158th regt. of inf., Paderborn; 159th regt. of inf., Mühlheim.

13th brig. of cav., Münster: 4th regt. of Cuirassiers "von Driesen" (Westph.), Münster; 8th regt. of Hussars "Emperor Nicholas of Russia" (Westph. No. 1), Paderborn.

14th division, Düsseldorf.

27th brig. of inf., Cologne: 16th regt. of inf. "Count von Sparr" (Westph. No. 3), Cologne; 53rd regt. of inf. (Westph. No. 5), Cologne.

28th brig. of inf., Düsseldorf: 39th regt. of Fusiliers (Lower-Rhen.), Düsseldorf; 57th regt. of inf. "Duke Ferdinand of Brunswick" (Westph. No. 8), Wesel.

14th brig. of cav., Düsseldorf: 11th regt. of Hussars (Westph. No. 2), Düsseldorf; 5th regt. of Uhlans (Westph.), Düsseldorf.

7th brig. of field-art., Münster: 7th regt. of field-art. (Westph. No. 1), Wesel; 22nd regt. of field-art. (Westph. No. 2), Münster; 7th bat. of the train (Westph.), Münster.

Attached to the corps are: 7th regt. of foot-art. (Westph.), Cologne; 7th bat. of rifles (Westph.), Bückeburg; 7th bat. of pioneers (Westph.), Deutz.

EIGHTH ARMY CORPS, COBLENZ

15th division, Cologne.

29th brig. of inf., Aix-la-Chapelle : 40th regt. of Fusiliers "Prince Charles Anton of Hohenzollern" (Hohenzoll.), Aix-la-Chapelle ; 65th regt. of inf. (Rhen. No. 5), Cologne.

30th brig. of inf., Coblenz: 28th regt. of inf. "von Goeben" (Rhen. No. 2), Ehrenbreitstein; 68th regt. of inf. (Rhen. No. 6), Coblenz.

15th brig. of cav., Cologne: 8th regt. of Cuirassiers "Count Gessler" (Rhen.), Deutz; 7th regt. of Hussars "King William I." (Rhen. No. 1), Bonn.

16th division, Treves.

31st brig. of inf., Treves: 29th regt. of inf. "von Horn" (Rhen. No. 3), Treves; 69th regt. of inf. (Rhen. No. 7), Treves.

32nd brig. of inf., Saarbrücken: 30th regt. of inf. "Count Werder" (Rhen. No. 4), Saarlouis; 70th regt. of inf. (Rhen. No. 8), Saarbrücken.

80th brig. of inf., Treves: 160th regt. of inf., Bonn; 161st regt. of inf., Treves.

16th brig. of cav., Saarbrücken: 7th regt. of Dragoons (Westph.), Saarbrücken; 7th regt. of Uhlans "Grand Duke Frederick of Baden" (Rhen.), Saarbrücken.

8th brig. of field-art., Coblenz: 8th regt. of field-art. "von Holtzendorff" (Rhen. No. 1), Saarlouis; 23rd regt. of field-art. (Rhen. No. 2), Coblenz; 8th bat. of the train (Rhen.), Ehrenbreitstein.

Attached to the corps are: 9th regt. of foot-art. (Schleswig-Holstein), Ehrenbreitstein; 8th bat. of pioneers. (Rhen.), Coblenz.

NINTH ARMY CORPS, ALTONA

17th division, Schwerin.

33rd brig. of inf., Altona: 75th regt. of inf. (Hanseat. No. 1), Bremen; 76th regt. of inf. (Hanseat. No. 2), Hamburg.

34th brig. of inf. (Grand-Duchy of Mecklenb.), Schwerin: 89th regt. of Grenadiers (Grand-Duchy of Mecklenb.), Schwerin; 90th regt. of Fusiliers (Grand-Duchy of Mecklenb.), Rostock.

81st brig. of inf., Lübeck: 162nd regt. of inf. (Hanseat. No. 3), Lübeck; 163rd regt. of inf., Neumünster.

17th brig. of cav. (Grand-Duchy of Mecklenb.), Schwerin: 17th regt. of Dragoons (Mecklenb. No. 1), Ludwigslust; 18th regt. of Dragoons (Mecklenb. No. 2), Parchim.

18th division, Flensburg.

35th brig. of inf., Flensburg: 84th regt. of inf. "von Manstein" (Schleswig), Schleswig; 86th regt. of Fusiliers "The Queen's Own" (Schleswig-Holstein), Flensburg.

36th brig. of inf., Rendsburg: 31st regt. of inf. "Count Bose" (Thür. No. 1), Altona; 85th regt. of inf. "Duke of Holstein" (Holstein), Rendsburg.

18th brig. of cav., Altona: 15th regt. of Hussars "Queen Wilhelmina of the Netherlands" (Hanov.), Wandsbeck; 16th regt. of Hussars "Emperor Franz Joseph of Austria" (Schleswig-Holstein), Schleswig.

9th brig. of field.-art., Altona: 9th regt. of field-art. (Schleswig), Itzehoe; 24th regt. of field-art. (Holstein), Schwerin; 9th bat. of the train (Schleswig-Holstein), Rendsburg.

Attached to the corps are: 9th bat. of rifles (Lauenburg), Ratzeburg; 9th bat. of pioneers (Schleswig-Holstein), Harburg.

TENTH ARMY CORPS, HANOVER

19th division, Hanover.

37th brig. of inf., Oldenburg: 78th regt. of inf. "Duke Frederick William of Brunswick" (East-Fries.), Osnabrück; 91st regt. of inf. (Oldenb.), Oldenburg.

38th brig. of inf., Hanover: 73rd regt. of Fusiliers "Fieldmarshal Prince Albrecht of Prussia" (Hanov.), Hanover; 74th regt. of inf. (Hanov. No. 1), Hanover.

19th brig. of cav., Hanover: 19th regt. of Dragoons (Oldenb.), Oldenburg; 13th regt. of Uhlans (Royal Hanov. No. 1), Hanover.

20th division, Hanover.

Artillery Firing.   27th Regiment of Field Artillery (Nassau).

39th brig. of inf., Hanover: 79th regt. of inf. "von Voigts-Rhetz" (Hanov. No. 3), Hildesheim; 164th regt. of inf. (Hanov. No. 4), Hameln.

40th brig. of inf., Brunswick: 77th regt. of inf. (Hanov. No. 2), Celle; 92nd regt. of inf. (Bruns.), Brunswick.

20th brig. of cav., Hanover: 16th regt. of Dragoons (Hanov. No. 2), Lüneburg; 17th regt. of Hussars (Bruns.), Brunswick.

10th brig. of field-art., Hanover: 10th regt. of field-art. "von Scharnhorst" (Hanov. No. 1), Hanover; 26th regt. of field-art. (Hanov. No. 2), Verden; 10th bat. of the train (Hanov.), Hanover.

Attached to the corps is: 10th bat. of pioneers (Hanov.), Minden.

ELEVENTH ARMY CORPS, CASSEL

22nd division, Cassel.

43rd brig. of inf., Cassel: 82nd regt. of inf. (Hess. No. 2), Göttingen; 83rd regt. of inf. "von Wittich" (Hess. No. 3), Cassel.

44th brig. of inf., Cassel: 32nd regt. of inf. (Thür. No. 2), Meiningen; 167th regt. of inf., Cassel.

22nd brig. of cav., Cassel: 5th regt. of Dragoons "von Manteuffel" (Rhen.), Hof-Geismar; 14th regt. of Hussars "Landgrave Frederick II. of Hesse-Homburg" (Hess. No. 2), Cassel.

38th division, Erfurt.

76th brig. of inf., Erfurt: 71st regt. of inf. (Thür. No. 3), Erfurt; 95th regt. of inf. (Thür. No. 6), Gotha.

83rd brig. of inf., Erfurt: 94th regt. of inf. "Grand Duchy of Saxony" (Thür. No. 5), Weimar; 96th regt. of inf. (Thür. No. 7), Gera.

11th brig. of field-art., Cassel: 11th regt. of field-art. (Hess.), Cassel; 27th regt. of field-art. (Nassau), Mayence; 11th bat. of the train (Hess.), Cassel; 11th bat. of rifles (Hess.), Marburg.

TWELFTH ARMY CORPS, DRESDEN
(ROYAL SAXON NO. 1)

23rd division (Royal Saxon No. 1), Dresden.

45th brig. of inf. (Royal Saxon No. 1), Dresden: 100th regt. of inf. (Saxon Grenadiers No. 1—Body-Guards), Dresden; 101st regt. of inf. "Emperor William, King of Prussia" (Saxon Grenadiers No. 2), Dresden.

46th brig. of inf. (Royal Saxon No. 2), Dresden: 102nd regt. of inf. (Saxon No. 3) "Prince-Regent Luitpold of Bavaria," Zittau; 117th regt. of inf. (Saxon No. 12), Dresden.

23rd brig. of cav. (Royal Saxon No. 1), Dresden: Regt. of Horse-Guards (Heavy Regt. No. 1), Dresden; 17th regt. of Uhlans "Emperor Franz Joseph of Austria" (Saxon No. 1), Oschatz; squadron of mounted rifles (Twelfth army corps).

32nd division (Royal Saxon No. 3), Dresden.

63rd brig. of inf. (Royal Saxon No. 5), Dresden: 103rd regt. of inf. (Saxon No. 4), Bautzen; 178th regt. of inf. (Saxon No. 13), Kamenz.

64th brig. of inf. (Royal Saxon No. 6), Dresden:

108th regt. of rifles (Fusiliers) "Prince-Regent George," Dresden; 12th bat. of rifles (Saxon No. 1), Freiberg; 13th bat. of rifles (Saxon No. 2), Dresden.

32nd brig. of cav. (Royal Saxon No. 3), Dresden: 18th regt. of Hussars "The King's Own" (Saxon No. 1), Grossenhain; 19th regt. of Hussars "The Queen's Own" (Saxon No. 2), Grimma.

12th brig. of field-art., Dresden: 12th regt. of field-art. (Saxon No. 1), Dresden; 28th regt. of field-art. (Saxon No. 2), Pirna; 12th bat. of the train, Dresden.

Attached to the corps are: 12th bat. of pioneers, Dresden; 7th and 8th comp. of railway troops, Berlin.

THIRTEENTH ARMY CORPS, STUTTGART
(ROYAL WÜRTEMBERG)

26th division (Royal Würtemb. No. 1), Stuttgart.

51st brig. of inf. (Royal Würtemb. No. 1), Stuttgart: 119th regt. of inf. "Queen Olga" (Würtemb. Grenadiers No. 1), Stuttgart; 125th regt. of inf. "Emperor Frederick, King of Prussia" (Würtemb. No. 7), Stuttgart.

52nd brig. of inf. (Royal Würtemb. No. 2), Ludwigsburg: 121st regt. of inf. "Old Würtemberg" (Würtemb. No. 3), Ludwigsburg; 122nd regt. of inf. "Emperor Franz Joseph of Austria" (Würtemb. No. 4), Heilbronn.

26th brig. of cav. (Royal Würtemb. No. 1), Stuttgart: 25th regt. of Dragoons "Queen Olga" (Würtemb. No. 1), Ludwigsburg; 26th regt. of Dragoons "The King's Own" (Würtemb. No. 2), Stuttgart.

27th division (Royal Würtemb. No. 2), Ulm.

53rd brig. of inf. (Royal Würtemb. No. 3), Ulm: 123rd regt. of inf. "King Charles" (Würtemb. Grenadiers No. 5), Ulm; 124th regt. of inf. "King William I." (Würtemb. No. 6), Weingarten.

54th brig. of inf. (Royal Würtemb. No. 4), Ulm: 120th regt. of inf. "Emperor William, King of Prussia" (Würtemb. No. 2), Ulm; 127th regt. of inf. (Würtemb. No. 9), Ulm; 180th regt. of inf. (Würtemb. No. 10), Tübingen; 126th regt. of inf. "Grand Duke Frederick of Baden" (Würtemb. No. 8), under Fifteenth army corps.

27th brig. of cav. (Royal Würtemb. No. 2), Ulm: 19th regt. of Uhlans "King Charles" (Würtemb. No. 1), Ulm; 20th regt. of Uhlans "King William I." (Würtemb. No. 2), Ludwigsburg.

13th brig. of field-art. (Royal Würtemb.), Ludwigsburg: 13th regt. of field-art. "King Charles" (Würtemb. No. 1), Ulm; 29th regt. of field-art. "Prince-Regent Luitpold of Bavaria" (Würtemb. No. 2), Ludwigsburg; 13th bat. of the train (Würtemb.), Ludwigsburg.

Attached to the corps are: 13th bat. of pioneers (Würtemb.), Ulm; 4th comp. of the railway troops (Royal Würtemb.), Berlin.

FOURTEENTH ARMY CORPS, CARLSRUHE

28th division, Carlsruhe.

55th brig. of inf., Carlsruhe: 109th regt. of inf. (Baden Grenadiers No. 1—Body-Guards), Carlsruhe; 110th regt. of inf. "Emperor William" (Baden Grenadiers No. 2), Mannheim and Heidelberg.

56th brig. of inf., Rastatt: 25th regt. of inf. "von Lützow" (Rhen. No. 1), Rastatt; 111th regt. of inf. "Margrave Ludwig William" (Baden No. 3), Rastatt.

28th brig. of cav., Carlsruhe: 20th regt. of Dragoons (Baden No. 1—Body-Guards), Carlsruhe; 21st regt. of Dragoons (Baden No. 2), Bruchsal.

29th division, Freiburg in Baden.

57th brig. of inf., Freiburg: 113th regt. of inf. (Baden No. 5), Freiburg; 114th regt. of inf. "Emperor Frederick III." (Baden No. 6), Constance-Hohenzollern.

58th brig. of inf., Mühlhausen: 112th regt. of inf. "Prince William" (Baden No. 4), Mühlhausen; 142nd regt. of inf. (Baden No. 7), Mühlhausen.

29th brig. of cav., Colmar: 14th regt. of Dragoons (Kurmärck.), Colmar; 22nd regt. of Dragoons "Prince Charles" (Baden No. 3), Mühlhausen; one squadron of mounted rifles.

39th division, Colmar.

82nd brig. of inf. (rifles), Colmar: 4th bat. of rifles (Magdeburg), Colmar; 8th bat. of rifles (Rhenish), Schlettstadt; 10th bat. of rifles (Hanover), Colmar; 14th bat. of rifles (Mecklenburg), Colmar.

84th brig. of inf. (rifles), Lahr: 169th regt. of inf. (Baden No. 8), Lahr; 170th regt. of inf. (Baden No. 9), Offenburg.

14th brig. of field-art., Carlsruhe: 14th regt. of field-art. (Baden No. 1), Carlsruhe; 30th regt. of field-art. (Baden No. 2), Rastatt; 14th bat. of the train (Baden), Durlach.

Attached to the corps are: 14th regt. of foot-art. (Baden), Strasburg; 14th bat. of pioneers (Baden), Kehl.

FIFTEENTH ARMY CORPS, STRASBURG

30th division, Strasburg.

59th brig. of inf., Saarburg: 97th regt. of inf., Saarburg; 136th regt. of inf., Dieuze.

60th brig. of inf., Strasburg: 99th regt. of inf., Zabern; 143rd regt. of inf., Strasburg.

85th brig. of inf., Strasburg: 105th regt. of inf. "King William II. of Würtemberg" (Saxon No. 6), Strasburg; 171st regt. of inf., Bitsch; 172nd regt. of inf., Strasburg.

30th brig. of cav., Saarburg: 11th regt. of Uhlans (Brandenb. No. 2), Saarburg; 15th regt. of Uhlans (Schleswig-Holstein), Saarburg.

31st division, Strasburg.

61st brig. of inf., Strasburg: 126th regt. of inf. "Grand Duke Frederick of Baden" (Würtemb. No. 8), Strasburg; 132nd regt. of inf., Strasburg; 138th regt. of inf., Strasburg.

62nd brig. of inf., Hagenau: 60th regt. of inf. "Margrave Charles" (Brandenb. No. 7), Weissenburg; 137th regt. of inf., Hagenau.

31st brig. of cav., Strasburg: 15th regt. of Dragoons (Siles. No. 3), Hagenau; 9th regt. of Hussars (Rhen. No. 2), Strasburg; one squadron of mounted rifles.

15th brig. of field-art., Strasburg: 15th regt. of field-art., Strasburg; 31st regt. of field-art., Hagenau; 15th bat. of the train, Strasburg.

Attached to the corps are: 10th regt. of foot-art., Strasburg; 13th bat. of foot-art., Ulm; Com. of the pioneers of the fifteenth army corps; 15th bat. of pioneers, Strasburg; 19th bat. of pioneers, Strasburg.

SIXTEENTH ARMY CORPS, METZ

33rd division, Metz.

65th brig. of inf., Mörchingen: 17th regt. of inf. "Count Barfuss" (Westph. No. 4), Mörchingen; 144th regt. of inf., Mörchingen.

66th brig. of inf., Metz: 98th regt. of inf., Metz; 130th regt. of inf., Metz.

33rd brig. of cav., Metz: 9th regt. of Dragoons (Hanov. No. 1), Metz; 13th regt. of Dragoons (Schleswig-Holstein), Metz.

34th division, Metz.

67th brig. of inf., Metz: 67th regt. of inf. (Magdeb. No. 4), Metz; 131st regt. of inf., Metz.

68th brig. of inf., Metz: 135th regt. of inf., Diedenhofen; 145th regt. of inf. "The King's Own." Metz.

86th brig. of inf., Metz: 173rd regt. of inf., St Avold; 174th regt. of inf., Metz.

34th brig. of cav., Metz: 6th regt. of Dragoons (Magdeb.), Diedenhofen; 14th regt. of Uhlans (Hanov. No. 2), St. Avold.

16th brig. of field-art., Metz: 33rd regt. of field-art., Metz; 34th regt. of field-art., Metz; 16th bat. of the train, Fohrbach.

Attached to the corps are: 8th regt. of foot-art. (Rhen.), Metz; 12th regt. of foot-art. (Royal Saxon), Metz; 2nd regt. of Royal Bavarian foot-art., Metz; 16th bat. of pioneers, Metz; 20th bat. of pioneers, Metz.

SEVENTEENTH ARMY CORPS, DANTZIC

35th division, Graudenz.

69th brig. of inf., Graudenz: 14th regt. of inf. "Count Schwerin" (Pom. No. 3), Graudenz; 141st regt. of inf., Graudenz.

70th brig. of inf., Thorn: 21st regt. of inf. "von Borcke" (Pom. No. 4), Thorn; 61st regt. of inf. "von der Marwitz" (Pom. No. 8), Thorn.

87th brig. of inf., Thorn: 175th regt. of inf., Graudenz; 176th regt. of inf., Thorn.

35th brig. of cav., Graudenz: 5th regt. of Cuirassiers "Prince Frederick Eugene of Würtemberg" (West-Pruss.), Riesenburg; 4th regt. of Uhlans "von Schmidt" (Pom. No. 1), Thorn.

36th division, Dantzic.

71st brig. of inf., Dantzic: 5th regt. of Grenadiers "King Frederick I." (East-Pruss. No. 4), Dantzic; 128th regt. of inf., Dantzic.

72nd brig. of inf., Deutsch-Eylau: 18th regt. of inf. "von Grolman" (Posen No. 1), Osterode; 44th regt. of inf. "Count Dönhoff" (East-Pruss. No. 7), Deutsch-Eylau; 152nd regt. of inf., Deutsch-Eylau.

36th brig. of cav., Dantzic: 1st regt. of Hussars (Body-Guards No. 1), Dantzic; 5th regt. of Hussars "Prince Blücher von Wahlstatt" (Pom.), Stolp; one squadron of mounted rifles.

17th brig. of field-art., Dantzic: 35th regt. of field-art., Graudenz; 36th regt. of field-art., Dantzic; 17th bat. of the train, Dantzic.

Attached to the corps are: 11th regt. of foot-art., Thorn; 15th regt. of foot-art., Thorn; 2nd bat. of rifles (Pom.), Culm; 2nd bat. of pioneers (Pom.), Thorn.

EIGHTEENTH ARMY CORPS, FRANKFURT-ON-THE-MAIN

21st division, Frankfurt.
    41st brig. of inf., Mayence: 87th regt. of inf. (Nassau No. 1), Mayence; 88th regt. of inf. (Nassau No. 2), Mayence.
    42nd brig. of inf., Frankfurt: 80th regt. of Fusiliers "von Gersdorff" (Hess.), Wiesbaden; 81st regt. of inf. (Hess. No. 1), Frankfurt; 166th regt. of inf., Hanau.
    21st brig. of cav., Frankfurt: 13th regt. of Hussars "King Humbert of Italy" (Hess. No. 1), Mayence; 6th regt. of Uhlans (Thür.), Hanau.
25th division (Grand-Duchy of Hesse), Darmstadt.
    49th brig. of inf. (Grand-Duchy of Hesse No. 1), Darmstadt: 115th regt. of inf. (Grand-Duchy of Hesse No. 1—Body-Guards), Darmstadt; 116th regt. of inf. "Emperor William" (Grand-Duchy of Hesse No. 2), Giessen; 168th regt. of inf. (Grand-Duchy of Hesse No. 5), Offenbach.
    50th brig. of inf. (Grand-Duchy of Hesse No. 2), Mayence: 117th regt. of inf. (Grand-Duchy of Hesse No. 3—Body-Guards), Mayence; 118th regt. of inf. "Prince Carl" (Grand-Duchy of Hesse No. 4), Worms.
    25th brig. of cav. (Grand-Duchy of Hesse), Darmstadt: 23rd regt. of Dragoons (Grand-Duchy of Hesse No. 1—Dragoon-Guards), Darmstadt; 24th regt. of Dragoons (Grand-Duchy of Hesse No. 2—Body-Guards), Darmstadt.

25th regt. of field-art. (Grand-Duchy of Hesse), Darmstadt; 3rd regt. of foot-art. "Grand Master of Field-Ordnance" (Brandenb.), Mayence; 11th bat. of pioneers (Grand-Duchy of Hesse), Mayence; 25th bat. of the train (Grand-Duchy of Hesse), Darmstadt.

NINETEENTH ARMY CORPS, LEIPSIC
(ROYAL SAXON NO. 2)

24th division (Royal Saxon No. 2), Leipsic.
    47th brig. of inf. (Royal Saxon No. 3), Leipsic: 139th regt. of inf. (Saxon No. 11), Döbeln; 179th regt. of inf. (Saxon No. 14), Leipsic.
    48th brig. of inf. (Royal Saxon No. 4): 106th regt. of inf. "Prince George" (Saxon No. 7), Leipsic; 107th regt. of inf. "Prince Johann George" (Saxon No. 8), Leipsic.
    24th brig. of cav. (Royal Saxon No. 2), Leipsic: Regt. of Carabiniers (Heavy Regt. No. 2), Borna; 18th regt. of Uhlans (Saxon No. 2), Leipsic.
40th division (Royal Saxon No. 4), Chemnitz.
    88th brig. of inf. (Royal Saxon No. 7), Chemnitz: 104th regt. of inf. "Prince Frederick August"

(Saxon No. 5), Chemnitz; 15th bat. of rifles (Saxon No. 3), Wurzen.
    89th brig. of inf. (Royal Saxon No. 8), Zwickau: 133rd regt. of inf. (Saxon No. 9), Zwickau; 134th regt. of inf. (Saxon No. 10), Leipsic; 105th regt. of inf. "King William II. of Würtemberg" (Saxon No. 6).

32nd regt. of field-art. (Saxon No. 3), Riesa; 12th regt. of foot-art. attached to the Sixteenth army corps.

FIRST ROYAL BAVARIAN ARMY CORPS, MÜNICH

1st division, Munich.
    1st brig. of inf., Munich: Regt. of inf. (Body-Guards), Munich; 1st regt. of inf. "The Kings Own," Munich.
    2nd brig. of inf., Munich: 2nd regt. of inf. "Crown Prince," Munich; 16th regt. of inf. "Grand-Duke Ferdinand of Toscana," Passau; 1st bat. of rifles, Straubing.
    1st brig. of cav., Munich: Regt. of Heavy Riders No. 1 "Prince Charles of Bavaria," Munich; Regt. of Heavy Riders No. 2 "vac. Crown Prince Archduke Rudolph of Austria," Landshut.
2nd division, Augsburg.
    3rd brig. of inf., Augsburg: 3rd regt. of inf. "Prince Charles of Bavaria," Augsburg; 20th regt. of inf., Lindau.
    4th brig. of inf., Ingolstadt: 10th regt. of inf. "Prince Ludwig," Ingolstadt; 13th regt. of inf. "Emperor Franz Joseph of Austria," Ingolstadt.
    11th brig. of inf., Neu-Ulm: 12th regt. of inf. "Prince Arnulf," Neu-Ulm; 15th regt. of inf. "King Albert of Saxony," Neuburg.
    2nd brig. of cav., Augsburg: 2nd regt. of Chevaulegers "Taxis," Dillingen; 4th regt. of Chevaulegers "The King's Own," Augsburg.
    1st brig. of field-art., Munich: 1st regt. of field-art. "Prince-Regent Luitpold," Munich; 3rd regt. of field-art. "Queen's Mother," Munich; 1st bat. of the train, Munich.

Attached to the corps are: 1st regt. of foot-art. "vac. Bothmer," Ingolstadt; bat. of railway troops, Munich; 1st bat. of pioneers, Ingolstadt.

SECOND ROYAL BAVARIAN ARMY CORPS, WÜRZBURG

3rd division, Nuremberg.
    5th brig. of inf., Regensburg: 11th regt. of inf. "von der Tann," Regensburg; 21st regt. of inf., Fürth.
    6th brig. of inf., Nuremberg: 14th regt. of inf. "Hartmann," Nuremberg; 19th regt. of inf. "King Humbert of Italy," Erlangen.
    3rd brig. of cav., Nuremberg: 1st regt. of Chevaulegers "Emperor Nicholas of Russia" Nuremberg; squadron of mounted rifles (Second army corps); 6th regt. of Chevaulegers "Prince Albrecht of Prussia," Bayreuth.
4th division, Würzburg.
    7th brig. of inf., Würzburg: 5th regt. of inf. "Grand-Duke Ernst Ludwig of Hesse," Bamberg; 9th regt. of inf. "Wrede," Würzburg; 2nd bat. of rifles, Aschaffenburg.
    8th brig. of inf., Bayreuth: 6th regt. of inf. "Emperor William, King of Prussia," Amberg; 7th regt. of inf. "Prince Leopold," Bayreuth.

1st and 2nd Regiments of Railway Troops.

4th brig. of cav., Bamberg: 1st regt. of Uhlans "Emperor William II., King of Prussia," Bamberg; 2nd regt. of Uhlans "The King's Own," Ansbach.

5th division, Landau.

9th brig. of inf., Landau: 17th regt. of inf. "Orff," Germersheim; 18th regt. of inf. "Prince Ludwig Ferdinand," Landau.

10th brig. of inf., Metz: 4th regt. of inf. "King William of Würtemberg," Metz; 8th regt. of inf. "Pranckh," Metz.

12th brig. of inf., Zweibrücken: 22nd regt. of inf., Zweibrücken; 23rd regt. of inf., Landau.

5th brig. of cav., Dieuze: 3rd regt. of Chevaulegers "Duke Charles Theodore," Dieuze; 5th regt. of Chevaulegers "Archduke Albrecht of Austria," Saargemünd.

2nd brig. of field-art., Würzburg: 2nd regt. of field-art. "Horn," Würzburg; 4th regt. of field-art. "The King's Own," Augsburg; 5th regt. of field-art., Landau; 2nd bat. of the train, Würzburg.

Attached to the corps are: 2nd regt. of foot-art., Metz; 2nd bat. of pioneers, Speyer.

While this book was being published the organization of the German army underwent far-reaching and important changes, which are minutely treated in a supplementary article by Major-General von Specht. As may be seen from the preceding classification and distribution of the army, the number of the army corps has been raised from twenty, as stated in the chapter on organization, to twenty-three. The new eighteenth corps was formed out of the eleventh corps, while the latter was replenished by some regiments of the fourth and tenth corps. The thirty-seventh and thirty-ninth divisions have been organized from parts of the fourteenth corps. The Saxon contingent is augmented by a new army corps, the second Saxon, while Bavaria will also be represented by a new corps, the third Bavarian. This is to be formed by the recently-organized fifth Bavarian division, which consists of three brigades of infantry and one brigade of cavalry. The innovation goes into effect on October 1st, 1899. The two newly-formed divisions of the frontier corps, the first and the fourteenth, are intrusted with special duties of frontier service in case of war. The new organization of the field-artillery, as treated in the supplementary article, was not introduced in the preceding chapter, as it goes into effect on and after October 1st, 1899. Each army corps' strength is given with only one brigade of field-artillery, comprising two strong regiments of from three to four detachments. In the future each division will be represented by one brigade of field-artillery. The brigade will comprise two smaller regiments, with two detachments of three batteries and about seventy-two guns.

THE GENERAL STAFF OF THE GERMAN ARMY

Prussia's victorious campaigns during the years 1864 and 1866, and particularly the immense success achieved by German arms during the war with France (1870–71) have attracted the attention of the nations to the conduct and operations on the field of the Prussian and German armies in these campaigns. They have also won for the name of von Moltke, chief of the German general staff, a world-wide fame. But it was not only the magnitude of the success which gained such renown for the German army and its leaders; the unfailing certainty, swiftness, vigor, and decisiveness of the warfare, together with the rapid and uninterrupted succession of brilliant victories, also became objects of admiration and wonder, and still continue to be so.

On the other side of the Atlantic, especially in the United States of North America, the new home of so many Germans, the glorious deeds of the German nation under arms were hailed with the greatest enthusiasm. But with the eagerness of all European countries to improve upon their military institutions, after the Prussian-German model, the United States was so happily situated in its geographical and political environment, as to be free from European complications and able to look complacently on the military projects of the Old World. The events of the year 1898, however, in connection with the war with Spain, so victorious to the American nation in its results, but exacting so many sacrifices, with its lessons, admonitions, and consequences, have altered the condition of affairs in the New World to such an extent that a consideration of the organization of the German general staff does not seem to be untimely.

Like the entire German army, the German general staff is organized on the basis and after the model of the Prussian staff, the latter naturally forming the principal part, only augmented by the general staffs of Bavaria, Würtemberg, and Saxony. The Prussian general staff, like the Prussian army, had a small beginning. It is the lot of the general staff, which means the staff, the help, or support of the general, according to the saying of the prominent military author von Clausewitz, to "transform the commanding general's ideas into orders, not only by conveying them to the troops, but still more, by perfect-ing details, and thus saving the general all unnecessary trouble." Frederick the Great, in fighting his famous battles of Rossbach and Leuthen with but 30,000 men, had no need of a special staff. He gave his generals the necessary orders either verbally or in writing, while he personally selected and trained the few aides-de-camp he needed. With the increase of the army the necessity arose for a larger staff of well trained and qualified assistants. Soon after the Seven Years' War, Frederick the Great established the "quartermaster-general staff." It consisted of one quartermaster-general, one quartermaster, and fourteen quartermaster-lieutenants. Out of this developed, in 1857, the Prussian general staff under the guidance of judicious men, especially under the direction of General von Moltke. The organization then reached that importance and efficiency so fully demonstrated in the great wars of 1864–66 and 1870–71.

The German general staff now consists in time of peace of one chief of staff, 4 quartermasters-in-chief, (lieutenant-generals), 30 colonels and generals-in-chief, 83 staff officers, and 91 captains,—in all 209 officers. This, with an average of 20 officers serving in the capacity of railroad commissioners, gives a total of 229 (225–230) Prussian officers. Besides these, there are 24 Bavarian, 11 Saxon, and 7 Würtemberg (42) officers, or a grand total of the general staff in time of peace of from 267 to 271 officers. Of this number, from 180 to 190 officers form the general staff of the army proper, 110 to 120 of whom belong to the general staff of the troops, while from 70 to 80 are assigned to the great general staff.

In order to understand the number, classification, and organization of this institution, it must be borne in mind that in the Prussian and German army not the entire staff of officers assigned to a general is identified with the general staff. There is a distinction made between the adjutancy and the general staff. It is the duty of the adjutants to superintend the discharge of the entire verbal and written regulations of the service in the different branches, including those who have charge of the rosters, lists, petitions, and matters pertaining to the reserve and to pensions. It is the task of the general staff officers to attend to all matters relating to the movement, quartering, engagement, and mobilizing of the troops, and to warfare in general. This accounts for the relatively small number of the general staff officers on a peace footing of almost 560,000 noncommissioned officers and men.

The placing of the army on a war footing naturally increases the number of the general staff officers. To the active German army at the beginning of the war of 1870–71 were assigned 200 general staff officers. The number was increased, however, during the progress of the war and to such an extent that the present number of the general staff officers assigned to the active army is about 250. This increased supply is secured by the character of the entire organization and by the manner of replenishing the general staff. Its nursery is the war academy established at Berlin in the year 1810, and designed to familiarize a number of officers belonging to the different branches of the service, and at the same time specially adapted to its requirements, with the higher branches of military science; and by such means to enlarge and increase their knowledge of tactics, and to educate and quicken their judgment of military affairs at large. The schedule of instruction comprises statistics, war history, tactics, fortification, siege operations, sketching, surveying and drawing, general staff service, and training in travel, means of communication, civil government, political economy, public and international law, military sanitary law, general history, general and physical geography, mathematics, geodesy, natural philosophy, chemistry, French and (optional) Russian, Polish, and English.

Officers having shown practical proficiency during a period of three years of service may apply for entrance examination. The regular course lasts for three years. During the yearly courses is sandwiched in some service with other branches of troops. The final examination decides the matter of the further employment of the officer either as instructor at one of the military schools, or in the army's service as adjutant or on the general staff. Those of superior mental and physical qualifications are selected to serve on the latter, and are furthermore trained and approved in some command under the general staff, lasting for a period of from one to two years. By this arrangement only the best of the selected officers are taken into the general staff. Out of the 400 who annually study at the war academy only 120 as a rule take the final examination, of which only a proportion of from six to ten are assigned to the general staff. A further training takes place either on the great general staff, or in the service connected with the commands of the troops (army corps and divisions), so that by an expedient change each officer of the general staff receives a thorough education in every branch of the general staff's work. By the yearly training travels and by employment at the great manœuvres of the army, as well as by theme compositions, literary lessons, and verbal recita-

tions, the efficiency of the general staff officer is constantly fostered, tested, and approved. Of special benefit has been the following out of the principle not to make the general staff an exclusive body or caste, in which the officer advances from the rank of lieutenant to that of general. By the temporary transferring of the staff officers to the front, a practical knowledge of the service is continually maintained. By this method the eye and ear of the officer are trained to the actual condition of the army and to the wants of the common soldier. By this process the officer's ability to handle and direct the troops is not founded upon routine knowledge merely, but upon practical experience, fostered and stimulated by study. According to this, every officer of the general staff must have successfully trained and handled a company, a squadron, or a battery for the period of one year, and that later on he must again have been intrusted with the command of a battalion or a regiment, and with the handling and the command of still larger bodies of troops, before he advances to the higher grades of the general staff, the rank of a chief, or that of a general. By this arrangement a further gain is assured in that a number of officers, academically and practically trained in the duties of the general staff, are to be found attached to the different branches of the service, and competent to reënter in sufficient numbers the ranks of the general staff in time of war.

This careful selection and training of the general staff officers is necessitated by the importance and the extent of the task falling to the lot of an efficient general staff. To be fully equal to this task the organization of the general staff is expediently fitted. Accordingly the latter is classified in the general staff proper and in the great general staff.

It is the function of the general staff of the troops to attend to all matters which formerly fell to the general staff proper, namely, those touching the movement, quartering, and engagement of the troops, and to the drawing up, working out and enforcing of orders for the strategical and tactical disposition of the commanders. For this purpose are assigned — the administration of the larger fortresses excepted — some general staff officers to the divisions, one to each; to the army corps, two to each corps, and three to each in war time. At the head of all stands the chief of the army corps' general staff. This officer is at the same time chief of the entire staff of the general command (of the army corps) and is invested with far-reaching authority in consequence of the great responsibility connected with the position.

To the general staff of the army corps also falls the laborious task of the mobilization of the army corps, the drawing up of the plan of mobilization proper, the establishment and enforcement of which requires the coöperation not only of the military but also of the civic authorities and especially of those of the railroad bureau

Railway Troops Practicing at the Tempelhof Drill Grounds.

in each corps district. But even with this, the functions of the general staff of the troops do not stop. Other things become incumbent on the same. It is of the utmost importance to prepare thoroughly in time of peace for the mobilizing of the army in time of war, its transportation and assembling, in fact to prepare for all warlike operations. Hence it is a matter of great moment to be constantly and well informed of the political and military affairs of other countries, with a knowledge of their armies and fortified places. This includes the task of ascertaining, if possible, all probable designs of the enemy, to prepare and receive the best possible and most accurate material in the way of maps, not only of Germany but also those of other countries, necessary for all eventualities. That the fulfillment of these tasks requires a continuous cultivation and application of the different branches of military science in conjunction with their auxiliary sciences is obvious. At the same time it is easy to understand that the extent and heterogeneousness of this labor call for a necessary division. Consequently, just after the Napoleonic wars at the beginning of this century, those officers not detailed to the command of the troops, but assigned to the Great Headquarters of the Prussian army, were massed at a central place in Berlin. At this place the "Great General Staff" in its different departments treats the various branches falling to their lot.

The Central division treats of personal and administrative affairs.
 First division, of Russia and Scandinavia.
 Second division, of Germany.
 Third division, of France and Western Europe.
 Fourth division, of the fortresses (Russia's excepted).
 Fifth division, of Austria, Italy, and the Balkan States.
 Sixth division, of manœuvres, training travels of the general staff, and the affairs pertaining to the war academy.
 Seventh division, of the Russian fortresses.
 Eighth division, of England, America, Asia, Africa, and Australia.

These divisions, to each of which are detailed several general staff officers and sub-officers in course of training, are directed by a chief (general or colonel). Several sections are placed under the direction of a quartermaster-in-chief (lieutenant-general). At the head of the imperial survey is a quartermaster-in-chief who has charge of the trigonometrical, topographical, and cartographical divisions, the latter including also the chamber containing the war-plans.

Only the sixth division and the historical division, which includes the war records and the library, are under the immediate supervision of the chief of the general staff. In this are included the war academy, the railway brigade, the bureau of the military railroads, and the commission of the railway lines. In regard to the latter, it is worth mentioning that the railroad division deals with everything connected with the military transportation. For this purpose the imperial railroads (analogous to the bureau of railroad districts) are divided into lines, presided over, in time of peace, by line commissions. These commissions comprise a general staff officer and a railroad official of high rank, whose duty it is to be constantly prepared for and ready to supervise the transportation of the troops, and to provide the necessary material and depot facilities for immediate use in time of war. To secure the necessary scope for the fostering of the military sciences and their auxiliaries, also to afford specially gifted and talented officers a deeper study and knowledge of the different military sciences, without being interrupted by troop service, all these officers are assigned to a special division. To this belong—besides the historical division, and the library and the war records—all the officers detailed to the survey of the empire, namely to the trigonometrical, topographical, and cartographical divisions. At the head of the entire general staff, including the various organizations, stands the chief of the army's general staff. The previous statement will make it clear that this place can be filled only by a man of superior qualification, including thoroughness in all branches of military science, one who combines with a long experience clearness and acuteness of judgment and great will power, the genius of a tactician and a strategist—the capacity to weigh carefully and venture fearlessly—and who finally will be able to foster and develop the supreme organization of the general staff by his educational methods. A man, with such gifts, and so situated, will be enabled to show his best and highest qualifications and efficiency when his mind is free to soar above all distractions and encumbrances. Accordingly the chief of the general staff of the Prussian and German army, while unincumbered in his entire sphere of activity in peace and in war, is subject only to the authority of the commander-in-chief, the King of Prussia and Emperor of Germany, to whom he submits immediately all projects, reports, and statements, and whom he attends in war time at the army's headquarters.

The general staff of the other great continental armies, namely those of Russia, France, Austria, and Italy, is organized like the Prussian-German staff, with the single exception that they exceed Germany in the number of its officers: Russia has 726, France 580, Austria 476 (in war time 550), and Italy 253 general staff officers. In none of these countries, however, is the chief of the general staff invested with such absolute acting authority as in Prussia. The latter country having taken the important step, in wise anticipation and foresight, to establish the institution of the general staff over the army in the year 1821, has, therefore, precedence over the

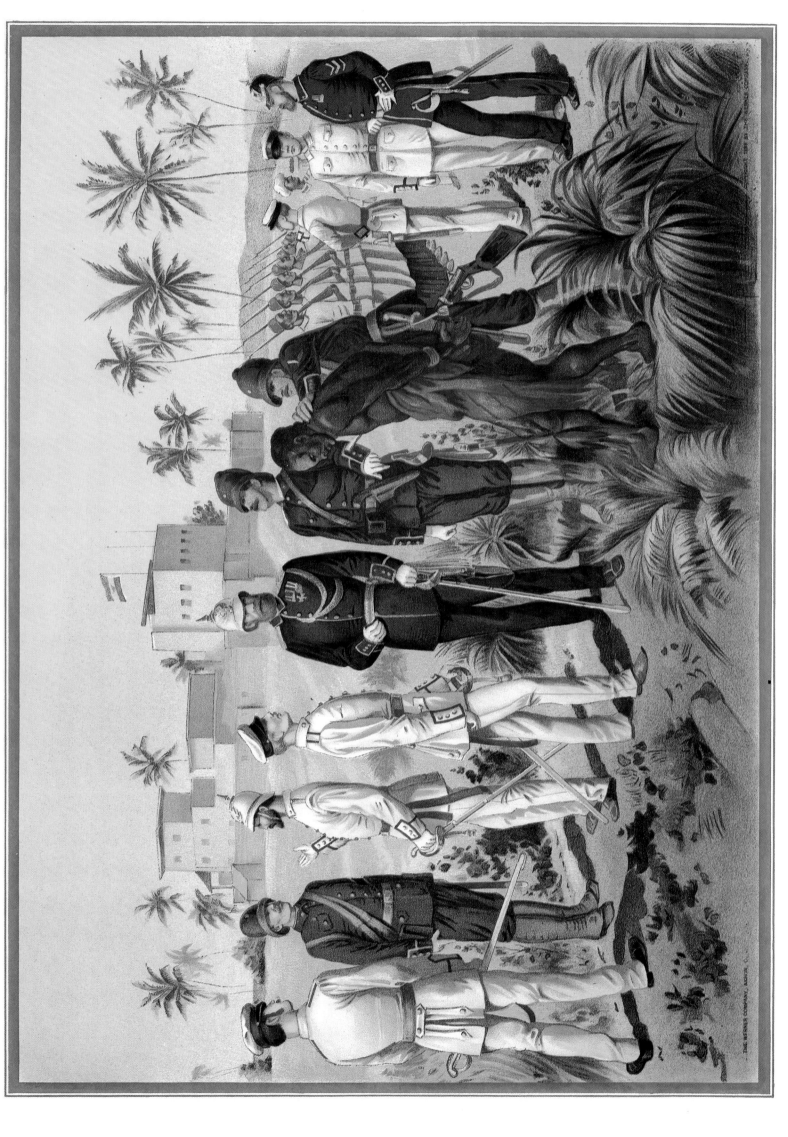

Paymaster (Undress)   Hospital Attendant (Fatigue)   Surgeon (Undress)   Lieutenant (Undress)   Commander (Full Dress)   Lieutenant (Fatigue)   Captive Mafiti Chief   Corporal (Fatigue)   Askari (Soldiers)   Sudanese (Trumpeter)   First Sergeant (Full Dress)

Sergeant (Undress)   Artificer (Undress)

The Colonial Troops of German East-Africa.

other nations. It has, moreover, opened to the Prussian-
German general staff a career of development and
achievement, which has contributed in no inconspicuous
manner to the glorious deeds of war achieved by Prussia
and Germany.

THE TRAINING OF NONCOMMISSIONED OFFICERS AND MEN

THE organization and composition of the German army, described in the preceding chapters, represent, as it were, the framework of the picture which may be said to surround every German fit to bear arms; the picture itself is seen in the vitality and strength of the organization set forth. Organization and composition create the preliminary conditions; the efficiency of the army, however,—apart from mental and physical capacity,—will, in a great measure and under general conditions, depend on the proper training of the troops. For this reason, special attention is bestowed in the German army upon the men's training. The superior officers of all ranks work to this end with indomitable zeal, energy, and faithfulness; even the Emperor's watchful eyes are constantly directed towards its fostering and development.

All branches of the service are governed by strict rules. These govern the drill and fatigue duty, the fencing, riding, driving, swimming, and shooting practice of the soldiers, and also the time given to gymnastics. Rules are laid down in a simple, clear, and concise form for the different branches of the service,—the infantry, cavalry, field and siege artillery, the pioneers, and the railway and telegraph troops. The strict enforcement of these rules is attended to by all superiors. They cannot be altered in any way, save by the Emperor, who, in the capacity of commander-in-chief, looks to their timely enforcement and fitting development.

The enrolment of the recruit takes place usually at the beginning of October. His training, after he has been bathed, measured, weighed, and clothed, commences at once, and his pedigree is taken down, with all other necessary facts about him. The commander of the company, rightly called its chief or head, whether of a company, squadron, or battery, then shoulders the responsibility of seeing to the man's individual, and to the company's entire, training. He assigns this duty to the lieutenant of the company. Under his personal and constant guidance and direction the service is performed according to a well-prepared schedule and in such a manner that every detail receives the closest attention.

The individual training, which commences about this time, takes place in sections of from twelve to sixteen men and is looked after by a noncommissioned officer of recruits, to whose assistance two or three privates of a previous year are assigned. The exercises begin without the use of a rifle and consist of light gymnastics. They serve to evenly develop the body of the young, often stiff and awkward, recruit, to harden his muscles, to enable him to acquire a free and energetic use of his limbs. This is preparatory to the recruit taking up the subsequent and real drill, which consists of the proper handling and use of the rifle and bayonet, and the various gymnastic apparatus made use of in his training.

With the exercises on the drill-ground and in the gymnasium, begins the instruction of the soldier in the Gelände (a staked-off and specially-designed manœuvre ground). Here the recruit pursues his exercises, drills, and other operations in order to gain the proper idea of their warlike use and purpose.

By such means the soldier receives a training which eminently fits him for all emergencies in the soldier's real life. He is then carefully and minutely instructed in what is likely to be new to him, namely, the use of firearms. He learns the aiming drill, and how to hold, carry, and use a rifle. This instruction is continued throughout the first year, so that the recruit learns to be familiar with his weapon; how to take aim with it in all positions of the body, and in every formation of ground whereon he is drilled. In addition to this varied drill he learns how to estimate distances.

Hand in hand with this practical training, goes instruction, beginning with the recruit's first day, in the moral duties and obligations of the soldier. He has defined to him the nature of his oath of fidelity to the colors, and of other matters pertaining to a soldier's duties. This is followed, in about three weeks after enrolment, by the swearing in of the recruit. This solemn act takes place after a preliminary church service in the presence of the high officials of the garrison; at Berlin it takes place under the eye of the Emperor. When the Emperor is present he addresses the recruit to be sworn in, admonishing him of his duties, reminding him of his pledge of fidelity, and of the high military virtues of a soldier, including piety, love of honor, and obedience.

The theoretical instruction covers all branches of the service and is greatly facilitated by every man receiving an illustrated book of instruction. The men without means are furnished one at the expense of the company. The book contains rules for the conduct of the soldier on and off duty. Its contents are imparted by a non-commissioned officer. The most important subjects, however, are treated by a higher officer, especially those touching the duties of a soldier in war time, the articles of war, the knowledge and use of the rifle, the rules governing the aim of the rifle, and musketry in general. In order not to forget details, and to make the soldier self-dependent and well-adapted for regular service, instruction is given in mending and scouring. The proper care of the body and the observation of all sanitary rules are also made special subjects of instruction.

While the recruit is being thus trained, the advanced training of the men belonging to the second year is proceeded with, and is generally directed by an older officer. The musketry service and the exercises in distance measurement are continued. The drill in the patrol service, especially that of the patrol leaders, for the purpose of reconnoitring the enemy, which is represented by opposing columns, is energetically followed. In connection with this, the training of the individual soldier is improved upon by further drills and courses of gymnastics, also by additional theoretical instruction.

At the end of this period of training (generally four months after the enlistment of the recruit), an inspection of the older soldiers by the commander of the battalion takes place. The inspection of the recruits, however, is performed by the regimental commander, mostly in the presence of the higher officials. This inspection tests the soldier, in explicit form, in all branches of the service, and in such a way that every individual's knowledge is practically and theoretically vouched for.

After this, the recruit — in the capacity of a young soldier — is mustered into the company according to his height. Now the second period of training commences. The recruit is instructed in company, in drill, and in engagement manœuvres; this takes place both on the drill-ground and on the manœuvre ground. The training is personally superintended by the captain of the company, and includes training in shooting, the most important part of the service. The soldier's achievement in this line is most important, and his proficiency decides, in great measure, his future. Here, too, at the conclusion, inspection by the regimental commander takes place, at which the company is tested in the carrying out of unexpected orders.

The recruit is now ready to receive his training in the battalion, which usually lasts from four to five weeks. The commander of the battalion is here himself the in-

structor, and directs and trains his four companies in the various battalion dispositions and movements. In the evolutions pertaining to the engagement drills he directs all movements by his own orders.

To what extent these exercises have been successful, and how they have served to make the battalion a vital and energetic instrument ready to be used by the commander in all emergencies in the field and for all missions, is again ascertained and verified by the inspecting commander in presence of the chief of the brigade, division, or corps, at the end of the time assigned to the battalion instruction.

When the training in battalion drill is concluded, the training in tactical matters ceases, and the drill-ground is left. Only in the forenoons, when the battalion presents itself for guard service and garrison duty, are the exercises pertaining to garrison duty gone through with. At the same time the carriage and bearing of the individual soldier is approved anew and tested by individual drill. The remainder of the time from the middle of May to the middle of August is used for musketry exercises, marching, drill, and picket duty, in connection with the reconnoitring and patrol service, and for exercises in the construction of rifle-pits. During this time exercises on a larger scale take place in marching, active fighting, and in advance guard-duty by day and night.

Musketry service is especially cared for, good marksmanship receiving the special notice of the Emperor. The company of the army corps which shows the greatest efficiency at the end of the year is distinguished by a badge, which is fastened to the left coat sleeve, while the captain of the victorious company is decorated with the Order of the Red Eagle.

Special stress is laid upon this important branch of military education, and captains of companies are held solely responsible for the company's accurate marksmanship. The practice shooting at the target-butts, with special tasks for each class, is followed by the training on the manœuvre ground. This begins with the shooting by each individual soldier, at stationary, moving, and disappearing objects, and at a distance to be guessed at. This practice is brought to a close by a shooting-drill with bullets, in regular order of battle, and in formations of companies and battalions, under special orders, at defined targets in the manœuvre ground.

In the meantime the exercises in gymnastics, and in fencing and swimming, proceed with uninterrupted progress. The men are theoretically well-instructed about their conduct on the march and during field engagements, in quarters and in camp. Surgeons also give necessary directions to the men as to the treatment to pursue when one of their number is sunstruck or wounded. Finally, the rules governing furloughs, and all matters pertaining to the reserve and Landwehr, are

Detachment of Balloon Troops. Cavalry Attack on a Balloon Detachment.

impressed on the mind of the soldier. This part of the training time is concluded by an inspection in gymnastics and in fencing. The test in swimming and in theoretical instruction is under the supervision of the regular commander, as is also the inspection of the shooting on the manœuvre ground.

Generally about the middle of August the Fall manœuvres commence with regiment and brigade drills, and are concluded by the manœuvres of regiments, brigades, divisions, and army corps, opposing each other.

Concurrently with the described course of training of the infantry (the army's chief branch of service), the training of the other arms of the service is conducted. In the cavalry, the training on foot is supplemented by exercises on horseback. The efficiency of the individual rider is followed out with painstaking care and the utmost zeal. This is done to perfect the rider and enable him surely and easily to overcome every obstacle he may meet; he thus learns to ford lakes and rivers, and, with perfect control of the horse, knows how to handle his weapons—the sabre and lance—in offence and defence against any adversary, either on foot or horseback. This, of course, cannot be accomplished by a short service of two years. Hence a three years' service in the cavalry and horse artillery is necessary. This longer time of probation enables the cavalry —which is equipped with the carbine for independent work at the front and on the flanks of the army—to receive the necessary training with the firearm for engagements on foot.

In the artillery the training in gunnery is the main point. To make this arm of the service equal to the task which falls to its lot, it is of the utmost importance that the guns reach their firing position over the most difficult country with the greatest speed. This is done to enable them to deploy quickly and accurately, and to open and continue firing with absolute fearlessness and composure.

The high requirements of batteries and divisions of artillery necessarily demand the most painstaking and comprehensive training. Every single piece of ordnance is brought into use and inspected in regard to its manning and service, and as to its efficiency in action. Practice is given in overcoming great obstacles, such as tapering ditches, steep elevations, precipitous slopes, by every single gun. The spirit to excel in gunnery is kindled to its highest pitch by conferring marks of distinction on the chief gunners, and by awarding shooting badges to those noncommissioned officers and men of the company who excel in marksmanship in the army corps. The cavalry is likewise stimulated to the highest pitch of achievement in shooting and drill by respective marks of distinction.

In these two arms of the service a scrutinizing inspection takes place by the higher commanders at the close of the different periods of the training. This is concluded by larger drills and manœuvres of troops, in which, at the end of the military year, infantry, cavalry, artillery, and the special branches of the army take part. Here the individual soldier becomes inured to exertion and the exactions of warlike marches, made in deep columns and in conjunction with cavalry and artillery. He learns by experience the manner of fighting in coöperation with other arms of the service; and how to conform his conduct in active engagement, while, at the same time, he makes use of and calls into exercise every instruction and detail of training that has been imparted to him. He acquaints himself alike with the ordinary and the unaccustomed and severe tasks, with the lot of the individual soldier on picket duty, directly following, it may be, a most tiresome march or a galling engagement. He finally learns the self-denial and restraint exacted of every soldier, high or low, when unavoidable difficulties arise at the assembling, the quartering, and the feeding of the massed troops.

With these warlike exercises and experiences the training of the soldier is completed. He will victoriously stand the test, if he, on his side, has taken advantage of all opportunities, however exacting, and if his superiors have succeeded in infusing in him the true martial spirit. But, inasmuch as the tasks imposed on every soldier in war time are so severe and far-reaching, effecting the highest efficiency on the part of the soldier, the entire German army, after the well-tested model of the Prussian army, recognized the training of the individual as the paramount and fundamental principle of success. Hence, all rules and efforts of the superiors and commanders of all ranks are so directed as to educate the individual soldier to the understanding of the virtues of piety, love of honor, fidelity, obedience, order, and punctuality, thus enhancing his readiness for and efficiency in war. In this sense of the word, not the schoolmaster, but the noncommissioned officer and the officer of the German army have become the instructors of the nation under arms.

In accordance with the aforesaid, the force of noncommissioned officers forms a most important part of the German army.

It would be impossible, without the most faithful and energetic activity on the part of the noncommissioned officers together with the relatively small force of higher officers, which is not materially increased in war-time, to reach the necessary goal in the training and education of the privates. The often heard "hue and cry" in the ranks of the anti-national parties about occasional cases of ill-treatment in the army will give way before the cooler judgment of every sensible person. In sober, dispassionate reasoning they will not underestimate the extent of character, self-restraint, and thorough knowledge required of the noncommissioned officer, still in the bloom of youth (from 20 to 30 years old), necessary to adequately fit him for the responsible task, made

9th Battalion of the Military Train (Schleswig-Holstein).

doubly difficult owing to the great dignity and tact which he must show in his daily contact with subordinates, a task which exacts no small measure of versatility in every department of the service.

Hence the utmost care is devoted to the training of the noncommissioned officers. The efficiency of the captain of the company is rightly measured by his capacity to replenish his body of noncommissioned officers with excellent material and to raise it to the highest efficiency. The noncommissioned officers are therefore instructed especially, by the chief of the company, in all branches of the service. They are trained in their general and special functions, and employed, according to their competency, for the delivery of verbal and written orders in the field service or in engagements. They are intrusted with written and verbal reports and orders, and are also educated and instructed in commanding and directing the firing line during all phases of the engagement.

Side by side with the schools of the company, in which, during the winter months, the soldiers in need of assistance in reading and writing, especially those not conversant with the German language, are instructed, is the regimental or "capitulanten" school, which looks after the advanced instruction in every regiment, from October until April. Geography and history, orthography and German composition, arithmetic in proper form and dimension, are taught by officers and hired civic teachers. By instruction in civil service and by the working out of written orders and reports, the "capitulanten" and noncommissioned officers are prepared in every direction. The instruction is for the purpose of fitting them, independently, for all the functions of the service, and also of preparing them for minor offices of the government or corporations, which they can claim after leaving the military service.

To facilitate the entrance into such offices, every noncommissioned officer receives, after a service of twelve years (that is, after meeting all legal requirements for a claim to a minor civil office), a bounty of 1,000 marks. It is to be hoped that the future of those noncommissioned officers who have proved faithful in the military service will be further secured by an additional increase of salary and other emoluments.

With this brief consideration regarding the matter of providing for the noncommissioned officers, the subject of the training and education of the noncommissioned officers and men is exhaustively treated. It is now only left to dwell somewhat longer on the very important question of the training of the officers—the commanders of the German army.

THE TRAINING OF THE COMMANDERS

BY

MAJOR-GENERAL VON SPECHT

TACTICAL DUTIES AND TRAINING IN LONG DISTANCE
RIDES, MANOEUVRES, TRAVELS OF THE GENE-
RAL STAFF AND THE WAR-GAME

IT WAS the dictum of that famous master of battles, Napoleon I, that to command a superior force at a given point, and at the critical moment of the fight, meant victory. He will be victorious who is equal to the occasion, grasping the opportunity by a brilliant use of higher tactics, called by Bonaparte, *la grande tactique*. But what unusual tasks does the fulfillment of this duty entail! What avails the greatest generalship or the highest strategy, when the hand which should guide the vital instrument, the army, in a thorough—nay, masterly—manner, is missing! History is replete with instances of the story that even well-disciplined and brave armies have had to succumb to the superior leadership of the enemy.

With an army in rags and half-starved, but inspired by patriotic fervor, Napoleon Bonaparte laid the foundation of his military fame by the genius he displayed in the campaigns of 1796–1797 in Italy, paving for himself the road to the imperial throne of France. After the patriotic fire was extinguished and the old veteran troops and the efficient and experienced officers had succumbed in the direful war with Russia in 1812, even Bonaparte's brilliant strategical talent, which once more shone forth with great lustre in his defensive campaign of the year 1814, could not avert his downfall. The master succumbed, because the sword he wielded was improperly forged; because the army, which embraced a hundred thousand young conscripts, was not equal to the task. The great wars of 1866 and of 1870–1871 also fully demonstrated that the greatest bravery displayed in the field cannot make good the blunders committed in the handling and leading of the troops. Both the Austrian and French armies succumbed to the German forces, not alone because of the more efficient training of their officers and men, but in consequence of the better organization and preëminently superior generalship of the Prussian and German armies. This superiority is not due, however, to an ingenious idea rising flash-like in the mind of the commander-in-chief; the success depends on the proper execution of the idea. Only that commander can expect success who is sure of his orders being promptly and accurately executed. To insure the latter, the general staff must understand not only how to transform the commander's ideas into practical commands, but every leader, from the general down to the youngest officer, must be able to thoroughly grasp the intention and meaning of all orders issued. He must be trained and accustomed to execute every order with perfect obedience and never-failing promptitude. He must at the same time strive to overcome. by the aid of all human possibilities, every difficulty that blocks his progress. With an iron will, nay, even by staking his own life on the fulfillment of his duty, must he see that the aim and purpose of the order are secured. Under no circumstances, in executing the order, must he depart from its explicit mandate, even when a change in the situation would seem to call for the exercise of private judgment.

To attain the acme of absolute obedience. of unflagging energy and resolution. combined with responsible and spontaneous acting, the training, schooling, and education of the officers of all ranks are objects of concern in the German army.

For the minor engagements and in the advance-guard drills, beginning with company drills and progressing into battalion and regimental drills on the manœuvre grounds, a specific scheme of war is laid out by two parties, each opposing the other. The commanders on both sides, namely, the lieutenants, captains, and staff officers, receive verbal or written orders directing them to make the necessary disposition thereof, the soundness, accuracy, and expediency of which are tested. The execution is also thoroughly supervised and minutely commented upon by the commanding officer at the close of the exercises. The greatest stress is laid upon the nature, form, and character of the order issued. It must have the qualities of military brevity, precision, clearness, and perspicuity in order to be fully understood. This, however, will not alone suffice. During the military exercise special attention is bestowed upon and the greatest efforts are made to see that the orders are issued from the proper place, excluding all expediences which do not conform with the rules of war. It occasionally happens in battle that all commanders, even the regimental commander, are put *hors de combat* when they, without stringent necessity, disobey the rules and expose themselves on horseback at the outset of the fight or on the firing line.

Besides these continual exercises for the training of the higher commanders, a special course of training for the officers of inferior rank, namely, the captains and lieutenants, is held annually in every regiment. By this course even the youngest officer receives a chance to be independently tested and approved in the solving of tactical problems. The tasks, together with those issued to the opposing forces, are handed in written form to the lieutenants by the battalion commanders, and to the captains by the regimental commanders. A proportionate number of troops, including, if possible, some detachments of other branches of the service corresponding with the garrison's strength, are placed at the disposal of each officer. This has special reference to the older officers, for whom these so-called "practical duties of the officer" (other than the theoretical duties, described later on) not only serve as drills, but also as tests of their ability to advance to higher positions. The advance to these higher positions is conditioned by the efficiency and qualifications shown at these exercises. For this purpose, namely, to awaken keen perception, judgment, tactical perspicuity, presence of mind, and resolution on the part of the officers, emergency or surprising situations are resorted to in the form of unexpected reinforcements of their own columns or of those of the enemy. By this method of procedure each respective commander is given an opportunity to exemplify the qualifications requisite for any and every emergency. When these exercises are of an important nature, those officers of the battalion and the regiment who are off duty attend as spectators. At the conclusion, the officer who has been conducting these exercises assembles about him the officers who have been executing his commands and with them he enters upon a discussion of the various exercises in which they have been engaged. This is followed by an additional comment by the higher officers present, including the regimental, brigade, and division commanders, upon the more difficult tasks performed. This is done for the purpose of further accentuating the difficulties involved in these essentially instructive tactical duties. Finally, every one of the respective officers is requested to give a minute report of the execution of his order—either by a sketch made with colored pencil on a report map, giving a minute description of the manœuvre-ground and the engaged troops, or by a detailed written report containing an appropriate skeleton-sketch. All these matters are commented upon in written form by the superior officers present.

On a larger scale, but for a similar purpose, namely, to train officers of a higher rank than the battalion commanders in the leading of the troops, and also to test their qualification, exercises are prepared for the troops in the manœuvre drills. These manœuvres differ only in the number of the troops employed and in the character of the duties involved. Their form and nature, improved upon by a process of development in the Prussian army during a period of one hundred and fifty years, has become a standard and a model in the German army. The origin of the manœuvres can be traced back to the drills by which Frederick the Great prepared his small army for the great task before them. Frederick's father, the "soldier king" Frederick William I, aided in a most efficient way by Prince Leopold of Anhalt-Dessau (the Old Dessauer), laid the foundation for a most systematic training of the troops in all details, including a rigid discipline. The King left to his great successor on the throne an army which needed only a more elaborate training in tactical matters and the manifestation of intellectual genius on the part of the commanders to make it unequaled. This problem was brilliantly solved by the king's great son, Frederick II. On the drill-grounds near Potsdam, Spandau, and Berlin, the King personally drilled his troops during the years 1745–1756. The exercises lasted about twelve days each. With these well-disciplined troops, Frederick II victoriously resisted half of Europe in the Seven Years' War. After the King had accomplished his object and secured peace for his dominions, the drill-grounds were no longer barred to the public but were opened to spectators, even to those representing foreign armies. This custom has been retained and is in vogue at the present time. After the custom pursued by the German army, the Great Powers send representatives to the manœuvres of the European armies. Those of the German army, are often personally attended by the sovereigns of Russia, Austria, and Italy. These larger drills begin in September with smaller so-called "detachment" drills under the leadership of the brigade commander, preceded by exercises which take place in the formation of regiments and brigades of different arms on the manœuvre-grounds, and which last for several days. To those detachments a brigade of infantry is assigned, further augmented by one or two regiments of cavalry, in addition to one regiment of artillery and some columns of pioneers and telegraph troops. Formed into two sections— called "detachments"—these mixed troops drill, opposing each other, for four or five days. In this undertaking they follow out first, the "general idea," which defines an ordinary war status, and secondly, the "specific idea," by which special daily tasks are assigned to each section. After a march in warlike array, or after the taking and the subsequent fortifying of a captured position, an engagement ensues which determines with which side the victory rests. This is followed by both parties placing pickets for the protection of their respective positions. These outposts bivouac, while the other troops take up their regular quarters, but are subject to "alarms," that is to a call to arms over night.

The "detachment" or brigade drills are followed by drills of the divisions, at which the divisions, like the brigades, oppose each other for from four to five days, under the leadership of the division commanders. In some cases the commander assembles his entire division and leads it personally into an engagement with the enemy, which is distinguished for this purpose by marked flags.

The division manœuvres are succeeded by those of the army corps, at which the divisions, under the leadership of the general in command, operate one against the other, and at which, generally on a special day, the entire army corps is directed against an enemy, indicated in some special manner.

In all these exercises the bearing and behavior of the troops on the march and in the engagements, and their conduct when bivouaced and on picket-duty, are closely scrutinized and made the subject of strict supervision. The paramount object of the exercises, however, is the training of the commanders. The detachment drills afford ample opportunity to the regimental commanders and the older staff officers of all arms to receive a proper training in commanding mixed troops, while the younger staff officers are thus afforded a good training in picket and miscellaneous duty. The division and corps manœuvres serve for the purpose of training the older regimental and brigade commanders, especially the division commanders, in the duties falling to their lot in time of war. They likewise serve to improve their qualifications and to increase and test their efficiency. At the conclusion of these various exercises the mounted officers are gathered around the commander, for the time being the commander-in-chief, at the signal "officers' call," for the purpose of a mutual criticism. As at the previously described lesser exercises, the respective duties and their execution are commented on, including the assigned tasks. The situation at the end of the engagement is clearly defined, while new manœuvres for the day following are planned. The newly assigned commanders have to issue the necessary orders at once. The formal withdrawing of the opposing force, including the placing of pickets, closes the day's drill. Underlying these exercises, especially the large manœuvres with their important aims and purposes, is the fundamental principle that the commander shall not be influenced in the least in the fulfillment of his tasks, but be accorded perfect freedom of action. On the other hand, the highest value is attached to the correct, independent, and resolute acting of the commanding officers, and to their ac-

curate knowledge of the manœuvre-ground and the designs and movements of the enemy, as well as to the proper tactical employment of the different troops engaged.

According to the important nature of these larger drills, which exercise a great influence on the army at large, and their significance as they affect the military career of the higher officers, special pains are taken to place the judgment and decision of the officers who command the drills and manœuvres on a sound and impartial basis. The commander cannot at the same time attend to the advance guard, the bulk of the army, and the flanking columns. He cannot watch with a critical eye the center and the wings of the battle line, neither can he superintend the operations which take place on picket duty both by day and by night. Further, and chiefly, the fact has to be taken into consideration that the success of all these warlike exercises can be estimated only, as they exclude, as a matter of course, the use of bullets and thrusting weapons, and allow only bloodless bayonet attacks and cavalry charges. Inasmuch as by this procedure the effect of the warfare does not become apparent by actual losses, the decision becomes dependent on purely conjectural methods. On this account, there are attached to the commander's staff assistants in the capacity of referees. These referees at the smaller drills are captains and staff officers, while at the larger manœuvres generals are intrusted with this duty. The referees conjecture the effect of the infantry and artillery fire, direct the attention of both parties to the same, and regulate, if necessary, the retreat of one side or the other. The referees are also invested with authority to declare entire columns of troops partially or totally disabled, and to decide, while taking all circumstances into consideration, the success or failure of the attacks made by infantry and cavalry. The troops have to submit without protest to the decision of the referees, who are recognized by a white sash worn around the coat sleeve. The arbitrators inform the commanders on both sides of the decisions made, while at the same time they personally report all details to the chief commander. The reports are subjected to exhaustive discussion and criticism, which take place at the conclusion of the exercises. Of special importance, naturally, is the function of the referees at the great manœuvres, at which several army corps oppose each other, and the extent of the fighting lines is measured by miles.

The origin of these great manœuvres, formerly called "King's manœuvres," and now known by the name of the "Emperor's manœuvres," is to be traced back to the great reviews at which Frederick the Great severely tested the skill of the army corps of the different provinces. Following his illustrious example, the Prussian King held annually a great review of one of the provincial army corps, in connection with drills lasting several days and called "King's manœuvres." The corps of the Guards, stationed at Berlin and Potsdam, did not take part in these exercises, however, as it was subject to the constant surveillance and inspection of the Prussian King.

Since the years 1866 and 1870–1871 the Prussian-German army has gradually risen from a strength of fifteen to nineteen, and finally to twenty-three army corps, and the inspection of one army corps, occurring annually, became insufficient. The practice in vogue to-day is to detail each year from two to four army corps to these great manœuvres. By this method a desirable succession is established which, comprising a period of seven to eight years, enables the commander-in-chief to test the entire German army in its training and readiness for war.

This privilege, accorded to the German Emperor by the imperial constitution, was exercised with unfaltering faithfulness by the old Emperor, William I, and practiced up to the time of his demise. Emperor William II has followed the illustrious example with a commendable energy, which is crowned by the best results. The "Emperor's manœuvres," taking place every September, are planned in the most elaborate manner and with the utmost care by the chief of the army's general staff. The outlines are tested and approved by the Emperor.

The manœuvres are ushered in by the so-called "Emperor's parade or review," which his Majesty orders in the case of each army corps detailed to take part in them. The scheme calls for methodized railway transportation, and a concentration of the different army corps in the direction of the territory designed for the manœuvres is effected. War-marches toward the landing-point of the two armies opposing each other are instrumental in assembling the army for these manœuvres. The assembling and advance of the army are covered by cavalry divisions, each from two to three brigades (or from twenty to thirty squadrons) strong, and under the leadership of specially selected commanders. These meet at different points some days previous. The cavalry divisions perform the tasks falling to their lot in war time, namely, of veiling the army's advance, establishing its lines of contact with the enemy, and covering the flanks of the army, while, at the proper time, they have to appear in the battle, often deciding the fate of the day by momentous charges. These charges are often led by the Emperor personally, who also assumes command of the army, changing sides between the two parties often even on the same day.

The carrying out of these manœuvres corresponds with that of the corps manœuvres previously described, with the one exception that they are conducted on a larger scale. The Emperor, who shows a special interest in the exercises, after hearing the reports of the chiefs of the general staff and of the referees, assumes the function of final critic. Surrounded by his generals and commanders, his presence lends a significance to the manœuvres. This is further enhanced by the regular attendance of the German Empress, of the German and other sovereigns and princes, likewise by the representatives of foreign armies. The exercises are also of value in a political aspect, since, by means of the festivities arranged by the cities and provinces in connection with the manœuvres, the German Emperor and Empress come into personal contact with all classes of the German people. In a military sense, however, the manœuvres are of the utmost importance.

The efficiency of the army's general staff, employed almost in its entirety, is tested in a most comprehensive manner. The capacity of the railroads is often taxed to the utmost, and the supplying of the troops with provisions from established military depots gives ample opportunity for the commissariat to prove its efficiency. The entire sanitary department of the army, including the field hospital service, likewise receives a most rigid test at these manœuvres. In addition, there are called into action the telegraph and balloon troops, and the corps charged with the employment and construction in the field of military signals, field bridges, military railroads, and fortifications of every description. The fact that all important technical, tactical, and strategical questions involved in the manœuvres become subject to the review and approval of the Emperor and the higher generals of the army, fully demonstrates the importance attained by the ".Emperor's manœuvres." It would, therefore, be in keeping with the military ideal if the entire German army could be concentrated annually in groups of several army corps each stationed respectively in the North, South, East, and West of the empire. By this procedure an opportunity would be afforded to the entire general staff, and also to all commanders up to the commanding general and army inspector, to practice warfare on a large scale, by one entire army operating against another. The enormous expense necessitated by such an undertaking presents, however, insurmountable barriers. For the purpose of enabling the general staff officers, whose ranks supply the greater part of the higher commanders, to practice annually warfare on a large scale, even without the employment of troops, and to improve upon the training of the officers in the functions necessary for the operation of the army, a scheme of travel for the general staff is instituted.

These travels are undertaken, generally in the summer preceding the manœuvres, by the officers of the great general staff, and are superintended by the chief of the army's general staff. They are performed by two separate parties, the ranks of which, from the commander of an entire army down to the commanders of the army corps and divisions, including the cavalry divisions with their respective staff, are filled by general staff officers, according to rank and age. All preliminary work for the concentration of the army is prepared in an explicit and warlike manner by the chief of the general staff, who, in the capacity of commander-in-chief, defines the general war scheme, and gives special directions to every higher commander, assigning at the same time to each one the duties involved in the operations. The plan of operation, the mapped out railroad and march routes, the necessary orders for the assembling of the army, and the survey of the troops' quartering, are thoroughly and carefully treated in all their details, subject, however, to the approval of the higher commander. After this, the latter, in company with all officers, repair to grounds selected for the operations. Here, by means of marching orders, marked and recorded in a special book, and by the instructions designed to cover the engagement, the necessary measures and movements are discussed from day to day. At the conclusion, the probable decision of the final encounter in the battle and of the entire operations are agreed upon by the higher commander. This decision is based on all the preceding directions, movements, dispositions, and orders, taking into consideration at the same time all circumstances, such as the manœuvre territory and also the partial success of the preceding day.

What amount of experience, practice, and instruction is entailed in such travels of the general staff, will become evident by this outline, especially when it is borne in mind that higher commissioners and surgeons are detailed to attend these exercises with their respective orders. A final and thorough discussion of all the assigned tasks and the entire course of the operations by the general staff, in the presence of the assembled participants, winds up the exercise.

Travels of a similar character, only on a smaller scale, take place annually for the purpose of training the general staff of the troops, and are superintended by the chief of the army corps' general staff.

Aside from the entire force of the corps staff, staff officers, and captains and lieutenants of all branches of the service are detailed to make these travels and are intrusted with appropriate tasks, in order to train them efficiently for the higher commands.

The travels of the general staff preëminently serve the purpose of exercising the officers of this grade in the tasks which have to be performed in the field with the utmost accuracy, and also of training them for their future duties as commanders. At the same time it is obvious that the officers of the different branches of the service are in need of further training, in order to prepare them for the duties of higher positions, and therefore more time has to be accorded them than the drills during the summer months and the fall manœuvres allow.

For this purpose the so-called "travels for tactical training" and long distance rides are designed. These are performed under the supervision of the commanders of the troops (regimental commanders and independent battalion commanders), and generally take place in the fall, at the conclusion of the manœuvres, and last till the following spring. Their tasks, as a rule, do not exceed the scope accorded to the detachment (brigade) exercises, which were described as introductory to the larger fall drills.

The momentous duties falling to the lot of the cavalry divisions in war time, namely, to veil the deployment and to cover the front and flanks of the army, require, obviously, a special preparation on the part of the assigned commanders and sub-commanders. For this purpose specific exercises are ordered annually, which are executed by cavalry and artillery officers, and are called "travels for the cavalry's training." These travels are undertaken over well-defined and previously laid out routes, and resemble, in their plan and execution, the travels of the general staff, that is, the exercises without the employment of troops.

Nor are the great importance and decisive effects of feats of horsemanship achieved by some cavalry officers to be underestimated. Mounted on fleet horses and riding through swamps, rivers, woods, and over mountains, by day or by night, they establish connection between far separated army columns, while at the same time they convey important orders or bring back valuable reports and information about the traversed territory, which bear witness to keen observation and correct military judgment on the part of the officer.

In order to find out and train officers best adapted for this task, long distance rides take place annually in every army corps, according to a special decree of the Emperor. In these tasks, assigned by the generals in command, the staff officers, and captains and lieutenants of cavalry take part. The officer who wins distinction in these long distance rides is rewarded by a prize, which is presented by the Emperor to the successful rider in every army corps.

The careful and elaborate training of the German officer is, however, not limited to the practical exercises hitherto described. The winter months are made use of diligently to further the officers' instruction and culture in the science of war. In the first place the "theoretical problems," which have to be solved by the first and second lieutenants every winter, serve for this purpose. They are generally assigned by the battalion commander, according to the age and qualifications of the officer, and are selected to incite individual study in all branches of knowledge and investigation. These so-called "winter tasks" are thoroughly criticized in writing by the battalion commander, and afterward by the regimental commander. The best exercises are submitted for further approval to the higher commanders, including the general commanding the army corps, and are thoroughly tested and duly commented upon by the latter. By this method, talented and industrious officers receive an opportunity which is sometimes of great importance, to gain the attention of their superiors, and their favorable notice.

Probably in no calling is the gift of free, clear, and emphatic address of more significance than in that of officers. To make them equal to this task and to develop the necessary faculties to the utmost, lectures are given every one or two weeks during the winter months, at which officers of all grades attend. These lectures are orally delivered, not read from manuscript, by older members of the military profession, captains and staff officers. These discourses are known as "garrison lectures" at larger places, and are attended by all the garrison officers. The themes are either self-chosen or are assigned by the commanders. They treat on all branches of science, giving preference, of course, to the science of war.

The oldest and largest gathering for the purpose of promoting military science by a regular lecture course, is the "military society" at Berlin. Having been in existence for over one hundred years, this society summons the officers, especially the older ones of the Berlin garrison, to a monthly lecture. This lecture is usually delivered by a general or a staff officer and is attended by the highest generals and even princes, very often, indeed, by the Emperor himself.

With the previously described exercises and lectures the methods of training the officers are not entirely exhausted. The military drills may approximately represent war in time of peace by means of their ingenious design and exactions, but, on the other hand, they never can fully set forth the stern picture of war. The effect of the clash of weapons and the momentous results of the conflict, achieved often by heroic bravery, daring prowess, and burning enthusiasm, are missing. While these great factors and momentous occasions cannot be realized in time of peace, there are, on the other hand, faculties, which can be developed and improved upon, nay, almost brought to the goal of perfection, at an opportune time. These are a quick and correct reading of maps and plans, expertness in drawing up dispositions and orders which have to combine military brevity with great distinctness in every detail, at the same time avoiding all superfluous verbiage. The officers in training must further exemplify the possession of a fundamental knowledge of the tactical use of all arms, with reference to their proper employment in the field.

With a due recognition of the above facts and with a view to further improve the tactical training of the officers, an exercise has been introduced in the German army which is called "the war-game." This exercise was invented by a Prussian officer about sixty years ago, and since then has been gradually improved upon to such an extent that as a medium of instruction, it is in vogue, not only in the German army, but in those of foreign nations.

The game is based on the following principles: On a large board, manœuvres, consisting of marches, engagements, and picket-drills, are executed with small colored figures, or checkers, by which the troops are represented. Those taking part in the play are divided in two sections. The different parts are assigned to the commanders and sub-commanders, and, suiting the circumstances, down to the captains of companies, squadrons, or batteries. This war-game embraces the manœuvres and travels of the general staff. The higher commander lays down first, the "general idea," designing the war scheme at large, and secondly, the special ideas, according to which he assigns the respective tasks to the commanders of both parties. As at the manœuvres and the travels of the general staff,

all arrangements, covering the dispositions and orders pertaining to the railroad transportation, the quartering and marching of the troops, and their engagement, are carefully perfected in a military manner. After this preparatory work is finished, tested, and discussed by the higher commander, the play commences on the board. The diagram is traced out on a scale of 1:12500 or 1:6250, showing all details important in military service. The diagram is sometimes executed in the form of relievo maps. As soon as the order for the movement of the troops, their transportation and marching is given (these operations being explained at the outset on maps giving a general view), the checkers representing the troops come into play. These checkers are distinguished by different colors, generally blue and red, and are used on the board accordingly.

The different branches of the service and the tactical unities of the troops are marked by forms and signs in a way that skirmish lines, companies, battalions, squadrons, and batteries are easily recognized. The position of pickets, quarters, bivouacs, marching columns, with the advance and rear guards, and detached bodies of troops on both sides of the army, are minutely represented on the board by an adequate number of checkers. The necessary orders are given on the spot, either verbally or in writing, and, at the proper time, all reports of a more important nature are entered with military precision on report maps. The movements of the troops, computed accurately by time and space, also by the rate of travel common to the different branches of the service, are pointed out by corresponding moves of the checkers. The following will exemplify the preceding statement: The higher commander, previous to the advance of the army, despatches, early in the morning, a patrol, under the lead of a cavalry officer, for the purpose of reconnoitring the enemy. The time of the officer's departure is written down, together with the direction which he is to take, and also the time in which he can reach the assigned point of his route on the manœuvre ground, from which he can overlook and watch the enemy. The time at which the report of the patrol officer will reach the higher commander, and how far the latter has advanced with his marching columns by this time, are also reckoned. Again the higher commander consults his watch and accurately ascertains, by the aid of his assistants, the lapse of time between giving his final orders and the receipt and execution of the same by the troops. By this method of procedure the very minute is ascertained when the troops will have been enabled to reach the proper point for entering upon an engagement with the enemy. According to this plan and method, the checkers representing the troops are put in order or placed on the proper squares on the board, corresponding with the given dispositions and orders.

At the beginning of the game the checkers are moved while hidden from view. The higher commander discusses the game with the competitors in a way that each can watch only his own troops. At the moment, however, that the movements come into a common range of sight, the checker board is uncovered, while the exercise is brought to an issue, adhering throughout to a detailed and warlike consideration of the situation. Every offensive and defensive move is accurately measured according to time and space. The effect of the weapons is judged and measured as at the manœuvres; all attacks are decided by the higher commander and his impartial referees. To allow some scope to moral influence and the fortune of war (other chances being even), the ultimate decision is sometimes determined by the use of the dice-box. This method of arriving at a decision, formerly more in vogue than at the present time, was obviously instrumental in giving the name of "war-game" to these exercises, so peculiar in their nature. The earnest, practical character of the game will be evident from the account here given. The great, fervid zeal which permeates the German army in the fulfilling of its duties, is reflected also in the manner of performing this branch of the training. It is no uncommon occurence, to find, even in the dead of night, new reports and orders issued touching the situations of the game to be played on the next evening. These are sent to the lower commanders by their superior officers, asking for an immediate drawing up of dispositions or orders, to be returned in written form by the bearers.

That the exercise cannot be performed in its entirety, while limited to a few hours play of a winter evening, is obvious. It often thus happens that several evenings are required to play the game. It will be understood that the duration of the game depends more or less on the character of the plot and the necessary scope accorded for its solution. In this respect a distinction may be made between tactical, strategical, and siege war-games, according to the peculiar nature of the exercises, defined either by the engagement of smaller or larger detachments up to brigades, divisions, and army corps, or by a battle between an army corps and a whole army or by the assault upon a fortress and its defence.

Of the lesser exercises, superintended by the battalion commanders, junior officers, down to the youngest lieutenant, are employed, while the exercises on a larger scale, held under the eyes of the regimental and brigade commanders, are participated in by the older officers and staff officers. In the exercises of the army corps and armies, however, the general staff and higher commanders take an interesting part. Frequently the officers of the neighboring garrisons are called together at the headquarters of the division commanders and of the general in command for the purpose of playing a war-game. The exercises which take place at the garrisons of Potsdam and Berlin in the presence of the Emperor, who often joins in the game, are played on a large scale. The foregoing illustrates the value set upon these exercises.

The discussions evoked by the game and touching important tactical problems, as well as the instructive comments of the higher commander during its progress and at its finish, give enhanced interest to it and to the players. The foregoing characteristics of the game will verify the fact that the proper and expedient management of these exercises is beset with great difficulties, requiring a large amount of military science and knowledge, combined with a great deal of perception, foresight, and mental versatility, in order to impart to the game an increasingly exciting, interesting, and instructive fervor. At the same time, the higher commander, while superintending the progress of the game, is afforded an opportunity of developing and exemplifying his military qualifications. The exercises thus serve the purpose of preparing the higher commanders for the task which falls to their lot at the larger drills and manœuvres. The war-games resemble in character and execution the travels of the general staff and the manœuvres. They supplement them, though most expediently, without causing any expense worth mentioning to the government or to the various bodies of officers, or without creating any errors or mistakes, which eventually have to be made good by the exertion and effort of the troops. They are instrumental in imparting a higher efficiency in the training of the officers of all ranks, and especially in instilling a closer study and a more thorough knowledge of the field-service ordinance (regulations touching the training of the troops for field service and the larger drills), and of the instructions for the higher commanders. These war-games will, at all times and most fittingly, serve their purpose, if they are undertaken and executed in the proper spirit,—the spirit which is fundamental in the case of all exercises pertaining to the training of the officers, namely, to enlarge the intellectual horizon of the officers and to prepare them for the higher commands. The attainment of this goal is warranted by the untiring vigilance, the unfaltering faithfulness, and the intelligent and energetic efforts on the part of the superior officers of all ranks. The commander-in-chief of the army, the Emperor, who combines high intelligence with rare energy, looks likewise with incessant care to the uniform enforcement of all rules pertaining to the field-service ordinance throughout the entire German army.

The fundamental principle which underlies all these rules is to exact from every soldier the putting forth of his whole faculties of body and mind, to demand preëminently a resolute acting, and to impress on the mind of every one — the highest commander as well as the youngest soldier — the idea that omission and negligence is to be considered a greater offence than a mistake made in the selection of the proper means.

SUPPLEMENT TO THE ORGANIZATION, COMPOSITION, AND STRENGTH OF THE GERMAN ARMY

BY

MAJOR-GENERAL VON SPECHT

THE organization, composition, and strength of the German army underwent important changes, due to laws passed by the Imperial Diet, at the solicitation of the German military authorities, on March 16th, 1899.

1. From the year 1893 there was in every regiment of infantry one battalion established at only half its strength. These half-battalions were gradually raised to their full strength of from two to four companies. By forming the four battalions into regiments, in the year 1897, two new regiments of infantry were added to each army corps. This process, in course of time, gave to each army corps two infantry brigades, which thus comprised three instead of two regiments. By this procedure the army corps, which hitherto consisted of two, now consisted of three divisions, and this created difficulties in regard to their handling and mobility in case of war. It thus became a matter of necessity to organize a new army corps from parts of those army corps which consisted of three divisions, a result brought about by the creation of the new regiments. It was likewise found expedient to muster into divisions the newly-formed regiments which belonged to the army corps stationed on the eastern and western frontiers of the empire, and consisting of two divisions. This was done for the purpose of assigning special duties of frontier service to these divisions, at the same time leaving intact the organization of the army corps. According to this, a new corps was added to the Prussian army, the eighteenth, with its command at Frankfort-on-the-Main, while the kingdom of Saxony has now, aside from the twelfth, the nineteenth corps, with its command at Leipsic. Bavaria will be represented by an additional army corps, the third Bavarian, with its command at Nurenberg. The two frontier corps, the first East-Prussian and the fourteenth of Baden, are to be augmented each by one division.

2. These newly-organized forces called only for three additional regiments of cavalry, and for a small increase of foot-artillery and pioneers.

3. The most important changes, however, were effected in the organization and composition of the field-artillery. By a gradual increase of the field-artillery, necessitated by events which took place after the war of 1870-71, the detachments and batteries of the field-artillery regiments became unlike in numbers to such an extent that some regiments showed as many as four detachments

and twelve batteries.

As a matter of fact, there belong to one battery equipped for war, besides six guns with gun-limbers drawn by six horses, eight ammunition wagons, each drawn by six horses, three provision wagons, and one portable forge. Each field-battery, therefore, consists of eighteen wagons with 108 horses. A regiment of nine to twelve batteries comprises, besides the horses of the officers, of the noncommissioned officers, and the necessary baggage and provision wagons with their horses, 162 to 216 army vehicles with from 972 to 1,296 horses. The preceding statement will make it clear that such masses are too bulky and unwieldy to be efficiently trained in time of peace by one man — the commander of the regiment. It would also be impossible for the commander properly to supervise all the necessary material in time of war, to bring it to the proper efficiency, and to guide it in battle and on the firing-line with the necessary precision and promptness. A due consideration of this matter led to expedient and timely changes. The regiments which were too large were severally reduced in size, but collectively increased in numbers. In order to remove every disproportion, all regiments of the field-artillery were placed on the same footing, that is, they had two detachments each of three batteries; in other words, each regiment had six batteries. By this action still another point was gained. Each army division, the chief tactical unity of the army and the battle, consisting of the three branches of the army's service, is now equipped uniformly with the necessary number of batteries corresponding to the great importance of artillery, which now often decides the fate of the day. To each army division one brigade of field-artillery, not, as formerly, one regiment of field-artillery, is detailed. The standard of each German division, of which two form one army corps, is now two infantry brigades of two regiments each, and one cavalry brigade and one artillery brigade of two regiments each.

By this innovation the German army has attained great efficiency and uniformity, and the German artillery has received an effective increase of eighty batteries. Included in the latter are a number of new howitzer-batteries, which lend material assistance in operations against an enemy protected by entrenchments or by cover of any description. They are expected to supplement, by their curved fire, the direct fire of the other batteries.

4. A similar improvement became necessary with regard to the troops which maintain communication with the army in the field. The motive which actuated the government in putting a proposal for this purpose before the Imperial Diet, is thus stated: "The progress in all branches of technics manifests itself in their various employment in warfare. The railway and balloon troops require a large increase in numbers, if a sufficient and competent *personnel* is to be secured for employment in the event of war. Neither can the establishment of new formations for the field-telegraph service be delayed any longer. With the increase of the army's forces, their handling without adequate telegraphic communication is out of the question. The field-telegraph service requires a body of thoroughly reliable operators who must be trained exclusively for those functions, and who are yet lacking." (The pioneers formerly received an additional training in these duties.)

In recognition of all these facts, the Imperial Diet granted the proposed establishment of three telegraph battalions and also an increase of balloon and railway troops. The placing of the railway brigade and the telegraph and balloon battalions under one bureau of inspection, embracing all troops which maintain the communications of the army, was agreed upon without opposition.

5. The proposition of the government, which called for an increase of the peace-footing of the infantry, the army's principal branch of service, did not meet with the entire approval of the Diet. The infantry, which is subject to the greatest toils of the campaign, and which usually suffers the heaviest loss in battle, ought to have been treated with more consideration in the changes effected throughout the army. In order to strengthen the battalions of a lesser count, as well as those which are stationed on the frontier and have to be ready for immediate service in time of mobilization, the number of men should have been increased. This increase appears all the more necessary as the strength during the recruit's period of training has been considerably reduced by the introduction of the shorter time of service —two years instead of three.

The proposed increase of the army on a peace-footing from 479,229 men (officers, noncommissioned officers, and one-year volunteers excluded) to 502,506 men was cut down to 495,500, with the provision, however, that a further increase shall be granted in case of necessity.

The changes made in the German army may thus be summarized:

1. The number of army corps is to be raised from twenty to twenty-three, by three additional corps, which gives the German Empire twenty-two, in place of nineteen, army corps districts. The army, therefore, consists of seventeen Prussian army corps, including those subject to Prussia's administration (Corps of the Guards), first, second, third, fourth, fifth, sixth, seventh, eighth, ninth, tenth, eleventh, eighteenth, fourteenth, fifteenth, sixteenth, and seventeenth corps; three Bavarian corps (first, second, and third); two Saxon corps (twelfth and nineteenth); one Würtemberg corps (thirteenth).

2. The strength of the different branches of the army's service is as follows:

625 battalions of infantry (an increase of 1).
482 squadrons of cavalry (an increase of 13).
574 batteries (an increase of 80).
38 battalions of foot-artillery (an increase of 1).
26 battalions of pioneers (an increase of 3).
11 battalions of engineer troops (an increase of 4).
23 battalions of the military train (an increase of 2).

3. The peace-footing of the army is raised from 479,229 men to 495,500 men, an increase of 16,271.

The changes mentioned under paragraphs 1 and 2 went into effect on the first day of April, 1899. The increase stated under 3 will become law on October 1st, 1899, and will be enforced accordingly.

A general scrutiny of the character of the changes made will demonstrate their importance. The management of the army's training in time of peace, its passing by mobilization from a peace-footing to a war-footing, and the handling of the various organizations to attest their readiness and efficiency for war operations are facilitated by the changes. The tactical unities—the divisions— have become more independent and efficient for actual service by the addition of a strong body of artillery. capable of being easily and efficiently handled.

The prompt communication between the different parts of the forces in the field, which is of the utmost importance, has been facilitated by the increase and the reorganization of the troops which maintain communication. The army's readiness for war in general has been materially enhanced by the innovation which has taken place. Throughout Germany the increase of the Fatherland's defensive strength, brought about by the energetic efforts of the German Emperor, was hailed with enthusiasm and approval by every loyal citizen. But also to other nations the following words, which characterize the intention of the German government in formulating its propositions, are significant and important: "The events of the Spanish-American war have demonstrated with great clearness that the lack of a careful and systematic preparation for war in time of peace is followed by most disastrous consequences. No nation desiring to maintain its reputation and integrity among the Powers can afford to dispense with these preparations. Hence the principle will always prevail in the future that a strong, well-organized army is the best foundation of a government, and at the same time the best safeguard of peace."

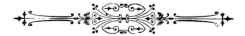

THE GERMAN NAVY

HISTORICAL SKETCH OF THE NAVY

THE history of Germany's sea-power dates far back into the Middle Ages. When the first Crusaders had taken the city of Tarsus they were joined by a fleet of Frisian and Flemish pirates, who wanted to do penance at the Holy Sepulchre. This took place in the year 1097. In 1147 a number of Frisian, Flemish, and Rhenish mariners gave manly assistance to the Portuguese in the capture of Lisbon, previous to their taking part in the great crusade under the leadership of Conrad III. At the beginning of the thirteenth century, during the era of the fifth crusade. Germany's sea-power was at its height. Oliverius, the brave and pious canon of Cologne, had succeeded in gathering together a great army of Crusaders near the Lower Rhine, in Westphalia and Frisia, the citizens of Cologne alone having equipped more than 300 vessels. The Counts William of Holland and George of Wied having been elected commanders of the fleet, the Crusaders put to sea in May, 1217, and reached the harbor of Acre in the following April, after great hardships; here they joined the Knights Templars in their expedition against Damiette in Egypt. At the siege of the latter town they erected on two of their ships a high wooden tower with a drawbridge for the purpose of storming the immense obstruction made of chains put across the Nile by the defending Saracens. After a hot fight the Frisians scaled the enemy's tower from their floating fortress, repulsed the Saracens, and cleared the river of its obstructions. Later on the towers of the boat-bridge at Damiette were destroyed by the same siege-machine, so that the town proper could be taken by storm, which event occurred November 5th, 1219.

In the twelfth century the city of Lübeck began to rise as an emporium of commerce. Having been destroyed by fire in 1152, Henry the Lion rebuilt the town. granting it many privileges and elevating it to a bishopric. In the year 1188 it was declared a free imperial city by Emperor Frederick Barbarossa. At that time the ships of Lübeck trafficked with the island of Gothland. Intercourse with Wisby, the capital of the island, was instrumental in forming the first federation of German merchants in foreign countries, giving a great impetus to the German trade on the Baltic Sea. The Teutonic Order was established by Crusaders from Lower Saxony at Riga. Here the influence of the German sea-power was strongly felt, and Riga became the centre for the spread of German culture throughout the Baltic provinces.

In the fourteenth century the severe conflicts of the German sea-towns with Denmark led to their incorporation with the Hanseatic League. About the year 1350 the league became a solid organization, with Lübeck as its soul and body.

The Danish King, Waldemar III, having captured the German emporium at Gothland in 1361, the Hansa cities determined to seek revenge on him for violating the treaty.

In May, 1362, the fleet under command of John Wittenborg, the burgomaster of Lübeck, stormed and captured Copenhagen and sacked the town. But, while they besieged the strong fortress of Helsingborg, Waldemar attacked the defenseless fleet, capturing twelve of the largest vessels and forcing the Hanseatic land-army to abandon the expedition. The brave but incautious Wittenborg atoned for his neglect by the loss of his head. The truce of the year 1362, recognizing the Danish possession of Gothland, having come to an end, the whole German Hansa bestirred itself, and, at a diet of the league at Cologne (1367), resolved to prosecute the war against Denmark. The mustered forces of the Osterlings (eastern division) and Westerlings (the western or Dutch division) raided the coast of Schonen, captured and destroyed Copenhagen and Helsingör and sacked the Danish and Norwegian ports. King Waldemar had to take to flight and was compelled to sign the ignominious treaty of Stralsund in the year 1370. By this treaty the Hanseats obtained possession of all the fortified seaports of Schonen. It was also stipulated that henceforth no King should ascend the throne of Denmark without the consent of the Hansa towns and that their privileges should be expressly confirmed. The treaty of Stralsund marks the zenith of the power and prosperity of the Hansa League, the strength of which was broken by internal dissensions and strifes. The piracy, brought about by the long wars, and practiced especially by the "Vitalienbrüder" and "Lickendeeler," greatly injured the trade of the Hansa cities. The Hanseatic trading vessels being compelled to sail in squadrons, their commerce suffered immensely by this method and likewise by the sound-duties levied by the Danish King, Eric, in 1425. This action was deemed by the Hansa tantamount to a cause of war. After three expeditions (1427-1429) had been sent forth King Eric was forced to make peace and to abandon the sound-duties.

Dissensions between the Westerlings (Dutch) and the Osterlings continued to weaken the great confederation, only Lübeck exercising its old influence for a limited period, of which the well-known historian, Æneas Silvius, afterwards Pope Pius II, writes: " Lübeck's influence is so commanding that three mighty kingdoms of the North accept or reject their rulers at its will."

The dissensions between the Osterlings and Westerlings were readily perceived by England, which power was not slow to grasp the advantages thus offered. King Henry VI, while favoring his old hosts, the merchants of Cologne, suffered Count Richard of Warwick, the royal governor of Calais, to attack 28 Lübeck merchantmen in the year 1458. The latter repulsed the attack, but in so doing lost six ships, and were unable to secure any compensation for such loss. During the reign of Edward IV some German merchants were illtreated and plundered at their London quarters, known as the Steelyard, or Guildhall, from sheer English jealousy. This outrage prompted the Hansa to suspend commerce with England, and to grant complete freedom of action to the " Vitalienbrüder," the pirates of the German Ocean, against the ports of England.

In the year 1472 the Hanseatic fleet, commanded by the brave freebooter Paul Beneke, harried the English coast, and captured many vessels. In 1474 Edward IV was compelled to sign a peace treaty, by the terms of which the Osterlings recovered their old privileges and an indemnity of £10,000 sterling. The latter term, it may be said in passing, is an abbreviation of Osterling.

Of the great countries beyond the sea, discovered at that period, Germany received none, the empire having then no adequate navy. Indeed, according to an imperial decree of 1512, no German trading company was allowed to transact business with a foreign country. Venezuela, which was forfeited as a pledge by Emperor Charles V as an hereditary fief to the princely Welsers of Augsburg, and subdued almost completely by the latter, was lost. They could not hold their possession for lack of German naval protection, being dependent on the arbitrary actions of Spain and Portugal.

Once more Lübeck's sea-power rose, shining forth in brilliant lustre. Allied with Dantzic, Rostock, Wismar, and Stralsund it gave support to the Swedish King, Gustavus Vasa. Christian II, King of Denmark, was dethroned and the island of Bornholm was pledged to Lübeck, as war indemnity, for a period of fifty years. But, alas! princely, social, and religious affairs of a particular nature interfered with Lübeck's endeavor to regain naval predominance on the Baltic.

The valiant burgomaster, Jürgen Wullenweber, who had subdued the entire kingdom of Denmark and had also crippled the Danish, Swedish, and Dutch commerce, was repudiated by his own fellow-citizens in a shameful manner merely from petty jealousy. This brave man was condemned to death and was executed at Brunswick September 29th, 1537, whilst the Council of Lübeck sanctioned the infamous sentence. The Hansa's sea-power suffered eclipse with the death of Wullenweber.

The energetic commercial people of England took advantage of the Hansa's weakness and selfish greed, and had the charters of the German merchants annulled by their rulers. The Hanseatic towns having aided in the equipment of the Spanish armada by supplying it with provisions, Queen Elizabeth in 1589 ordered a whole fleet of Hanseatic merchantmen brought up at the mouth of the river Tagus, and the Germans to be driven out of their guildhall at London. After that, the Hanseatic merchants were looked upon as harmless weaklings and were compelled to obtain their part of the trade by intrigue, barter, or entreaty.

During the reign of the Emperor Ferdinand II the Hansa League missed its chance to regain lost power, fearing, in the spirit of narrowmindedness, that the Emperor might become too powerful. Wallenstein organized an imperial navy at Wismar, receiving from the Emperor, in 1628, a commission as " General of the ocean and the Baltic Sea and Captain-General of the Armada, then in course of construction." Only the city of Stralsund offered a stubborn resistance to the imperial forces, forming at the same time an alliance w' ʰ the Swedish King, Gustavus Adolphus. Having acquired Stralsund, the King established a firm foothold on the Baltic Sea and got possession, in the course of time, of the bishoprics of Verden, Bremen, Wismar, the island of Rügen, and almost all of Pomerania.

At a council of the Hansa League, convened at Lübeck in 1630, the emissaries of the different Hanseatic towns declared themselves unable to continue the confederation. Without further parley the proud league was dissolved, only Lübeck, Bremen, and Hamburg deciding to assist each other in case of emergency. The fundamental evil of the league lay in the defects incident to its imperfect organization. These were lack of harmony, selfish greed in individual members, and the sad want of a national government, i. e., the firm hand of an Emperor, powerful at sea, and able to wield and direct its great powers. At the close of the Thirty Years' War, Denmark, with Schleswig-Holstein and Oldenburg in its possession, controlled the entrance to the German harbors, Bremen, Hamburg, and Lübeck. Sweden held the countries lying between the Elbe and Weser, and the coasts of Mecklenburg and Pomerania; Rostock alone preserving its independence. The duchy of Prussia, Dantzic excluded, was subject to Poland.

Frederick William of Brandenburg, the Great Elector, possessed at the beginning of his reign only a strip of the Pomeranian coast with the only seaport, Kolberg, the open unprotected roadsteads of Stolp and Rügenwalde, and the little seaport of Pillau as a fief of Poland. After having been invested by the treaty of Oliva in 1660 with the sovereignty of the entire Prussian coast, the resolute Elector resolved to create a powerful navy and to make his seafaring dominions rich and prosperous by trade with foreign countries.

The Brandenburg flag, a red eagle on a white field, for the first time flew from privateers sent out to

Captain.   Commanding Admiral.   Assistant-Surgeon.   Naval Cadet.

cripple Swedish commerce. The Swedes having made inroads into Brandenburg, the Elector, with the design of destroying Swedish commerce, hired, through the agency of the Dutch merchant, Raule, ten Dutch frigates, upon which he hoisted the Brandenburg flag. In a short time twenty-one well-laden vessels were captured, and in four weeks the Swedish flag disappeared from German waters.

In the summer of 1676 the Elector closed another contract with Raule for the equipment of five frigates and six sloops to cut off the Swedes from Pomerania. Raule joined, at Copenhagen, a Danish and a Dutch auxiliary fleet under the command of Admiral Cornelius Tromp. At the naval battle fought near Bornholm on June 5th, in which the Swedes were utterly routed, Raule captured the *Leopard*, a vessel of 22 guns, and a fire-ship of 8 guns, and brought his prizes into the seaport of Colberg. His squadron also rendered good service at the blockade of the Pomeranian coast and captured many valuable prizes.

In the year 1678 Raule had to provide a fleet of 210 large and 140 smaller vessels for the transportation of the Brandenburg troops to the island of Rügen. This was effected under convoy of the united Dutch and Danish fleets commanded by Admirals Tromp and Juël. After the capture of Rügen, Raule's ships blockaded the inland waters of Rügen, an operation which secured the surrender of the towns of Stralsund and Greifswald.

By the treaty of St. Germain, signed on the 29th of July, 1679, the Elector was deprived of all the advantages gained over the Swedes, who had been almost driven from Pomerania. By this treaty the sea-power of the Elector, heralded by flattering promises, came to naught. In the same year a new agreement was drawn up between the Elector and Raule to last six years. It stipulated for the equipment of eight vessels, with a crew of 400 sailors, officers included, and also for the construction of twelve war vessels and two fire-ships at the shipyard of Pillau. It was hoped to receive the necessary funds for the construction of Raule's fleet from Spain, which country owed the Great Elector subsidies to the amount of 1,800,000 thalers, the payment of which had been in arrears since the year 1674. Spain, however, refused the money, and without any reason. But the Elector was not the man to be trifled with and his announcement, made at Madrid, "that he would try different methods to get his money," was followed by deeds. On the 14th of August a Brandenburg squadron consisting of the vessels *Frederick William*, *Kurprinz*, *Dorothea*, *Red Lion*, *Fuchs*, *Berlin*, and the fire-ship *Salamander*, with 165 guns, manned by 38 officers, 481 sailors and 180 marines, under command of Claus von Bevern, put to sea to watch near Dunkirk for the convoy of Spanish merchantmen sailing from Ostend to Cadiz.

On September 18th, the Brandenburg vessels overhauled a Spanish ship of 28 guns, the *Carolus Secundus*, with a cargo of costly lace and fine linen. Captain Cornelius Raes cruised with the other three ships, heading for the West Indies, to capture a Spanish fleet laden with silver. On April 20th, 1681, three frigates, the *Princess Marie*, *Wasserhund*, and *Eichhorn*, under Captain John Lacher, left the port of Pillau to cruise in the English channel and from there to proceed in the direction of the West Indies. Raule promised the Elector "to tackle the Spaniards within two months, so that they never should forget it." As a support to Lacher, in June and July three additional great frigates followed, the *Fuchs*, *Frederick William*, and the *Carolus Secundus*, the name of which had been changed to the *Margrave of Brandenburg*. After having joined Lacher in the Straits of Dover, Thomas Alders led his squadron into the Atlantic, heading for Cape St. Vincent, for the purpose of capturing the Spanish "silver fleet," which was on its way homeward from the West Indies.

This daring undertaking provoked the wrath of the Spanish government. It equipped, at the seaports of Galicia, twelve galleys and two fire-ships, which put to sea in September, under command of the Marquis de Villafiel, with the intention of driving off the Brandenburg ships and protecting the approaching "silver fleet."

On September 30th, Alders sighted the Spanish ships. Eager to encounter the long and anxiously expected silver galleys, he gave furious battle with his six small vessels to the vastly superior Spanish forces. After a hot contest, lasting over two hours, in which Alders lost ten men killed and thirty wounded, he drew off and made for the Portuguese harbor of Lagos, while the "silver fleet" safely reached the port of Cadiz. In spite of the undertaking having proved futile, its daring was not to be underestimated. The boldness shown by little Brandenburg in attacking the ships of a European sea-power excites to-day the same admiration and amazement it did at the time of the occurrence. Honorably the Brandenburg navy maintained its prestige on the ocean amidst great seafaring nations.

At this juncture the Great Elector resolved to replace the hired navy by one of his own, and also to acquire some colonial possessions. On January 1st, 1683, Major Otto Frederick von Groeben solemnly took possession of some territory lying on the west coast of Africa by hoisting the Brandenburg flag and erecting the fort "Gross Friedrichsburg," near the Cape Three Points on the coast of Guinea. Later on, two other forts were built, named "Dorothea," near Accadda, and "Brandenburg," near Taccarary. The Elector also acquired the island of Arguin in the bay of Arguin in the year 1685, where an old Dutch fort was rebuilt and thirty guns were mounted. A commercial agency was also established at the island of St. Thomas' in the West Indies. The death of the Great Elector, which took place May 9th, 1688, prevented the proper realization of his bold plans. His successor, Elector Frederick III, could not continue the fostering of the work; his whole energy was spent in the war going on with the French at that period. Only two frigates were equipped, which took a few prizes. King Frederick William I's efforts were all absorbed in the establishment of an efficient army; he

H. M. Armored Cruiser "Fürst Bismarck."

THE WERNER COMPANY, AKRON, O.

would not sacrifice a farthing for colonial enterprises. The king sold, in the year 1720, the entire colonial possessions for the sum of 6,000 ducats, and 6,000 guilders in shares, to the Dutch Company; in the year 1731 the agency formerly established at St. Thomas was likewise relinquished. Frederick the Great endeavored to raise the maritime commerce of his dominions. He created, under great difficulties, an "Asiatic" and a "Bengal" trading company, the success of which was frustrated by the jealousy of the English and Dutch. Having no adequate navy, the King could not guard his colonial interests against the inconsiderate encroachments of the former Powers. The Swedes threatening the fortress of Stettin in the year 1758, a small Prussian fleet, with a crew of 436 seamen, prevented the enemy from entering the Pomeranian inland waters. In September, 1759, this fleet encountered a vastly superior Swedish fleet in the Bay of Stettin. In the battle which ensued the Swedes lost 3 ships and 120 men, and were prevented from entering the harbor.

After peace had been concluded, the Prussian war vessels were altered into trading vessels, and the Prussian flag disappeared from the high seas for a period of about a hundred years. In the stormy times of the year 1848 the German nation, in the belief that it had effected the unification of the Fatherland, asked for the immediate organization of a navy. The fact that little Denmark was able to blockade the entire German coast made the question of defence at sea a burning one. But, contemporaneous with the universal wish, there was a general misconception of the situation. Even though the necessary funds were forthcoming, the organization, equipment, and armament of a navy could not be effected at a moment's notice; little, therefore, was accomplished, in spite of the manifested feverish zeal.

In April, 1849, the German navy consisted of the following vessels:

2 steam frigates, the *Barbarossa* and *Archduke Johann*, each of 9 guns.
1 steam frigate, the *Hansa*, of 11 guns.
1 first-class steam corvette, *King Ernst August*, in course of construction.
3 additional steam corvettes, the *Lübeck*, *Hamburg*, and *Bremen*, each of 2 guns.
1 steam corvette, *Bonin*, in course of construction at Kiel.
1 sailing frigate, the *Deutschland*, of 32 guns.

With the latter, only three steam vessels, the *Barbarossa*, *Lübeck*, and *Hamburg*, were really available for active service. With these three ships Captain Bromme, formerly in the Greek naval service, made the only reconnoitring cruise ever undertaken under the federal flag, the colors of which were black, red, and gold. The cruise, made in the waters of Heligoland, was a futile one. The federal navy so hastily created was neither fit for service nor was it fit to survive; its dissolution was decreed by the federal Diet and the several ships were partly sold and partly auctioned off.

The navy created by the Schleswig-Holstein committee on naval affairs showed, however, a brilliant activity in the struggle with Denmark, lasting from 1848 to 1851. In the fight at Eckernförde, which took place April 5th, 1849, the Danish battleship *Christian VIII* was blown up by two Schleswig-Holstein land batteries of 10 guns, while the frigate *Gefion* was forced to surrender. The two ships carried 132 heavy guns. In all its engagements the Schleswig-Holstein navy succeeded in warding off the attacks of the vastly superior Danish forces upon the chief German seaports. After the surrender of the Elbe duchies to Denmark, this small navy soon ceased to exist.

In contrast with the inefficient work of the federal navy, doomed to ruin from the start, the Prussian navy developed itself slowly, but on a solid foundation. On March 1st, 1849, Prince Adelbert was appointed commander-in-chief of all Prussian war vessels. These consisted of 1 sailing corvette, the 2 mail-steamers, *Prussian Eagle* and *Elisabeth*, and 21 sloops, armed with 67 guns and with a crew of 32 officers and 1,521 men. At Stettin a naval depot, and at Dantzic a navy yard were established; while a naval corps, a marine corps, and a division of engineers were created in 1852. In 1853 a Prussian squadron, consisting of the *Gefion*, bought from the derelict federal navy, the *Amazon*, and the *Mercur*, set out on a naval expedition on the Atlantic to Madeira, and to the La Plata States and the West Indies. The expedition was commanded by Commodore Schroeder, formerly in the Dutch service. In 1853, Jahde bay was acquired from Oldenburg as a harbor on the German Ocean. In the following year, Prince Adelbert was appointed admiral of the Prussian coasts. About that time the organization of the dock-yards and marine corps was effected, and the marine reserve was put in an efficient condition. Besides the marine depot at Stralsund, a station command was established at Dantzic, the school of sea cadets was removed from Stettin to Berlin, and the reserve and landwehr were also organized.

During the years from 1859 to 1865, the Prussian navy was strengthened by additional vessels. These included the protected corvettes *Arcona*, *Gazelle*, *Vineta*, and *Nymphe;* the gunboats *Delphin*, *Blitz*, and *Basilisk*, the sailing brig *Hela*, together with the despatch-boat *Loreley*.

The navy suffered a great loss in November, 1861, by the foundering of the corvette *Amazon* off the Dutch coast. In this mishap 6 officers, 19 naval cadets, and 120 men were engulfed in a watery grave.

In the war of 1864, the Prussian navy, consisting of three large vessels and a number of gunboats, with about 70 guns, was no match for a Danish fleet of 18 war vessels, carrying 363 guns. Its activity was confined to a number of short and unavailing fights and attacks, such as the encounter which took place at Stubenkammer, under Captain Jachmann on March 17th, and that under Prince Adelbert against the Danish frigate *Tordenskjold*, in the waters of Rügen.

The Prussian vessels, *Prussian Eagle*, *Blitz*, and

Battalion of Marines on Picket Duty.

Basilisk, having returned from the Mediterranean, fought a battle on May 9th, 1864, in conjunction with the Austrian screw frigates *Schwarzenberg* and *Radetzky*, under Commodore Tegethoff, against the Danes near Heligoland. The Danish squadron consisted of the frigate *Niels Juël* and the corvettes *Heimdal* and *Dagmar*, — opposing 104 Danish guns to 98 guns of the allied Prussians and Austrians. The Austrian Commodore Tegethoff maintained a fierce fight for a time, but was compelled to withdraw, his flagship being set on fire by the enemy. Towards the close of the war, the Prussian gunboats gave active support in capturing the flotilla of the Danish Captain, Hammer, near the island of Föhr.

During this period the armed vessels *Arminius* and *Prince Adelbert*, and the unprotected corvettes *Augusta* and *Victoria*, were bought abroad; the corvette *Medusa* was completed at the navy yard at Dantzic in 1865. In the same year the marine station of the Baltic Sea was removed to Kiel, and a naval artillery service was created. In the years 1865–68 the protected corvette *Vineta* made a tour around the world, this being the first expedition of the kind made by a German war vessel.

In the war of 1866, only the gunboats *Cyclop* and *Tiger*, the side-wheeler *Loreley*, and the armed vessel *Arminius* came into action. They took the fortress of Stade by surprise and captured the enemy's batteries posted on the Elbe, Weser, and Ems.

With the creation of the North German confederation, the Prussian navy was merged into a North German federal navy. This took place July 1st, 1867. The confederation had to provide for the navy, to the service of which the entire seaman population was now liable. The flag of the North German navy was hoisted on all ships in service on October 1st, replacing the Prussian colors. The flag shows a black cross in a white field, in the centre of the cross the Prussian eagle, and in the upper inner quarter the German imperial colors,— black, white, and red,— with the iron cross. This flag has been retained in its entirety as the imperial war-flag.

In 1868 the navy received an additional increase of three large armed battleships, built abroad, the *König Wilhelm*, *Friedrich Carl*, and *Kronprinz*. In the same year the beautiful wooden screw corvette *Elisabeth* was launched, a masterpiece of German shipbuilding. This vessel made her first cruise in the Mediterranean to attend the opening of the Suez Canal and joined there the squadron which had escorted Crown Prince Frederick William to Port Said. In 1869 the harbor for men-of-war, situated on the Jahde, was opened and named Wilhelmshaven by King William. This took place on June 17th.

At the beginning of the Franco-German war the North German federal navy mustered only 3 armored frigates, 2 other armored vessels, 1 battleship, 3 protected and 5 unprotected corvettes, 8 first-class and 14 second-class gunboats, 3 side-wheel steamers, and 7 sailing vessels, with a total crew of 162 officers and 3,650 men. Of these the two protected corvettes *Arcona* and *Hertha*, the unprotected corvette *Medusa*, and the first-class gunboat *Meteor*, were abroad. The opposing French fleet consisted of 232 war vessels ready for warlike operations, of which 33 were armored. It was formed into two squadrons; the Baltic squadron comprised 5 armored frigates, 2 armored corvettes, 2 despatch-boats and 1 yacht, with a total crew of 4,000 men. Its entire armament included 70 heavy and many light guns. The French squadron stationed in the German Ocean consisted of 7 armored frigates, 2 unprotected frigates, and 2 despatch-boats, of 87 guns, with a total crew of 4,000 men.

As a matter of course, the German navy contented itself with the defence of the coast, the attacks upon which by the French squadrons were unavailing.

On August 17th, 1870, while on a reconnoitring cruise, an unimportant engagement took place between the German flotilla stationed at Stralsund (consisting of the *Grille* and three first-class gunboats under Admiral Jachmann), and the French Baltic squadron. During the night of August 22nd, the *Nymphe*, under Captain Weikhmann, made a sortie from the harbor of Dantzic against three French battleships anchored in the bay. The ship succeeded in approaching the enemy without being noticed and delivered two broadsides into the French vessels, which replied with only a few shots. The German ship safely drew back into the harbor. The French soon left their moorings on the Prussian coast. In September the French Baltic squadron withdrew from Baltic waters, so dangerous to navigation, and joined the squadron stationed near Heligoland, in the German Ocean, which was blockading the mouths of the Elbe, Weser, and Jahde. No engagement followed.

The corvette *Augusta*, under Captain Weikhmann, which left in December, succeeded, however, in capturing three French vessels laden with provisions and ammunition at the mouth of the river Gironde. The vessel was later on penned up by a French squadron in the Spanish harbor of Vigo, and had to stay there till the war was ended.

On November 9th, the gunboat *Meteor*, commanded by Lieutenant-Captain Knorr, encountered the French despatch-boat *Bouvet* near Havana. The German vessel was of 347 tons and 320 horsepower, and had an armament of three rifled guns, one of 5.9 in. and two of 4.7 in. with a crew of 62 men. The *Bouvet* was a vessel of 700 tons and 600 horsepower, with a steaming power twice as great as that of the *Meteor*. Her armament consisted of one 6.1 in. gun, two 4.7 in. guns and four swivel-guns; the crew numbered 85 men. At noon on November 9th the *Meteor* left the harbor of Havana to meet her adversary, that had taken to the open seas twenty-four hours previous. After a lapse of about thirty minutes, the vessels drew near each other—to within 2,000 yards. The French having fired eight shots, which, however, fell short, the distance between the vessels was reduced to about 1,000 yards. Knorr opened fire with his 4.7 in. bow gun and changed his course somewhat to the east, to bring his heavy 5.9 in. midship gun to bear upon his opponent. By this manœuvre Knorr exposed his broadside, of which Captain Franquet, the French commander, took instant advantage. He first tried to ram the German boat, but in this he was partly foiled; he was also to some extent puzzled by the adroit manœuvring of Captain Knorr. In the collision, the bow of the French boat stove in the larboard boats and injured the hurricane deck of the *Meteor*. It also turned away the projecting muzzles of the amidship and after-deck guns, preventing the discharge of the former and the further use of the latter. The *Bouvet's* foreyard broke off the foreyard and the mizzenmast of the German gunboat, and bent over the mainmast, while its iron cathead carried off the larboard shrouds. The gunboat was lying by, apparently disabled for the time being. Knorr, however, manœuvred about so skillfully that the mainmast, swinging to and fro, fell to the starboard like the foremast, and turned his boat in such a manner that the larboard guns were available for action.

While the Frenchman missed his chance, the *Meteor* fired the first shell from her 5.9 in. gun, striking the *Bouvet* amidship, near the water line, and enveloping her in a cloud of steam. The Germans hailed this decisive turn in the fight with a thundering hurrah. The Frenchman at once set sail for Havana, seeking in haste the protecting neutral zone, leaving the scene of action and the victory to the *Meteor*. Had the fight continued, the *Bouvet*, which had fired no shot after the collision, would have been forced to strike her colors. When the *Meteor* returned to Havana she was welcomed with rousing *vivas*.

The war on land, so successful to Germany, fully demonstrated that the lives of many brave soldiers could have been saved if a German navy had been in existence to prevent the importation of arms into France by America and England, especially the latter. Gradually, but effectively, the opinion prevailed in German countries that a strong empire needs an efficient navy in order to figure as a great Power among the nations.

After the title and dignity of an Empire were revived, on January 18th, 1871, the North German federal navy became the German imperial navy, but without a change of colors. It was now the duty of the empire to provide for a navy adequate to the Fatherland's position among the nations. Some changes in the organization of the navy were effected at this period. The naval ministry was replaced by the imperial admiralty in 1872; a naval station on the German Ocean was created at Wilhelmshaven, with a second marine division and a second navy-yard division. After this the naval academy was founded and amalgamated with the marine school at Kiel, followed by the establishment of a ship-boys' division at Friedrichsort. General von Stosch was appointed chief of the imperial admiralty. Prince Adelbert, the creator and first tutor of the navy, who

died June 1st, 1873, did not live to see the fruits of his work. In the same year the imperial diet granted the funds asked for by the government, namely 218,-500,000 marks, for the purpose of constructing the following navy, adequate to the position of the empire, to be finished in the year 1882: 8 armored frigates, 6 armored corvettes, 7 armored monitors, 2 armored batteries, 20 corvettes, 6 despatch-boats, 18 gunboats, 2 artillery training ships, 3 sailing vessels, 3 sailing brigs, and 20 torpedo-boats. The navy-yards at Dantzic, Wilhelmshaven, and Kiel were improved and enlarged. Admiral von Stosch energetically followed out his design to foster and promote home shipbuilding to such an extent that in a short time all ships could be built at German shipyards. Only the armored frigates *Kaiser* and *Deutschland* were launched from an English shipyard in 1874.

In the seventies, the active peace operations of the German navy began. In 1873, the battleship *Friedrich Carl* and the corvette *Elisabeth*, commanded by Commodore Reinhold Werner, were despatched to the Spanish Mediterranean coast, to protect the German residents at that place during an insurrection in Spain. According to maritime law, the Spanish government declared the vessels held by the insurgents in the harbor of Cartagena to be those of pirates subject to pursuit by all foreign powers. Under the guns of the rebel fortress Cartagena, the *Friedrich Carl* captured the Spanish despatch-boat *Vigilante*. Her crew was set free; the ship, however, was delivered over to the Spanish government. On August 1st, Werner forced the rebel vessels *Vitoria* and *Almansa* to surrender. The crew, 1,400 men strong, were landed; the two frigates, however, were delivered first to an English squadron, and later on to Spain. Werner's energetic action was praised in England as a daring deed, the equal of a glorious achievement at sea. Not so in Germany; there it was regarded in a totally different aspect. Werner was relieved of his command, receiving the commission of director-in-chief of the navy-yard at Wilhelmshaven.

During the disturbances, which took place in the Orient in 1876, and in which the German and French consuls of Saloniki were murdered by a mob, the Porte was compelled by a German squadron, consisting of four armored frigates under Rear-Admiral Batsch, to punish the murderers, and also the instigators of this act of violence.

In the years 1874–1876, the circumnavigation of the globe was effected by the protected corvette *Gazelle*, commanded by Captain Baron von Schleinitz. This was the first scientific expedition on a large scale ever undertaken by a German man-of-war.

In the year 1877, Prince Henry of Prussia, the brother of the German Emperor, entered the navy as a cadet on the sailing frigate *Niobe*. His name, since then so closely associated with the German navy, will continue to live in its history.

A great catastrophe befell the navy on May 31st, 1878.

The large new battleship *Grosser Kurfürst* was sunk in a collision with the *König Wilhelm*. This event took place near Folkestone in the English channel, and caused the loss of 269 men.

In the year 1879, during the war between Chili and Peru, the armored frigate *Hansa*, under Captain von Heusner, effected the release of the steamer *Luxor*, which had been attached contrary to law. The frigate also saved the seaport of Callao, where many German interests were at stake, from bombardment by Chili's fleet. On September 17th, 1881, the first great naval review was held by Emperor William at Kiel.

In the spring of 1883, when Admiral von Stosch stepped out of office, the navy consisted of the following ships: 7 armored frigates, 5 armored corvettes, 11 protected and 8 unprotected corvettes, 9 first-class gunboats, 1 armored vessel and 11 armored gunboats for coast defence, 10 torpedo-boats, 4 mine-layers, 1 second-class gunboat, 8 despatch-boats, 2 transport steamers, 12 schoolships, and several steamers for harbor and pilot service. In course of construction were 1 battleship, 3 corvettes, 1 first-class gunboat, 2 armored gunboats, and 1 torpedo-boat. General von Caprivi was appointed chief of the admiralty.

At this juncture Germany's naval power was efficient enough to resume the colonial policy dormant during a period of two hundred years. The colonial enterprises and commercial interests started at that time in countries beyond the sea, gave to the German navy in the eighties a chance to demonstrate its efficiency and the necessity of its existence. On July 4th, 1884, the annexation of Bageida in the Toga country was effected by H. M. S. *Möve*, Dr. Nachtigal officiating as imperial commissioner. The same ship hoisted the German flag at Kamerun, where Hamburg merchants had established commercial agencies since 1868. H. M. S. *Elisabeth* under Captain Schering, together with the *Leipzig*, took possession of some territory on the southwestern coast of Africa, acquired by the Bremen merchant Lüderitz in 1883. On August 7th, 1884, all territory from the northern banks of the Orange river to the 26th degree south latitude was placed under the protectorate of Germany. On the 12th of the same month, the entire coast, north of "Lüderitzland" and stretching to the Portuguese frontier at Cape Frio, was incorporated into the German colonial possessions by the gunboat *Wolf*. But Walfisch bay, claimed by England, was excluded from the deal.

In the South Sea, on November 3rd, 1894, Captain Schering secured, by means of the *Elisabeth* and the gunboat *Hyäne*, Matupi, the chief port of the Bismarck Archipelago, and the following day obtained possession of the harbor of Mioko. In the same month the territory lying on the coast of New Guinea, and now called "Kaiser Wilhelmsland," became subject to German rule, and the German flag was hoisted by the *Elisabeth* in the important harbor of Finch on November 27th.

During this period the navy suffered several losses.

In June, 1885, the corvette *Augusta* foundered in a terrible hurricane in the Gulf of Aden. The entire crew of 9 officers and 214 men were lost.

In August, 1885, a squadron consisting of the corvettes *Prince Adelbert*, *Stosch*, *Elisabeth*, and *Gneisenau*, under Commodore Paschen, anchored in front of the Sultan of Zanzibar's palace. The squadron was augmented on the 17th of the month by the corvette *Bismarck*, the flagship of Admiral Knorr, and later on by the gunboat *Möve*. The East-African company had previously purchased 2,500 miles of good inland territory. To make this colony self-supporting, an adequate strip of the coast land had to be procured. The Sultan, instigated by the English, tried by force to prevent this action. On December 20th, Admiral Knorr concluded an important treaty with the Sultan, by the terms of which the latter granted the strip of coast in question.

The occupation of a few of the Caroline islands (now [1899] purchased with the adjoining island groups, by Germany) by the *Iltis* in 1885 almost provoked a war with Spain, which nation claimed a prior title to the islands. The imperial chancellor, Bismarck, succeeded in averting warlike actions, however, by leaving the decision to the Pope. By papal arbitration Spain was granted possession of the islands with the stipulation that Germany would receive the privilege of free commerce, and the right of a coaling station upon one of the islands. In October, 1885, the Marshall Islands were annexed by the *Nautilus*, and in 1886 the Solomon Islands by the *Adler*.

At the festivities held in connection with the laying of the cornerstone of the Kaiser Wilhelm Canal on June 3rd, 1887, with the purpose of shortening the route between the Baltic and the German Ocean, and also of making the operations of the German navy independent of the enemy's action, the German naval forces were imposingly represented. Twenty-one German war vessels, of which seven were battleships and thirteen torpedo-boats, with a crew of 6,380, thundered forth their salute in honor of Emperor William. This was the Emperor's last naval review

Emperor William II ascended the throne on June 17th, 1888. From his earliest youth he gave evidence of great interest in the navy, which interest increased in intensity, as was manifested in the course of his reign by the untiring zeal and active concern displayed by him. In July of the same year the Emperor appointed Vice-Admiral Count von Monts chief of the admiralty, who, however, died shortly afterward and was succeeded by Vice-Admiral Baron von der Goltz. In March of the following year the admiralty was divided into two branches of service. One, the chief command of the navy, had to deal with affairs pertaining to the different commands, the other was the imperial naval bureau whose function embraced the administration of naval affairs. Since 1895 Admiral von Knorr has been the commanding admiral.

The blockade of the East-African coast, lasting from

Skirmish of a Landing Party of Marines.

November, 1888, to the fall of 1889, was undertaken in conjunction with England. This task fell to the lot of a squadron consisting of the cruiser-frigate *Leipzig*, the cruiser-corvettes *Carola* and *Sophie*, the cruisers *Möve* and *Falke*, and the despatch-boat *Blitz*, commanded by Rear-Admiral Deinhart. In this undertaking they were successful, as they were in the suppression of a rebellion of the Arabs on the mainland of German-Africa, which was effected by the coöperation of the German colonial troops with the marines. The squadron blockaded the coast from the fourth to the ninth degree south latitude, in order to suppress the slave trade carried on by the Arabs. Previous to this, on September 22nd, 1888, a corps of marines from the *Leipzig* had stormed Bagamayo. On January 29th, 1889, a body of marines from the *Sophie* drove the Arabs out of Dar-es-Salaam. On March 27th of the same year, some troops from the *Leipzig*, *Carola*, and *Schwalbe*, under Captain Hirschberg captured the town of Kondutschi, a notorious lurking place of the Arabs. On May 8th, some marines, in connection with the colonial troops under Captain Wissman, stormed the fortified camp of Chief Buschiri near Bagamayo, the enemy losing 80 killed. On July 8th, Pangani, and on the 10th, Tanga, were captured. On October 19th and 20th Lieutenant von Gravenreuth routed the Mafitis, led by Buschiri, and the rebel chief took refuge at Sadaani. This place was taken on November 8th, by marines from the *Carola*, *Schwalbe*, and the just arrived *Sperber*, in conjunction with 200 colonial troops. In May, 1890, the *Schwalbe* and the *Carola* took part in the capture of Kilwa, Lindi, and Mikindani, effecting a complete suppression of the rebellion.

By these engagements the navy indirectly won the English island of Heligoland for Germany; on July 1st, 1890, this island was exchanged for Witu and the surrender of the German protectorate of Zanzibar.

The protection of German interests on the Samoan islands cost many lives. In 1888, the cruisers *Olga* and *Adler*, and the gunboat *Eber*, were despatched to quell an uprising of the natives against the German settlers and merchants. In a fight near Apia with the rebels, who were amply provided with firearms by the Americans, 2 officers and 14 men were killed on the German side, while 37 men were wounded. A great disaster befell H. M. SS. *Olga*, *Adler*, and *Eber* in the harbor of Apia. In a terrific hurricane, March 15th, 1889, the *Adler* and the *Eber* foundered on the coral reefs, while the *Olga* escaped destruction only by running ashore. Five officers and 80 men met a watery grave.

In August, 1891, the *Leipzig*, *Sophie*, and *Alexandrine* were sent to protect the German residents at Valparaiso. Three hundred men of the squadron held two hills of the town, where most of the Germans lived, until the victorious opposing party had restored order in the town and guaranteed security to the Germans.

Fresh in the memory of every reader is the great naval review which took place at the opening of the canal connecting the German Ocean with the Baltic. Fifty-three foreign warships, representing sixteen nations, and surrounded by twenty-eight men-of-war and two divisions of torpedo-boats of the German empire, thundered forth their salutes to the German Emperor, as he laid the finishing stone of this gigantic undertaking at Holtenau. The Emperor named the canal "Kaiser Wilhelm Kanal" in honor of its founder. This event occurred on June 20th, 1895.

At the beginning of the Japanese-Chinese war the *Iltis* sailed for Corea, in order to protect the German consul at Seoul. During this cruise the ship saved 220 shipwrecked Chinese, who had taken refuge on the inhospitable island of Tak Shan. In April, 1895, the *Iltis* was called upon to protect the German steamer *Arthur*, lying at Tamsui, a harbor of Formosa. Some Chinese rebels had fired from the land-forts of Tamsui harbor upon the steamer, which had a sum of money on board belonging to the Chinese government. At this juncture the *Iltis* threw a few well-directed shells into the fort, one of them killing thirteen Chinese and scattering the others in all directions. On July 23rd, 1896, this ship went down in a typhoon near the cape of Sha-Tung, only ten of the crew being saved. With three cheers for their Emperor the gallant seamen sank beneath the surging waves.

In December, 1897, after some German missionaries had been murdered by a Chinese mob, German marines took possession of the harbor and fortified town of Kiau-Chou in China. This incident caused the German government to establish a firm foothold in China, in order to protect its imperial subjects, and also its important commercial affairs. Germany's object, however, was not to make war upon China, but to come to an agreement with the Chinese Emperor, by which Kiau-Chou could be leased for a period of ninety-nine years. To enforce Germany's demands, the Emperor, shortly before Christmas, sent a squadron to China. Prince Henry of Prussia, the Emperor's brother, who commanded one division of marines belonging to the above squadron, was intrusted with the political part of the mission.

During the Spanish-American war of 1898, it fell to the lot of the East-Asiatic squadron to protect the important commercial interests of the Germans living in the Philippines, and especially at Manila. This squadron consisted of the second-class battleship *Deutschland*, commanded by Prince Henry, her sister ship *Kaiser*, the flagship of Admiral von Diederichs, and the cruisers *Kaiserin Augusta*, *Irene*, *Princess Wilhelm*, *Gefion*, and *Cormoran*. This task led to unpleasant misunderstandings and somewhat complicated situations. The complaints preferred by the American Admiral, Dewey, against the commander of the German squadron of having violated the laws of blockade led to a remonstrance by the American ambassador at Berlin.

The German secretary of foreign affairs, however, assured the latter that all reports about intentional violation of the blockade were absurd, and furthermore, he declared that the presence of such a powerful German squadron in the harbor of Manila was absolutely necessary for the protection of the large number of Germans residing there. He also insisted that the action of the cruiser *Irene* against the insurgents at Subig bay, on July 7th, was justified and only instituted in behalf of humanity. It might be asserted that the German squadron in the whole affair did not show an intentional unfriendly feeling toward the Americans, strictly adhering to international law and usage; that on the other hand, the squadron never shirked its duty in protecting imperial subjects.

ORGANIZATION OF THE NAVY

IT SEEMED for a time as though the splendid success achieved by the German army in the war of 1870–71, and the efforts which were subsequently directed toward its further development under the consolidated empire, had absorbed all the interest and resources of the German people, and prevented any attempt to build a navy that should be truly representative of the country. It was only at the beginning of the eighties, and especially with the accession to the throne of the present Emperor, William II., that an active naval policy was inaugurated. It is largely due to the Emperor's persistent efforts that Germany now possesses the modern and efficient navy represented by the fine vessels of the *Brandenburg* class and by the *Kaiser Friedrich III.*, the *Fürst Bismarck*, the *Kaiserin Augusta*, and others of the new type. The organization of the navy, too, with all its details, is pre-eminently the work of the Emperor, who, with an ever watchful eye, endeavors to raise Germany to the position of a real sea-power, to enlarge her colonial possessions, and to foster and protect her foreign commerce in every quarter of the globe.

The army, together with the navy, constitutes the fighting strength of the German Empire. Both branches, though independent of each other, have coördinate jurisdiction. According to Article 58 of the Imperial Constitution, the whole of the maritime population of the empire, including the technical *personnel* and the artisans, are absolved from land duty, but are liable to service in the imperial navy. The organization of the marine comprises the Naval Cabinet, the General Naval Inspection Department, the Imperial Naval Administration, and the *personnel* of the navy.

The commander-in-chief of the navy is His Majesty, the Emperor and King, William II. Directly under his command is the Naval Cabinet at Berlin.

In the cabinet such matters are treated of as are not dealt with in the reports of the Admiralty's Staff, or in those of the Secretary of the Imperial Naval Administration. A rear-admiral acts as chief of the Cabinet, assisted by two captains. According to a Cabinet order of March 14th, 1899, the former chief command of the navy is abolished and replaced by the General Naval Inspection Department.

The Admiralty's Staff Department, which formerly formed a part of the chief command, becomes an independent organization, and is called the Admiralty's Staff of the Navy. This new organization is directed by an admiral as chief, and is located at Berlin. The chief of the Admiralty's Staff is placed directly under the Emperor. The authority exercised by the former admiral in command, in regard to matters which pertain to discipline and furlough, fall to his supervision. The Staff of the Admiralty not only transacts all routine business of the Admiralty, but has to do also with affairs concerning the ships abroad, both in a naval and political aspect. Directly placed under the authority of the Emperor are likewise the chiefs of the naval stations, the inspector of the navy's educational institutes, the chief of the first squadron, and the chief of the cruiser squadron. The inspector-general of the navy is also appointed by the Emperor.

The General Naval Inspection Department consists of an inspector-general, with the rank of an admiral, and the Admiralty's Staff at Berlin. This Staff is classified into a chief (rear-admiral), an adjutant (captain of corvette), and a departmental directory, composed of one captain, four captains of corvette, five captain-lieutenants, and one lieutenant. The commands of the naval stations covering the German waters (of which there are two, namely, the Baltic naval station at Kiel, and the North Sea naval station at Wilhelmshaven), are named the home stations. The foreign waters are divided into the Mediterranean station, the East-African and West-African stations, the East-Asiatic, the American, and the Australian stations. These are called the foreign stations. The commands of the ships abroad are independent and only subject to the Emperor's authority in all naval and political matters. The Emperor's orders are transmitted to these ship commands by the chief of the Admiralty's Staff.

The command of the Baltic naval station, located at Kiel, is composed of a chief of the station (admiral), of the chief of the staff (captain), and the admiral's staff. The latter is classified into two adjutants (a captain of corvette and a lieutenant), an assistant (captain of corvette), and a captain of the port. The chief of the station has one captain, two captains of frigate, and two captains of corvette at his disposal.

According to a cabinet order of May 23rd, 1899, there are placed under the command of the Baltic station the

The Brandenburg Squadron at Sea.

After Willy Stöwer

first marine artillery division at Friedrichsort, the first torpedo division at Kiel, and the first battalion of marines at Kiel. Subject to the above command are also the first marine inspection department at Kiel, embracing the first seamen division at Kiel (first and second detachments), and the first dock-yard division at Kiel.

The command of the North Sea naval station at Wilhelmshaven is composed of a chief of the station (vice-admiral), of a chief of the staff (captain), and of the admiral's staff. The latter comprises two adjutants (a captain-lieutenant and a lieutenant), a captain of corvette as assistant, and a captain of the port. The chief of the station has three captains of corvette under his control.

Under the command of the North Sea naval station are placed the second, third, and fourth marine artillery divisions, the second torpedo division, and the second battalion of marines at Wilhelmshaven. Subject to the same command is the second marine inspection, comprising the second seamen division and the second dock-yard division, both located at Wilhelmshaven. This innovation was evidently inaugurated in order to simplify the routine business, especially to secure expedition in the event of mobilization. The inspection departments, or the inspectors of the torpedo service, of the marine infantry, and the marine artillery, retain their functions as regards the training of their respective troops and the technical *personnel* of the navy. In all other matters, especially those pertaining to mobilization and to the reserve, the intermediate functions of the inspection departments cease to operate. The various bodies and organizations of the navy communicate directly with the commands of the Baltic and North Sea naval stations. They thus may be compared to the chief commands of the army, which, while themselves independent, are subject only to the authority of the Emperor.

The department of the torpedo service inspection, located at Kiel, stands likewise under the command of the Baltic naval station. This department has to provide for the proper training of the different crews in the use of the torpedo and the torpedo boats, and has to look to the readiness and perfection of the equipping material. At the head of the department is a vice-admiral in the capacity of an inspector. Included in this bureau are the command of the torpedo tests at Kiel, supervised by a captain, and the torpedo laboratory at Friedrichsort, which is superintended by a captain of corvette.

The department of the marine infantry inspection, with staff headquarters at Kiel, is also subject to the Baltic naval station. At the head of the department stands an inspector, who ranks with a regimental commander of the army. His functions include the supervision of the entire service of the sea battalions, of which the first is stationed at Kiel, and the second at Wilhelmshaven.

The department of the marine artillery inspection has its seat at Wilhelmshaven. It is placed under the command of the North Sea naval station. At the head of

the bureau is a rear-admiral in the capacity of an inspector. This department also embraces the supervision of the naval-telegraph school at Lehe and the commission of naval tests at Kiel.

The department of the naval-depot inspection is located at Wilhelmshaven. Its inspector has the rank of a captain. The bureau has to supervise the entire artillery, mine, and torpedo material for the coast-defence. The inspection is divided into four ordnance and mine depots, of which the first is located at Friedrichsort, the second at Wilhelmshaven, the third at Geestemünde, and the fourth at Cuxhaven.

The department intrusted with the inspection of the educational institutes of the navy has its seat at Kiel. This bureau has for its chief a vice-admiral. The Naval Academy and the Naval School, both at Kiel, provide for the scientific training of the naval officers and cadets. The Naval Academy has the following *personnel* of officials: One director, who ranks as vice-admiral; two members as board of directors, who rank as captain and captain-lieutenant; a chief of the bureau, and a librarian, who is a captain of corvette. The staff of teachers is composed of four captains. The Naval School at Kiel is superintended by a director, with the rank of a captain, while instruction is given by six officers, namely, one captain, two captains of corvette, one captain-lieutenant, and a captain of the first marine battalion. For the training of the deck officers and noncommissioned officers the deck-officers' school at Kiel is designed. A captain officiates as director, with a captain of corvette as teacher. The sailor-boy division at Friedsichsort is superintended by a captain. Subject to the inspection of the educational institutes are the government of Kiau-Chou and the third marine battalion located at Tsintau.

The German littoral is divided into six inspectorates, each supervised by a captain. The first inspectorate, comprising East- and West-Prussia, is located at Neufahrwasser. The second, embracing Pomerania and Mecklenburg, has its seat at Stettin. The third, taking in the coast of Schleswig-Holstein, is situated at Husum. The district of the Elbe and Weser stands under the inspectorate of Bremerhaven, while the sixth inspectorate, consisting of the district of the Jahde, the East-Frisian coast, and Heligoland, is located at Wilhelmshaven. The technical institutes of the navy are the navy-yards at Kiel, Wilhelmshaven, and Dantzic, the commission of ship tests at Kiel, and the naval observatory at Hamburg.

Each navy-yard is directed by a captain, in the capacity of director-in-chief, assisted by a captain of corvette. The duty of the navy-yard is to lay up in reserve and repair all the ships which are out of commission, to hold ready, and to equip and provision the ships that are to be put in commission, and to construct new vessels. The eight departments or bureaus, which are supervised either by civil officials or naval officers, are the provision, artillery, torpedo, navigation, shipbuilding, engine construction, harbor construction departments, and the bureau of administration.

H. M. First-Class Battleships "Kaiser Wilhelm II." and "Kaiser Friedrich III."

Members of the commission for ship tests are a presiding rear-admiral, one captain of frigate, and one captain of corvette. The naval observatory at Hamburg is directed by a secret counselor of the Admiralty. The bureaus intrusted with the clothing of the navy are under the supervision of the naval stations of the North Sea and the Baltic.

The entire administration of the navy is concentrated in the Imperial Naval Administration at Berlin. By a cabinet order of April 19th, 1899, the Naval Administration or the naval war ministry is organized analogous to the war ministry of the land army. The Administration directs the entire organization and development of the navy. It supervises the construction and equipment of the war ships, and keeps account of all expenditures made in behalf of the navy, the harbors, navy-yards, and the coast-defences in the rivers Jahde, Weser, and Elbe, and at Kiel.

The Imperial Naval Administration is directed by the naval secretary of state, who ranks with a rear-admiral. The secretary of state is responsible to the imperial chancellor in matters pertaining to the Administration, while in other affairs he is subordinate to the Emperor. The business of the Administration is conducted by a number of departments and bureaus. These consist of a central department, with a military section; a section pertaining to pension and legal affairs; and a section treating of the government of Kiau-Chou. The technical department consists of the old marine department and the bureau of construction. Another department is that of administration proper. The fifth is the ordnance bureau; the sixth treats of the *personnel* of the navy; the seventh is the nautical department; the eighth is the medical department; the ninth the justiciary department; and the tenth is the intelligence bureau.

The *personnel* of the German navy is liable to service both on land and at sea, and consists of two distinct branches,—those engaged in active service and the navy officials. The former are classified into officers and men.

The officers are divided into the following ranks: The corps of naval officers; the officers of the marine infantry; the engineers; the torpedo engineers; the surgeons; the ordnance, pyrotechnic, and torpedo officers. The corps of naval officers is classified according to the following ranks: Flag officers, staff officers, and subaltern officers. The first rank comprises six admirals, ranking with a general of the army; four vice-admirals, ranking with a lieutenant-general; and fifteen rear-admirals, having the rank of major-general. The second class, staff officers, is composed of forty-six captains, ranking with a colonel;

fifteen captains of frigate, ranking with a lieutenant-colonel, and seventy-one captains of corvette, who rank with a major. The subaltern officers are divided into captain-lieutenants, ranking with a captain of the army; lieutenants and sub-lieutenants, who rank with the first and second lieutenant of the army. The corps of naval officers is replenished by the naval cadets, who rank with the ensigns, wearing the silver knot, and by the junior cadets, who rank as pupils with the privates. The rank of the officers of the marine infantry is identical with that of the land army. The engineer corps is composed of the staff engineers, who rank with the captains of corvette; of the chief engineers, with the rank of a captain-lieutenant; of engineers and sub-engineers, who rank with the lieutenants and sub-lieutenants. The torpedo engineers corps is classed into torpedo chief engineers, torpedo engineers, and torpedo sub-engineers.

The ranks of the naval surgeons are as follows: The surgeon-general of the first class ranks with the captain or rear-admiral; the surgeon-general of the second class ranks with the captain of frigate. The chief surgeon of the first class has the rank of a captain of corvette; while that of the second class ranks with a captain-lieutenant. The assistant surgeon of the first class ranks with the lieutenant; that of the second class, with the sub-lieutenant, while the sub-surgeon classes with a noncommissioned officer wearing the silver knot.

The ordnance and pyrotechnic officers are divided into captains, lieutenants, and sub-lieutenants, while the torpedo officers are classified into captain-lieutenants, lieutenants, and sub-lieutenants. The chief paymaster of the navy ranks with the captain-lieutenant, the paymaster with the lieutenant, and the sub-paymaster with the sub-lieutenant.

The men are divided into noncommissioned officers and privates. The noncommissioned officers wearing the silver knot comprise the deck officers and noncommissioned officers of seamen, paymaster aspirants, sergeant-majors, cadets, signal masters, chief gunners, sub-surgeons, and one-year volunteer surgeons.

The noncommissioned officers of seamen comprise the boatswains, carpenters, helmsmen, stokers, masters, machinists, torpedo-machinists, gunners and torpedo-gunners, artificers, and mechanics. The deck officers are composed of the same classes, but of a higher rank.

The noncommissioned officers without the silver knot are the master's mates and mates, ranking with the sergeant and corporal. The men are classed as upper and ordinary seamen, divided into the classes of higher and lower seamen.

H. M. Fourth-Class Battleship "Aegir," and H. M. Third-Class Protected Cruiser "Gefion."

THE German marine, which has been described in the previous chapter, is classified into a land division and a division for service at sea. To the former belong:

1. The naval seamen divisions. The first of these has its garrison at Kiel, the second at Wilhelmshaven. Each division comprises two detachments, each of three companies. The normal strength of the two divisions is 1,433 deck and noncommissioned officers and 7,112 men. This contingent furnishes the crews for all ships in service.

2. The dock-yard divisions, of which the first is established at Kiel and the second at Wilhelmshaven. These supply the necessary complement of machinists, stokers, craftsmen, hospital attendants, clerks, and paymasters. Each division comprises five companies, which are numbered from one to five.

3. The marine-artillery divisions, which are employed in the defence of the seacoast and the harbors. There are four divisions of marine-artillery garrisoned at Friedrichsort, Wilhelmshaven, Lehe, and Cuxhaven. They number 2,013 men.

4. The ship-boy division. This division furnishes the necessary complement of noncommissioned officers, mates, and seamen of the imperial navy. The strength is 600, and the period of training lasts two years.

5. The torpedo-boat divisions, of which there are two—one at Kiel, the other at Wilhelmshaven. Each division is composed of three companies. They are classified as seamen and technical experts, and number 2,336 men.

6. The artillery, torpedo, and mine depot. This organization has to prepare and keep in seaworthy shape all the material necessary for naval and submarine warfare.

7. The marine infantry. This part of the navy consists of three sea-battalions, each of four companies. The first battalion is garrisoned at Kiel, the second at Wilhelmshaven, and the third at Tsintau (Kiau-Chou). The duty of the marine infantry is to defend the imperial harbors and to replenish the detachments of marines on battleships. This corps has been employed several times in the colonial service.

In 1894 one company was sent to the Kameruns, but did not see actual service. One company was stationed at Kiau-Chou, the newly-acquired German territory in China, and was raised to the strength of one sea-battalion—the third, as previously mentioned. The normal strength of the marine infantry is 168 noncommissioned officers and 1,206 men. The total strength of the men belonging to the navy is 19,680, of which 13,295 compose the crews, and the remainder are non-commissioned officers.

The uniform of the navy differs essentially from that of the land army. The tunic, overcoat, and helmet of the land army are represented by the jacket, shirt, over-coat, and cap of the naval troops. The material of the clothing is of a dark-blue color, the cut is uniform throughout all divisions, with the exception of the marine infantry. The ribbon around the cap and the buttons are the only marks of distinction. The seamen and dock-yard divisions, the seamen artillery, the torpedo and ship-boy divisions wear a cap with a ribbon and a black, red, and white cockade, a white or blue shirt, white or blue trousers, neckcloth, a jacket of dark-blue cloth with Brandenburg facings, gloves, and a dark-blue overcoat with a large lay-down collar. The uniform of the marine infantry consists of a tunic of dark-blue cloth cut similar to those of the land army, a jacket like the sea-battalions, a gray overcoat resembling that of the cavalry, and a shako with a bronze anchor, the imperial crown and eagle, and the German colors affixed. They are also equipped with a knapsack, cooking utensils, belt and sabretasche of black leather, and boots such as the land troops wear.

The German fleet is represented by the ships in service. The commander of a ship when in home waters, or when not forming a part of an active division, is subject to the station command; if a ship, however, is on service abroad in foreign waters, its officers become subject to the admiralty staff. A division consists of from three to five ships, which sail under an admiral in the capacity of chief of division. Two

divisions form a squadron, under an admiral as chief of the squadron, and several such squadrons form a fleet.

The fleet is classified according to the employment of the ships in time of war. At an early day Germany will have at her disposal the following vessels:

FIRST TYPE

7 first-class battleships.
3 second-class battleships.
7 third-class battleships.
10 fourth-class battleships.

SECOND TYPE

13 armored gunboats.

THIRD TYPE

1 armored cruiser.

FOURTH TYPE

10 second-class protected cruisers.
7 third-class protected cruisers.
9 fourth-class protected cruisers.

FIFTH TYPE

4 gunboats.

SIXTH TYPE

11 despatch-boats.

SEVENTH TYPE

14 training-ships.

EIGHTH TYPE

11 torpedo-division boats.
120 torpedo boats.

NINTH TYPE

10 ships for special use.
9 scout-boats.
3 station yachts.
12 dock-steamers.
5 pilot boats.
3 depot and fortification steamers.
3 sailing yachts.

TENTH TYPE

10 auxiliary cruisers of the Hamburg-American line and the North-German Lloyd of Bremen.

The navy-yards employed in the construction of the navy are the Imperial yards at Kiel, Wilhelmshaven, and Dantzic; the private yards ''Vulcan'' near Stettin, ''Germania'' at Kiel, and ''Waser'' at Bremen; also the private dock-yards of ''Schichau'' at Elbing and Dantzic.

All the German war vessels, with the exception of the two battleships, Kaiser and Deutschland, were built from German material and equipped with German guns. Since 1880 the material used in the construction is steel; older vessels show iron construction, while the use of wood has ceased entirely. All devices in ship-building are for the purpose of protecting the vessel against injury below the water line. The water-tight bulkheads, which divide the ship lengthwise into a number of independent water-tight compartments, aid in neutralizing the injury which the ship might receive when rammed. The use of longitudinal as well as transverse bulkheads above the armored deck adds much to the security of the ship when in danger of sinking, or in case of injury by shots. The outer row of cells is filled with cork, the second row remains empty and forms the cofferdam; while the rest of the space is occupied by the coal, provisions, and other ship material. There is also a system of drainage established for the purpose of removing leak-water, or of filling some compartments with ballast-water. The pipes connected with this system are conducted through the coats of the ship and are regulated by stop-cocks and stop-valves.

In order to protect the vital parts of the hull against shot and shell, the battleships are provided with armor. The armoring of war vessels has kept pace with the development of the iron industry as regards material, strength, and dimensions. Rolled iron was first used for the construction of armor plate. Later on experiments were made with toughened steel, a process which led to the introduction of plates having steel on the outer side and iron on the inside. At present armor plates of nickel-steel are preferred, while the armored ships of the latest construction are fitted with plates of Harveyized steel. In the modern battleship only the heavy guns are placed in strong steel turrets. The hull carries a continuous armor-belt from stem to stern and a strong armored deck, which protects the machinery, the ammunition rooms, and the magazine hatchways. The new second-class cruisers also have an armored deck, while the hatchways leading to the magazines below are sheathed with heavy armor. The despatch-boats of a later type have a similar protection, consisting of a strong steel deck. The smaller cruisers and the older despatch-boats are more lightly armored, but have water-tight bulkheads and a cell system; the engines are protected by the coal-bunkers and a proper sluice system.

The first-class battleships are the Kurfürst Friedrich Wilhelm, Brandenburg, Weissenburg, and Wörth, each of 10,033 tons displacement; Kaiser Friedrich III. and Kaiser Wilhelm II., of 11,081 tons; and Kaiser Wilhelm der Grosse, of 12,000 tons. The two latter are in course of construction.

The four ships of the Brandenburg type, and called the "Brandenburg squadron," consist of the Brandenburg, Weissenburg, Kurfürst Friedrich Wilhelm, and Wörth (flagship). They represent the chief fighting strength of the German navy. The following is the details of their construction: Displacement 10,033 tons; dimensions, length 380 feet, beam 64 feet, and 24 feet 7'

Practice with Captive Balloon on Board of Torpedo Boats.

inches draught; speed 17 knots. The ships carry a continuous nickel-steel armor-belt of 15.9 in. thickness amidships, sloping to 11¾ in. at the ends. The guns are placed in barbette-turrets, protected by overhead shields, which revolve with the guns. For protection against injuries by the ram, torpedoes, and mines, the ships have a double bottom reaching beyond the continuous armor-belt. On top of the latter lies a corkdam from stem to stern. The ship is divided in halves by a longitudinal water-tight bulkhead, while eleven diagonal bulkheads separate the double bottom into twenty-four water-tight compartments. On top of the armor-belt is the main deck, armored with 2.5 in. nickel-steel. Between the main deck and the gun-deck are two steel barbette-turrets of 11.9 in. armor; the third barbette-turret is mounted on a high forecastle deck and its guns are carried eight or ten feet higher than those in the central and aft barbettes. Close to the forward barbette is the armored conning tower. The whole ship's armor weighs about 3,200 tons. The main battery, consisting of six 11 in. guns, is placed in the three barbette-turrets; the two guns of the middle barbette are 35 calibre (29.5 feet) long, while the other four are 40 calibre (32 feet) long. The fire of all six guns can be brought to bear at an angle of 90 degrees. One broadside of the six guns delivers 3,373 pounds of steel. The secondary battery of the ship, placed below the two smoke-stacks, consists of six 4.1 in. rifles, which fire 37-pound shells provided with fuses at an angle of about 100 degrees. As each gun can be fired ten times in a minute, the secondary battery throws, in three minutes, from one side as many pounds of steel as one round of the six heavy guns. Near the forward barbette-turret are placed four 3.5 in. quick-firers, and aft of the military mast four after-deck guns of the same calibre. Each of these can be fired fifteen times in a minute; that is, in three minutes it fires 2,777 pounds of steel. The *Brandenburg*, therefore, delivers from one broadside 9,528 pounds of metal. Besides the above guns there are in the tops of each military mast four 0.28 in. machine-guns, and on the hurricane deck two boat-guns, which may also be used in an emergency. For the discharge of the 17.7 in. torpedoes six tubes are provided, namely, three on each side, lying above the armor-belt. The ship is also supplied with nets capable of warding off attacks by torpedoes. The ships of the Brandenburg squadron have twin-screw engines which are covered by the armored deck and separated by the water-tight bulkhead. The twelve boilers furnish with a natural draft about 9,000 horse-power, or with artificial draft 10,288 horse-power. The maximum speed is seventeen knots an hour. The normal coal supply is 800 tons.

The rudder of the *Brandenburg* is suspended and connects direct with the steering gear, which is manipulated by steam. Five steering gears direct the steering

of the ship from as many different points. The most important apparatus is placed in the conning tower, which is armored with 11.8 in. steel plates. The ship carries twelve boats, two of which are propelled by steam. One of these is fifty feet long, and has for armament a torpedo tube and a revolving gun. The rigging of the *Brandenburg* shows two steel military masts, at the lower platform of which electric searchlights are attached. Each ship of the squadron has a complement of 556 men. The fighting quality of the vessels equals that of the English ship *Barfleur* and the *Oregon* of the United States navy.

The most powerful battleship of the German navy is the *Kaiser Friedrich III*. This ship was launched from the navy-yard of Wilhelmshaven on July 1st, 1896. The vessel is 377 feet long, 65.6 feet wide, draws 25.9 feet, and displaces 11,081 tons. The armor consists of the best tempered steel which has thirty per cent. more resistance than common nickel-steel. The plates, furnished by the rolling mills of the Dillingen and the Krupp establishments at Essen, surpass all armor-plates made abroad. The *Kaiser Friedrich III*. has a continuous armor-belt, 6.5 in. wide and from 5.9 in. to 11.8 in. thick, covering four-fifths of the ship's length. The short aft of the ship is protected by an arched 2.8 in. armored deck. A 2.5 in. armored deck rests on the armor belt and protects the entire hull. The guns are placed partly in revolving steel turrets, partly in separate armored casemates. The main battery is protected by a 9.8 in. armor, and the secondary battery by a 5.9 in. armor. The heavy artillery consists of four 9.4 in. guns, which are 40 calibre (30.4 ft.) long. These guns are sufficient to pierce armor plates of any thickness used on battleships. A shell fired at a right angle will penetrate iron plates of 28 in. thickness and 9.4 in. to 10.2 in. steel plates. The powerful English battleships of 15,000 tons displacement carry an armor of only 10.2 inches. The secondary battery is strengthened considerably, as the ship mounts eighteen 5.9 in. rapid-firing guns of 40 calibre length, twelve 3.5 in. guns of 40 calibre length, twelve 1.4 in. and twelve 0.28 in. machine-guns. The ship can deliver from one broadside 148 shots per minute, representing 8,867 pounds of steel.

The artillery of the ship, which may be called a citadel-turret ship, is disposed on six decks. On the gun-deck are placed two 9.4 in. guns in a revolving turret giving a firing range of 270 degrees. In front of the aft turret the gun-deck is covered with high superstructures. In the corners of the four lower casemates are four 5.9 in. rapid-firing guns, the fire of which is limited to a range of 140 degrees. On the next deck, which is seven feet higher, are stationed fourteen 5.9 in. guns, six of which are in revolving turrets giving a fire range of 180 degrees. The other eight are disposed in casemates separated by armored partitions. Each of the guns

H. M. Dispatch Boat "Wacht" Turning Searchlight on H. M. Second-Class Protected Cruiser "Kaiserin Augusta."

can bring its fire to bear on objects which are at an angle of 130 degrees to the ship's course. On the third deck, in front of the forecastle, stands the second powerful revolving steel turret, in which are the other two 9.4 in. guns. Back of the steel turret is the forward conning tower, protected by 9.8 in. steel plates. Aft of the conning tower a long open deck rises, in the corners of which ten 3.5 rapid-firing guns are placed, protected by shields; there are also two 1.4 in. machine-guns without shields. On the fourth deck, the forward lower hurricane deck, we find four 1.4 in. machine-guns, and two rifled cannon of the same calibre on the aft hurricane deck, back of the aft conning tower. The fifth deck, the forward higher hurricane deck, carries two 3.5 in. rapid-firing guns. On the sixth, the tops of the military masts, 75 feet above the water-line, four 1.4 in. machine guns are posted. The twelve 0.28 in. machine guns are distributed over the ship at suitable places. The 9.4 in. guns fire either the short steel shells, weighing 352 pounds, or the long shells with a fuse attached, of 473 pounds. The charge is 209 pounds of brown gunpowder. The ship has six tubes for the discharge of the 17.7 in. torpedoes. The tubes are all submerged, except the one placed at the afterdeck, and discharge the torpedo below the water-line. The ship has triple-expansion engines; the three screws give 13,000 horse-power and a speed of 18 knots. The coal supply is 650 tons, and the complement is 655 men. The vessel is also equipped with six searchlights, and carries two military masts.

To the second-class battleships belong the *König Wilhelm* of 9,757 tons displacement, and the *Kaiser* and *Deutschland*, each of 7,676 tons displacement. The *König Wilhelm* was launched in the year 1868. She is a so-called battery-ship, the construction of which is obsolete on account of the limited concentration of the fire. At the time the ship was remodeled its circuitous armor belt was fitted with compound plates of 11.9 in. thickness. On top of the armor-belt are the long battery and the stands for the heavy guns of the gun-deck, armored with 5.9 in. plates. In 1895 the ship received a modern armored deck. The *König Wilhelm* is 354 feet long, 59 feet wide, with a draught of 25 feet, a displacement of 9,757 tons, and a speed of 14.5 knots. The coal supply is 800 tons. The armament consists of twenty 9.4 in. guns, one 5.9 in. gun, eighteen 3.5 in. rapid-firing rifles, and eight machine guns. The two forward military masts have each two tops; the shorter aft mast, as well as the forward masts, carries a platform with searchlights attached. The ship has an armored conning tower and eleven spars for manipulating the torpedo nets. The complement is 732 men.

The *Kaiser* and *Deutschland* were both launched at Samuda in 1874. They are 278 feet long, 62 feet wide, with a draught of 25.2 feet, and a displacement of 7,676 tons. Both ships have an armor-belt of 9.8 in.

thickness and a covered casemate (a shortened battery with blunt corners) which is protected by 8.8 in. armor. In the casemate are posted eight 10.2 in. guns, on the gun-deck eight 5.9 in. and twelve 1.9 in. rapid-firing guns, which are protected by revolving shields. Both vessels have military masts, in the tops of which machine guns are placed. They are also provided with search-lights, five torpedo tubes, and torpedo nets. The engines give 8,000 horse-power and a speed of 14 knots. The complement is 644 men.

To the third-class battleships belong the *Preussen* and *Friedrich der Grosse*, each of 6,770 tons displacement; the *Sachsen, Bayern, Württemberg,* and *Baden*, each of 7,400 tons; and the *Oldenburg* of 5,200 tons. The *Preussen* and *Friedrich der Grosse* are constructed of iron, with a length of 272 feet, a beam of 52 feet, and a draught of 24 feet. A 9.2 in. iron armor-belt from stem to stern protects the water-line. The two turrets which stand amidships on the gun-deck have a 10.2 in. armor; the conning tower is located on the great hurricane deck.

There are placed in the two turrets four 10.2 in. guns 22 calibre long, on the gun-deck one 6.7 in. afterdeck-gun and one 6.7 in. bow-gun 25 calibre long, which fire a steel shell of 117 pounds weight. Both ships mount ten 3.5 in. quick-firing guns of 30 calibre. The military mast has a steel top, armed with two 1.4 in. revolving guns. For the discharge of torpedoes four tubes are provided. The engines give the ships a speed of from 13 to 14 knots. In fighting qualities the Sachsen squadron ranks next to the Brandenburg squadron in the German navy. The four ships belonging to this squadron were built at German navy-yards, either imperial or private, namely, the *Sachsen* in 1877, the *Bayern* and *Württemberg* in 1878, and the *Baden* in 1880. They were originally called scouting corvettes, but have to be classified as citadel ships, inasmuch as more than one-half of the forward and after parts of the ship lacks the vertical armor. The ships have two tiers of plates abreast; on the outside a plate of 10 in. of rolled iron; back of this an equally thick tier of teak-wood, followed by a plate of 5.9 in. rolled iron and a 7.9 in. tier of wood, ending in a double iron skin. The vessels of the Sachsen squadron are of 7,400 tons displacement. They are 298 feet in length, 57 feet in width, and of 19.3 feet draught. Both the forward and after parts of the ship are protected by a corkdam and a cofferdam, which lie on the arched armored deck and join the lower edge of the vertical armor. In case of injury to the outer skin, the cork is expected to swell by the entering water, thus closing the aperture made by the shot. The hull is divided into one hundred water-tight compartments in order to prevent the ship sinking when injured by a torpedo or a ram. The ships of the Sachsen squadron are called low-board vessels, as their gun-deck rises only seven feet above the load water-line. The muzzles of the four 10.2 in. guns placed in the large central battery are about 17 feet above the load water-line; the two 10.2 in. guns in the forward barbette are mounted 3.3 feet higher. The barrel of the latter is only 22 calibre (18.7 feet) long; it weighs 17 tons and fires a steel shell of 412 pounds weight and a shell with a fuse attached of 356 pounds. The two bow-guns, which are placed in the forward barbette, have a range of fire of about 270 degrees. The guns of the main battery stand in the four corners of the large barbette and have a range of over 125 degrees. They are covered by a protective deck, on which are placed the quick-firing guns, and which serves at the same time as the hurricane deck. The heavy artillery delivers from one broadside 1,648 pounds of steel. The secondary battery numbers only six 3.5 in. rapid-firing guns of 30 calibre (8.4 feet) length, which are posted on the protective deck on top of the casemate. In each military mast two five-barreled 1.4 in. Hotchkiss revolving guns are placed. Five torpedo tubes are fitted into the hull, of which two discharge torpedoes amidships and one aft. The engines are twin screws and are separated by a longitudinal bulkhead. The boilers have been replaced by new ones and the speed is in consequence raised from 13 to 16 knots. The coal supply is 500 tons. One searchlight is attached at the forward smokestack, while the other is placed on the protective deck. All the vessels are provided with torpedo nets. The complement of each vessel consists of 377 men.

The fourth-class German ships, comprising the *Siegfried, Beowulf, Frithjof, Hildebrand, Heimdal, Hagen,* and *Odin,* each of 3,495 tons displacement, and the *Aegir* of 3,530 tons, serve the purpose of preventing the enemy from entering the mouths of the German rivers and from approaching the seacoast. The first four are assigned to the naval station on the German Ocean, while the other four belong to the Baltic naval station. The ships are 239 feet long, of 49 feet beam, and draw 17.7 feet of water. The arrangement of the water-tight compartments is similar to that of the *Brandenburg.* A corkdam and a cofferdam add to the security of the ship in event of injury near the water-line. The principal protection of the ship consists of a complete nickel-steel armor-belt, 8.2 feet wide, amidships 9.4 in. thick, and sloping to 7 in. at both ends of the vessel. On top of the armor-belt lies an arched armored deck, from 1.1 in. to 1.4 in. in thickness, protecting the powder and ammunition rooms. The four covered barbettes and the conning tower are provided with a 7.9 in. armor. The twin-screw engines give 4,800 horse-power and a speed of 16 knots. The three 9.4 in. guns (35 calibre long), which fire 32 in. long steel shells of 474 pounds, and a number of 3.5 in. quick-firing guns are disposed

either in revolving turrets or in superimposed structures.

The second type of war vessels are the armored gun-boats. The eleven boats of the *Wespe* class, which were built at the Weser yard of Bremen, are the *Wespe, Viper,* and *Biene,* launched in 1876, the *Scorpion* and *Mücke* in 1877, the *Basilisk* and *Chamäleon* in 1878, the *Crocodile* in 1879, the *Natter* and *Salamander* in 1880, and the *Hummel* in 1881. All these boats have a displacement of 1,109 tons, a length of 144 feet, a beam of 36 feet, and a draught of 10 feet. Each boat mounts one short 12 in. gun, the heaviest German naval gun, which fires a shell with a fuse attached of 725 pounds.

A circuitous armor-belt, of 8 in. in thickness, protects the hull, reaching from 2.3 feet below the water-line up to the gun-deck. On the latter, in front of the smokestack, stands the barbette in the form of a horse-shoe, provided with 8 in. armor, which rests on a strong layer of teak-wood. On the armor-belt lies an arched 1.9 in. armored deck. The armor plates and the hull are made of rolled iron. The water-tight bulkheads and compartments are arranged similar to those of the Sachsen type. The twin-screw engines, separated by a water-tight longitudinal bulkhead, furnish a 700 horse-power and yield a speed of about $9\frac{1}{2}$ knots. As protection against torpedo boats, each ship carries two 3.5 in. rapid-firing and two revolving guns. Back of the barbette stands the armored conning tower. Each boat is provided with one torpedo tube, placed near the bow, and a spur for close encounter. On account of their light draught these boats are especially fitted for the defence of the narrows between the islands of the German Ocean and the Baltic Sea. The armored gunboats received a further addition of two more vessels, in 1883 the *Brummer* and in 1884 the *Bremse.*

The third type of war vessels is represented by the armored cruisers, the forerunners of which were the frigates and corvettes. The powerful frigates, mounting about fifty guns, used to fight in the ranks of the ships of the line; the light frigates, however, known as cruisers, were represented by ships, which, on account of their good sailing and cruising qualities, were chiefly employed for scouting and reporting purposes, though in part also for destroying the commerce of the enemy. The oldest corvettes were very small vessels, which mounted less than twenty guns, and were employed for coast-defence. The first sailing frigate of the Prussian navy, the *Gefion,* which was captured from the Danes at the encounter of Eckernförde, differed very little in construction from the daring privateer-cruisers of the Great Elector.

The introduction of steam-power effected at first hardly any changes in the form and construction of the frigates. From 1868 to 1878 seven cruisers, formerly called covered corvettes, were launched. Of these cruisers, which were constructed entirely of wood, the *Elisabeth* was the finest. She had a displacement of

2,508 tons, a length of 216 feet, by 41 feet, and a draught of 18 feet. The armament consisted of twenty-six 5.9 in. guns of 22 calibre length. Additional frigates of the cruiser type were the *Leipzig*, the *Prince Adelbert*, and the vessels of the *Stosch* type, namely the *Bismarck*, *Moltke*, *Stosch*, *Blücher*, *Stein*, and *Gneisenau*, the latter, however, constructed of iron. All these ships lacked the necessary speed, also the practical disposition of the artillery, and especially any kind of armor. The German navy had only one armored cruiser, the old armored frigate *Hansa*, which was launched at the Dantzic yard in the year 1872. She had a displacement of 3,610 tons, a length of 223 feet, a beam of 45 feet, and a draught of 19 feet. The engines, of 2,000 horse-power, gave a speed of 12 knots. The armor-belt was 6.2 in., and the armored casemate 5 in. in thickness; the latter covered one-fourth of the ship's length. The introduction of rapid-firing guns of light and medium calibre made it urgent to abandon the old type of unprotected cruiser-frigates and to adopt the new type of armored and protected cruisers. In a modern navy only armored vessels are considered as first-class cruisers. They must be protected by an armored deck and by side armor, while the main battery guns are expected to be of at least 8.2 in. calibre. These vessels serve a double purpose, namely, alike in times of peace and of war to protect the interests of the native country in foreign waters, and when hostilities break out to engage the enemy's cruisers.

The only armored cruiser, which the German navy possesses, carries the proud name of *Fürst Bismarck*. This formidable vessel has a displacement of 10,650 tons, a length of 393 feet, a beam of 65 feet, and a draught of 25.7 feet. The engines, which are of 13,500 horse-power, give a speed of 19 knots. The coal supply is 1,000 tons. The *Bismarck* has a complete armor, 8 feet in width, and reaching on the water-line from stem to stern. The revolving turrets, the casemates, and the hatchways and scuttles are provided with nickel-steel plates from 7.9 in. to 11.9 in. in thickness. The armament consists of four 9.4 in. guns of 40 calibre length, disposed in the armored turrets, with a range of fire of 270 degrees. The secondary battery, comprising twelve 5.9 in. quick-firing rifled cannon 40 calibre long, is placed partly in the armored revolving turrets and partly in single casemates. The light artillery consists of ten 3.5 in. quick-loading guns 30 calibre long, ten 1.4 in. and eight 0.28 in. machine guns. The ship carries formidable additional weapons in the form of six torpedo-launching tubes for the firing of large torpedoes charged with 198 pounds of gun cotton. Five of the tubes are submerged; only the tube on the afterdeck is above the water-line so as to be out of the way of the rudder and the screws. On the top of the two military masts four searchlights are attached, while two more lights are stationed on the sides of the ship. The ship's complement is 565 men.

Cruisers which mount guns of at least 5.9 in. calibre and are provided with a protective deck, are called modern protected cruisers, and form the fourth type of the German war ships. They are classified either according to their tonnage or the calibre of their main guns. First-class protected cruisers, like the *Columbia* and *Minneapolis* of the United States navy, with a displacement of 7,475 tons, are not to be found in the German navy.

Of the second class of protected cruisers are the *Kaiserin Augusta* of 6,052 tons; *Irene* and *Princess Wilhelm*, each of 4,400 tons; *Hertha* and *Freya*, each of 5,628 tons; and the *Victoria Luise*, *Hansa*, *Vineta*, and two more boats, each of 5,628 tons; the latter five being in course of construction. These fast, but insufficiently protected, cruisers are necessary not only for service in foreign waters, but also for reconnoitring and reporting in naval warfare. In this respect these vessels fulfill the mission of the old cruising-corvettes, whose successors they are. Of protected cruisers, which answer every modern requirement, the German navy has five, as mentioned previously. The *Princess Wilhelm* was launched in 1887 at the Germania navy-yard of Kiel, and the *Irene* in 1888 at the navy-yard Vulcan of Stettin. Each ship has a displacement of 4,400 tons, a length of 308 feet, a beam of 45 feet, and a draught of 22 feet. The hull, which is constructed entirely of steel, carries an outer skin consisting of a double tier of wood lined with plates of yellow metal. The longitudinal and transverse bulkheads, which divide the ship into a number of water-tight compartments, are arranged similar to those in the modern battleships. Each vessel is equipped with a 3 in. steel armored deck which is capable of being lowered, forward and aft, to about six feet below the water-line. On the armored deck rests a cofferdam about eight feet wide. The engines are of 8,000 horse-power and give the ship a speed of over 18 knots. The coal supply is 700 tons. The armament of the vessel consists of four 5.9 in. guns, 30 calibre in length; eight 4.1 in. quick-firing guns, 35 calibre in length; and six 1.9 in. rapid-firing guns of 40 calibre length. The ship has a further armament of five torpedo-launching tubes. Beside these, each cruiser carries on its deck a small torpedo boat, propelled by steam and provided with a torpedo tube. The conning tower on the hurricane deck is armored, and is provided with two powerful searchlights. The complement of each ship consists of 365 men.

In 1892 the third protected cruiser of the second class, the *Kaiserin Augusta*, was launched. This vessel is the largest of the cruisers of this class. Her displacement is 6,052 tons; length 387 feet, beam 51 feet, and draught 22.5 feet. The hull is constructed of steel, with double tiers of wood and a metallic lining. The armored deck consists of two sets of plates, the upper set being 2.8 in., and the lower one 0.7 in. in thickness. The armored deck is highly arched and slopes forward and aft from 7 to 3 feet below the water-line. A circuitous cofferdam, 8 feet in height and 3.2 feet in width, extends from stem to stern of the armored deck. The cells of the cofferdam are filled with strips of cork glued together, which, independently of the water-tight compartments, add greatly to the security of the ship in case of injury. The *Kaiserin Augusta* has triple-screw engines which give her a nominal 12,000 horse-power. With artificial draught under the boilers and an atmospheric pressure of 1.18 in. the three engines furnish 15,152 horse-power and 501 additional horse-power to the auxiliary engines, which give the ship a speed of from $21\frac{1}{2}$ to 22 knots. The boat can be easily manœuvred. At a speed of 18 knots it can be stopped inside of one and a-half minutes, making only 437 yards from the time the command to stop is given. The normal coal supply, which, however, can be augmented, is 860 tons. The armament of the ship consists of twelve 5.9 in. guns of 30 calibre length, with eight 3.5 in. quick-loading guns of 30 calibre length. From one broadside a mass of projectiles weighing 4,663 pounds can be delivered in the space of one minute. The steel shell of the 5.9 in. gun pierces steel plates of 11.9 in. thickness. All the guns are protected by armor shields. The boat has five torpedo-dischargers, one placed at the bow and the other four amidships, and carries, in addition, a torpedo boat 50 feet long, and two electric searchlights. The complement of the *Kaiserin Augusta* is 418 men.

The *Freya* has a displacement of 5,628 tons, a length of 344 feet, a width of 46 feet, and a draught of 20.5 feet. The armament consists of two 7.2 in. guns of 40 calibre length, eight 5.9 in. quick-loading guns, and a number of small rifled cannon. The engines are of 10,000 horse-power and give the vessel a speed of from 18 to 19 knots.

All cruisers provided with a protective deck and mounting main guns of a calibre less than 5.9 in. are classified as third-class protected cruisers. The seven third-class cruisers are the *Gefion* of 4,109 tons, the *Gazelle* of 2,645 tons, and the *Arcona* and *Alexandrine*, each of 2,373 tons. The *Olga*, *Marie*, and *Sophie*, each of 2,169 tons, are used for training-ships. The *Gefion* was launched in 1893 at the Schichau dock-yard of Dantsic. She is constructed of steel and has a displacement of 4,190 tons, a length of 344 feet, a beam of 41 feet, and a draught of 19 feet. The ship is strengthened below the water-line with double planks, and has a metallic bottom. On the water-line lies a splint deck from 1 in. to $1\frac{1}{2}$ in. thick, as protection against the shell-splinters. The engines are protected by a 3.9 in. armor-cap made of nickel-steel, which rests on a layer of 5.9 in. wooden planks. The ship has also a corkdam, a cofferdam, and bulkheads. The engines furnish 9,000 horse-power and a speed of $20\frac{1}{2}$ knots. The coal supply is 770 tons.

The armament is composed of ten 4.1 in. quick-loading guns of 35 calibre length; six 2 in. rapid-firing guns of 40 calibre length; eight machine guns; and one 2.3 in. boat-gun. The *Gefion* can fire at objects lying at an angle of 45 degrees to the course of the ship 7,040 pounds of steel in three minutes. On each side of the upper deck a torpedo tube is fixed on a pivot, discharging torpedoes of 17.7 in. diameter. The ship has two electric searchlights, of which one is placed at the foremast. The complement is 302 men.

The fourth-class protected cruisers are the *Seeadler*, *Condor*, *Cormoran*, and *Geier*, each of 1,640 tons; *Falke* and *Bussard*, each of 1,580 tons; *Schwalbe* and *Sperber*, each of 1,120 tons; and one cruiser of 2,600 tons in course of construction. These cruisers belong to the naval station on the Baltic Sea, and were equipped at Kiel. They are designed for service in foreign waters. Two are employed for service on the western coast and two on the eastern coast of Africa, while two find their field of activity in the waters of Eastern Asia, and three are designed for the protection of the German colonies and settlements in the South Sea. The oldest of these cruisers are the *Schwalbe* and the *Sperber*; each has twin-screw engines of 1,500 horse-power and a speed of 14 knots. The coal supply of 250 tons is sufficient for a run of 3,000 miles at a speed of 12 knots. The boats are armed with eight 4.1 in. guns, five 1.4 in. machine guns and a torpedo gun, firing amidships. An electric searchlight is stationed in front of the smoke-stack on the hurricane deck. The complement of the boats is 116 men each. The *Bussard* and the *Falke*, launched in 1890 and 1891 at Kiel, are larger than the previously mentioned vessels. Their displacement is 1,580 tons; they are 268 feet long, 32 feet wide, and draw 16 feet. No other navy can boast such model cruisers. The twin-screw engines furnish 2,800 horse-power and give a speed of 16 knots. The four cruisers of a later date are larger than the *Bussard*. They displace 1,640 tons, and are, in construction, armament, equipment, and complement, on a parity with the *Bussard*.

To the fifth type of war vessels, which are called gunboats, belong the *Habicht* of 848 tons, the *Wolf* of 498 tons, and the *Jaguar* and *Iltis*, each of 895 tons. The two gunboats of the *Albatross* class, namely, the *Albatross* and *Nautilus*, which were launched at Dantsic in 1871, have a displacement of 716 tons, a length of 167 feet, a beam of 26 feet, and a draught of 10 feet. The single-screw engine, of about 600 horse-power, gives a speed of 10 knots. Each boat has four 4.6 in. guns and a complement of 69 men. The boats are employed in the scientific-survey service off the German coast. Smaller boats than the two described were built for service at the mouths of rivers and in the narrow waters of eastern Asia. Of these the *Iltis*, which foundered in a typhoon, was launched in 1877, and the *Wolf* and *Hyäne* in 1878. The boats are constructed of iron, and are 138 feet long, 25 feet wide, and draw 9.8 feet. The single-screw engine, of 340 horse-power, gives a speed of 9 knots. The coal supply is 100 tons, sufficient for a run of 3,000 miles at a speed of 8 knots. The *Hyäne* is armed with two 5 in. guns, one 3 in. gun, and three revolving guns, and is employed in the coast-survey service. Each boat has a complement of 85 men. Larger and better armed is the *Habicht*. This boat is 174 feet in length, 30 feet in width, and of 11 feet draught. The single-screw engine, of 600 horse-power, gives a speed of 12 knots. The armament is composed of one 5.9 in. gun, four 4.9 in. guns, and five revolving guns. The crew consists of 179 men.

A most interesting type of warship is the sixth one, the despatch-boats. Of this type there are the *Kaiseradler* of 1,700 tons, the *Greif* of 2,000 tons, the *Blitz* and the *Pfeil*, each of 1,382 tons, the *Wacht* and the *Jagd*, each of 1,250 tons, the *Zieten* of 975 tons, the *Meteor* and the *Komet*, each of 946 tons, the *Hela* of 2,003 tons, and one other boat in course of construction.

The despatch-boats are the reconnoitring and reporting ships of the navy. They are like the cavalry of the land army, and are termed the "eyes" of the fighting navy. The despatch-boats not only sail in the van of the fleet, in order to espy and report the enemy's position, but they are likewise employed for the destruction of torpedo boats, for which reason they are also called torpedo-boat destroyers. In the capacity of outpost ships they, in connection with the cruisers, have to patrol great tracts at sea in order to prevent hostile ships from breaking through the skirmish lines. At the same time these boats have assigned them the duty of breaking through the enemy's outposts for the purpose of ascertaining the strength of the opposing fleet.

The side-wheel despatch-boat *Kaiseradler* was launched at Kiel in 1876, and served for awhile as the imperial yacht, under the name of *Hohenzollern*. The boat has a length of 268 feet, a width of 32 feet, and a draught of 13 feet. The engines, of 3,000 horse-power, give a speed of 16 knots. The armament consists only of two 3.4 in. guns and six revolving guns. The *Greif* has a length of 318 feet, with a beam of only 31 feet, being the sharpest keeled vessel of the German navy. The twin-screw engines, of 5,400 horse-power, give the boat a speed of over 20 knots. The armament comprises two 4.1 in. quick-loading guns 35 calibre long, ten 1.4 in. revolving guns, and several torpedo tubes; the vessel has an axe-shaped bow for ramming. It has a complement of 151 men. The *Blitz* and the *Pfeil* are built of steel, their length is 246 feet, their width 32 feet, and their draught 13 feet, with a speed of 16 knots. The armament consists of six 3.5 in. quick-firing guns 30 calibre long, one submerged torpedo tube placed near the bow, and two electric searchlights for detecting torpedoes. The complement is 134 men. The *Wacht* and the *Jagd* have each a displacement of 1,250 tons, a

length of 275 feet, a beam of 30 feet, and a draught of 13 feet. They are provided with a steel-armored deck of 0.9 in. thickness. The twin-screw engines, of 4,000 horse-power, give a speed of 20 knots. The armament comprises four 3.5 in. rapid-firing guns 30 calibre long and three torpedo tubes. The complement is 140 men.

The *Meteor* and the *Komet* are the smallest of the despatch-boats. The former was launched at Kiel in 1890, the latter at Stettin in 1892. Each ship has a displacement of 946 tons, a length of 262 feet, a beam of 30 feet, and a draught of about 12 feet. They are provided with a 0.9 in. steel deck, also with a corkdam and a cofferdam. The armament consists of four 3.5 in. rapid-firing guns and three torpedo tubes. They are also equipped with two electric searchlights. The twin-screw engines of the *Meteor* furnish 4,500 horse-power and give a speed of 21 knots, while the engines of the *Komet*, of 5,000 horse-power, afford a speed of 23 knots. Each vessel has a complement of 115 men. The most modern German despatch-boat, the *Hela*, which was launched at Bremen in 1895, has a length of 344 feet, a beam of 48 feet, and a draught of 15 feet. The boat is built of the finest steel and is provided with a strong armored deck, a corkdam, and a cofferdam. The engines, of 6,000 horse-power, afford a speed of 23 knots. The water-tight compartments are arranged similar to those of the modern battleships; forty-five independent engines, with eighty-five cylinders, are needed to operate the ship's machinery and other mechanical contrivances. The *Hela* carries four 3.5 in. rapid-firing guns 30 calibre long, six 1.9 in. quick-firing rifled guns 40 calibre long, and four torpedo tubes. The ship's complement is 168 men.

The seventh type of warships is represented by the training-ships. These include the *Mars* of 3,333 tons, the *Charlotte* of 3,222 tons, the *Stosch, Stein, Moltke, Gneisenau,* and *Blücher*, each of 2,169 tons, *Nixe* of 1,760 tons, *Carola* of 2,169 tons, *Rhein* and *Ulan*, each of 498 tons, *Grille* of 350 tons, *Hay* of 203 tons, and *Otter* of 129 tons.

As long as the gun represents the most formidable weapon of naval warfare, the training of efficient gunners will constitute the navy's principal duty in time of peace. For this purpose the artillery training-ship *Mars* is designed. The vessel, which was launched in 1879, has a displacement of 3,333 tons, a length of 262 feet, a beam of 48 feet, and a draught of 19 feet. The ship mounts about 30 guns of almost every calibre used in the navy, ranging from the 8 in. and 9 in. gun to the 1.4 in. rapid-firing rifled gun. The complement of 697 men consists mostly of recruits, who have to serve on the vessel for a period of from three to six months. Specially gifted seamen are here trained for the functions of chief gunners on board the war vessels. The ship-boys, likewise, after having served their time on board of training-ships, receive a course of instruction in gunnery. Young officers, who aspire to the position of battery commanders, also take part in the practice with the guns.

Aside from these functions, the *Mars* does duty in artillery and technical experiments, which are made with newly-invented projectiles, caissons, etc. The vessel is, for this reason, of much significance to the navy in general. For the training of the gunners, who have to become versed in the handling of the quick-loading guns, the old cruiser-frigate *Carola* is assigned, having the iron gunboat *Hay* attached as tender.

Since the year 1877, the old cruiser-frigate *Blücher* has been employed as the torpedo training-ship. On board of this vessel the different crews are drilled in the use of the torpedo weapon. The ship is supplied with from eight to ten torpedo tubes, which are fitted into the hull, both above and below the load water-line, amidships, and on the bow and afterdeck. Here the different torpedo crews are trained in the technical and hazardous handling of the torpedoes, after which training they are employed on board of the war ships. Those officers who perform the functions of torpedo officers on battleships and cruisers, receive the adequate instruction on board of this vessel. The *Blücher*, at the same time, is employed as an experimental ship by a board of torpedo experts. This board consists of a staff of naval officers, who test and approve all inventions made in the line of torpedo warfare. Attached to the *Blücher*, as tender, is the *Ulan*. This vessel has a displacement of 377 tons, a length of 72 feet, a width of 25 feet, a draught of 10 feet, and a speed of 12 knots. The *Ulan* does service in towing torpedo targets, long rafts with submarine nets attached as targets, which the torpedo has to traverse on its run.

To the technical training-ships belongs the small steamer *Rhein*, which practices the laying of submarine mines. The mines are laid in waters off the seacoast, and, until fired off, are dangerous to an approaching enemy, inasmuch as they are invisible, lying quietly moored. The *Rhein* has a displacement of 498 tons, a speed of 9 knots, and a complement of 80 men. The small gunboat *Otter*, of 120 tons, is employed as tender for the commission of naval tests. This commission is composed of a staff of officers and technical experts, whose duties are to oversee and vouch for the speed tests of all new ships of the navy. They take down notes of observation and give the necessary hints for improvements in the case of deficiencies. For the training of the *personnel* necessary to replenish the force of naval officers, the two old cruiser-frigates *Stosch* and *Stein* are employed. These ships receive the naval cadets for a course of one year's training in naval warfare, after the latter have passed their entrance examinations at the Naval Academy of Kiel. During the summer time the cadet training-ships take part in the naval manœuvres which take place in home waters, while during the winter

months the vessels cruise in the Mediterranean, in the West Indies, or in other parts of the Atlantic Ocean.

The ship-boy training-ships provide for the training of an efficient and ample body of noncommissioned officers. Of these ships the *Nixe*, which was launched at Dantsic in 1885, is the newest; she has a displacement of 1,760 tons, a length of 177 feet, a beam of 41 feet, and a draught of 17 feet. The vessel is constructed of iron, after the fashion of the old covered-corvettes, and specially fitted for sailing; they usually make 10 knots with a favorable wind. The vessel has also a small steam engine of 700 horse-power, which gives a speed of about 6 knots. The armament is composed of eight short 4.9 in. guns and six revolving guns. The crew consists of 384 men. Though obsolete in type of construction, the training-ships have been recently used for the settlement of complicated situations, their employment being a case of necessity till the German navy is sufficiently equipped with modern ships. Fresh in the memory of most readers — to cite an instance of many — is the German-Haytian incident of December 6th, 1897. This affair was ended by the Haytian government yielding to the menacing attitude of two German training-ships, the *Charlotte* and the *Stosch*, and accepting the German ultimatum with all its conditions.

The eighth type of war vessels, represented by the torpedo boats, is the most modern and the most interesting type of all. The boats are classified into pole-torpedo boats and fish-torpedo boats. The former were successfully employed as early as in the United States' Civil War. These boats were very small and were called "Davids." Attached on the bow was a pole thirty-five feet long, with the torpedo fastened to it, which exploded by striking against the hostile ship. Well known in the annals of naval warfare is the attack which was made by Lieutenant Cushing on the battleship *Albemarle*. The exploit took place on the Roanoke River on the night of the twenty-sixth and twenty-seventh of October, 1864. By the explosion of a torpedo the *Albemarle* had an enormous hole made in her below the water-line and sank in a few minutes, while the torpedo boat also foundered in the upheaval of water caused by the explosion. During the Franco-German war the German navy had a great number of pole-torpedo boats, which had a speed of eight knots, but were not used for any operations against the enemy. The first torpedo boats fit for service were built in England. In Germany, the Schichau dock-yard of Elbing took the lead in torpedo boat construction. The superiority of the Schichau torpedo boats led to the introduction of their model into the English navy. The German torpedo boats are usually 100 feet long and 10 feet wide; with a draught of about seven feet and a construction of steel, they combine the greatest strength with the greatest lightness. The boats show little elevation above the water and their decks are completely covered. The latter, which is elliptical on the aft, while the forward part extending from the stem to the conning tower is a so-called whaleback, secures the boat more or less against shot and shell and against drenching by sea-water. On both sides of the stem the launching tubes project. The compartment lying directly below is used for the storing of the torpedo, the ammunition, and the apparatus for the launching of the projectile, which is effected by means of an air-pump. Adjoining this compartment are the quarters, which will accommodate twelve of the crew. The tower which stands above this compartment contains the steering gear, by which the boat is directed in its course. The roof of the tower carries a Hotchkiss revolving gun; separated by a water-tight bulkhead, the boiler-room follows next. Here, for inducing ventilation in bad weather, an engine is placed, which affords a pressure of two atmospheres. Separated by another bulkhead comes the engine-room. Near the hatchway leading down to this room stands the aft tower, which carries a 1.9 in. quick-loading gun. The room situate at the stern serves for the storage of provisions and other ship's material. The coal bunkers are placed on both sides of the boiler-room and afford, when filled, some protection to the boilers. On the afterdeck, back of the aft tower, a swivel torpedo gun is placed, which can fire toward both sides. Most torpedo boats are equipped with dynamos for electric lighting and searchlights, also with the Kaselonsky signal apparatus. The complement of a boat of about 90 tons displacement consists of 1 officer as commander, 1 machinist, 2 boatswain mates, 3 machinist mates, 4 sailors, and 4 stokers. In some respects the torpedo boats represent the cavalry in naval warfare. In connection with the despatch-boats they are engaged in the reconnoitring service. One of their greatest merits lies in the circumstance that a torpedo boat crew of 15 men can hold in suspense night and day the complement of a battleship consisting of 600 men. For an attack on a war ship from four to six boats are united, forming a torpedo-boat division, under the lead of a so-called torpedo-division boat. The weapon, which has effected a real revolution in the naval affairs of all nations, is called the Whitehead torpedo. The original inventor of this weapon is the Austrian naval officer Lupis.

The Whitehead torpedo consists of a cigar-shaped envelope of phosphor bronze from twelve to twenty-five feet long. Its motive power is compressed air; it is propelled by two two-bladed screws revolving in opposite directions about the same axis, and is maintained at a constant depth by horizontal rudders and on a straight course by vertical fans at an angle determined by experiments. In this respect the torpedo resembles a submarine vessel. The torpedo contains several compartments for its propelling, directing, and exploding mechanism. The forward compartment contains the ex-

ploding cartridge, which consists of a series of disks of wet gun cotton, perforated in their centres to receive the priming tube of dry gun cotton. The second compartment contains the immersion regulators which so control the horizontal rudders as to carry the torpedo down to a given depth and keep it there during its journey.

This chamber contains also a hydrostatic balance, a pendulum connected with the horizontal rudders, and a combination of springs, which, in connection with the pressure of the water on the hydrostatic piston, are to counterbalance each other, while the swinging of the vertical pendulum causes the rudder to be turned upward or downward until the torpedo comes back to an even keel.

Behind this chamber is the reservoir for compressed air and in the rear of that a three-cylinder brotherhood engine which this force sets in motion. Behind the machinery compartment comes the buoyancy chamber, the purpose of which is to bring the torpedo to the surface or to sink it. Then comes a compartment containing the bevel gear which causes the propellers to revolve in opposite directions, and finally the rudder supports and the rudders. The torpedo is started simply by placing it in a tube and lowering it till it is completely submerged. By a lever attached to the tube a valve is opened which allows the condensed air to enter from the reservoir into the engines, thus starting the torpedo on its journey. This form of launching is only practiced in torpedo batteries for coast-defence. On board of warships and torpedo boats, tubes are provided from which the torpedo is discharged either by condensed air or by a small charge of powder. The tubes are either submerged and built into the hull, in which case aim has to be taken by steering the ship, or they are placed above the water-line, adjusted for aiming in every direction. As a protection against this treacherous projectile, the battleships are provided with torpedo nets. As the explosion of a torpedo works destruction only when close to the ship, nets, consisting of steel rings, are fastened to the points of a number of spars 30 feet long, which stand off from the hull in a horizontal position and are suspended vertically in the water when the ship lies alongside. As the torpedo adheres to the nets without doing any harm, the torpedo boats are equipped with special explosives for the destruction of the nets. An adversary of a more dangerous character to the torpedo boats is to be found in the rapid-firing guns, and especially in the torpedo-boat destroyers. These boats are very fast and are called, in the German navy, torpedo-division boats, or sea-going torpedo boats. There are eleven of these boats in readiness, numbered D 1 to D 11. The boats, which were launched at the Schichau dock-yard during the period from 1887 to 1896, have a displacement of from 300 to 380 tons, a length of from 166 to 213 feet, a beam of 22 feet, and a draught of 6.7 feet. The twin-screw engines, of from 2,000 to

4,000 horse-power, give a speed of from 21 to 26 knots. The armament consists of from four to six 1.9 in. rapid-firing guns and of from three to four tubes, which are placed amidships on the upper deck of the modern and very fast boats.

The division boats have in front of their smokestack a large superstructure which carries the hurricane deck, a room provided with charts, and several other compartments, also an electric searchlight for use at night. The complement consists of about 40 men.

Of late the torpedo boats have been employed for highly interesting experiments with the captive balloon, which are commended by the prominent naval author, Willy Stöwer, in a treatise on the captive balloon in the service of the navy.

"An important feat of reconnoitring at sea could be seen at the lower end of the bay of Kiel, in the Baltic Sea. The detachment of balloon troops, stationed at Berlin, had to undergo a drill with a dragon-balloon of a new construction. Very interesting at these exercises, which lasted two weeks, was the employment of the balloon on board of torpedo boats. The construction of the new model is peculiar, differing from all those formerly in use. The balloon consists of two parts, namely, the main balloon, which is oblong in form and rounded at both ends, and of a smaller balloon, which is attached to the lower rear end of the larger one, and adheres to the latter like a pad. The smaller balloon serves somewhat as a helm to the main balloon, which, thus held in an oblique position, is prevented from swinging, and is steered in a straight course, even toward the wind. The gondola, which is independent of the guy-rope, affords a splendid point of perspective observation, securing great steadiness and accuracy. In order to transport the balloon from one locality to another, without lowering it and interrupting observation, torpedo boats were used, which are specially adapted for this purpose on account of their enormous speed. Even on water, experiments were made to move the windlass which operates the guy-rope of the balloon from one torpedo boat to another lying near its bow. The balloon with the windlass was likewise conveyed on shore from the boat in a short time. Both experiments were reported as highly succesful.

"In order to contrast the range of sight to be gained on the gondola with that afforded by the lighthouse tower, the balloon arose in the neighborhood of Bülk. There, at the northern end of the bay of Kiel, a light-house tower, ninety-six feet high, was erected. The range of sight gained on top of this tower covered a range of only fifteen sea-miles. The occupants of the gondola, however, were enabled, by the aid of good telescopes, to overlook the entire Danish waters. They could see beyond Copenhagen, on the east beyond the island of Rügen, and on the west over the German Ocean, lying west of Holstein. The warships moored in the waters of the Great Belt were readily recognized according to their types. Officers of the army and navy were practiced in observing and distinguishing the ships and their positions at sea from the balloon. To the navy the widening of the scope of sight is of great significance, as a due recognizance of the enemy is exceedingly valuable in warfare."

The ninth type of German war vessels is composed of ships for special use. These are the imperial yacht *Hohenzollern*, of 4,187 tons; the battleships *Kronprinz*, of 5,568 tons, and *Friedrich Karl*, of 6,007 tons; the armored vessel *Arminius*, of 1583 tons; and the corvette *Luise*, of 1,710 tons, which are used as harbor ships. The *Möve* of 848 tons, and *Albatross* and *Nautilus*, each of 716 tons, are employed in scientific survey work; the *Pelikan* of 2,360 tons and the *Eider* of 402 tons are transport-steamers.

His Majesty's yacht, *Hohenzollern*, is a masterpiece of German shipbuilding. The ship, which was launched at Stettin on June 27th, 1892, has a displacement of 4,187 tons, a length of 380 feet, a beam of 45 feet, and a draught of 18 feet. The twin-screw engines, of 9,000 horse-power, give the ship a speed of about 22 knots. The rigging shows three masts, each made of one piece of timber, the forward one of which carries a signal-yard. The flag-poles are mounted with tops displaying the emblem of the imperial crown. The armament consists of three 4.1 in. quick-loading guns 35 calibre long in time of war, and of eight 1.9 in. quick-firing guns in time of peace. All the guns, which are placed on the upper deck, are provided with shields for protection. A double bottom, holding many water-tight compartments and bulkheads, secures the ship in case of injury to the outer skin. The equipment of the interior ship is commodious and tasteful. For the imperial family a number of apartments is assigned, which all open out into the largest room, "the Blue Salon." A large dining room is located on the upper deck. On top of this is the highest deck, the so-called promenade deck, the after part of which is used as a smoking cabin. The complement of the ship is 307 men.

The two oldest armored vessels of the German navy, the *Arminius* and the *Prinz Albert*, were monitors. The former was launched at the Samuda dock-yard of London in 1864. It was of a low build and had a displacement of 1,583 tons, a length of 196 feet, a beam of 38 feet, and a draught of 12 feet. The entire hull was protected above the water-line by 4.7 in. iron plates and by 9.4 in. tiers of teak-wood. The two revolving towers have an armor of 4.7 in. thickness. In each tower are placed two guns of 8.3 in. calibre. The spur is short and nearly round. Later on the ship was equipped with revolving guns and torpedo tubes. The engine, of 1,200 horse-power, gives a speed of 10.5 knots. In 1892, the ship was struck from the list of warships, and is now employed as an ice-breaker for harbor use. The *Prinz Albert* was likewise ordered out of commission. The armored frigates *Friedrich Karl* and the *Kronprinz* were the first battleships of the North-German navy. Both were launched in 1867. The beautiful frigate, *Friedrich Karl*, which has a displacement of 6,007 tons, a length of 282 feet, a beam of 48 feet, and a draught of 23 feet, was launched at the dock-yard of La Seyne, near Toulon. The frigate *Kronprinz*, of 5,568 tons displacement, a length of 285 feet, a beam of 48 feet, a draught of 23 feet, and a speed of 13 knots, was launched at the Samuda dock-yard of London. Both ships carried an armored battery of 4.5 in. thick iron, and a circuitous armor-belt of 5 in. thickness. These boats did efficient service in the cause of the Fatherland, as was mentioned in the historical sketch of the navy. At present, the boats, in the capacity of harbor-ships, have a quiet and contemplative existence, and are employed for different purposes. The *Friedrich Karl* serves as a torpedo training-ship. The former corvette *Luise*, now used as harbor-ship, was launched in 1872. The ship, whose displacement is 1,719 tons, is 203 feet long, 35 feet wide, and draws 16 feet. The armament consists of six short 5.9 in. guns, two 4.7 in. guns, and four revolving guns. The crew numbered 238 men.

The *Möve*, *Nautilus*, and *Albatross* are used for the scientific survey of the coast. The *Möve* is employed in Australia, while the latter two are stationed for a like purpose in the Baltic Sea and in the German Ocean. The survey of the coast of the German Ocean, especially, has to be performed repeatedly, as the depth of the navigable water is subject to constant changes, caused by storms, undercurrents, and drifting ice.

Worthy to be mentioned under the class of ships for special service is the transport-steamer *Pelikan*. This ship, which was launched at Wilhelmshaven in 1891, has a displacement of 2,360 tons, a length of 259 feet, a beam of 38 feet, and a draught of 16 feet. The single-screw engine, of 3,000 horse-power, gives a speed of 16 knots. The armament, which is placed on the upper deck, consists of four 3.5 in. guns 39 calibre long, and four machine guns. The crew numbers 183 men.

Other dock and harbor vessels are the pumping steamers. These are employed in time of war for giving assistance to those vessels which spring large leaks when injured by the ram, shell, torpedo, or by the explosion of a submarine mine. The two pumping steamers, *Kraft* and *Norder*, have a displacement of 800 tons each. The engines, of 1,200 horse-power, can be used for extinguishing fires and for tug purposes. Steam tugs are used in time of peace and of war, for the moving and wheeling of disabled ships which cannot be individually manœuvred. The tugs employed at the three imperial dock-yards are the *Aeolus*, of 50 horse-power; the *Boreas*, of 380 tons and 900 horse-power; the *Notus*, of 600 horse-power; the *Zephir*, of 250 horse-power; the *Friedrichsort*, of 67 tons and 75 horse-power; the *Swine*, of 50 horse-power; the *Rival*, of 190 tons and 290 horse-power; and the *Motlar*, of 130 tons and 320 horse-power. The two boats, *Caurus* and *Jade*, are used for the transport of drinking water. In the pilot-service and in that of the transport of casks, the pilot-steamer *Wilhelmshaven*, the

pilot-schooner *Wangeroog*, and the cask-layer *Heppens*, are employed, while the *Schilling* and *Usedom* do miscellaneous service. There are also signal ships stationed for the purpose of showing the course of navigable water at the mouth of the river Jahde in the sound of Minsen, on the Genius banks in the river Jahde, and on the Adler grounds in the Baltic Sea.

The three sailing yachts, *Lust*, *Liebe*, and *Wille*, serve for the practice of the sailing sport, that is, for reviving the old seafaring spirit, and thus aid in promoting maritime efficiency. The yachts are from 47 to 52 feet long, and are used for drilling and racing by the officers of the harbors during the summer months.

As modern naval warfare demands many cruisers, all large navies endeavor in case of war to increase their number by enlisting the fast steamers of the commercial fleet, which are equipped accordingly, and are called auxiliary cruisers. These boats form the tenth type of war ships.

In the German navy four fast steamers of the Hamburg mail-boat line are selected for this duty in case of emergency. The ships are the *Fürst Bismarck*, of 8,874 tons and a speed of 20½ knots; the *Palatia* and *Patria*, each of 7,118 tons and a speed of 20 knots; and the *Augusta Viktoria*, of 7,671 tons and a speed of 19½ knots. The six fast boats of the North-German Lloyd chosen as auxiliary cruisers will, in all probability, be the *Lahn*, of 5,351 tons and a speed of 19½ knots; the *Saale*, of 5,267 tons and a speed of 17½ knots; the *Trave*, of 5,262 tons and a speed of 17½ knots; the *Aller*, of 5,217 tons and a speed of 17½ knots; the *Ems*, of 4,612 tons and a speed of 17½ knots; and the *Werra*, of 4,900 tons and a speed of 17½ knots. These ships, in case of war, would be equipped with a great number of quick-loading guns and machine-guns in order to fit them for active war service. As these fast-sailing steamers, however, lack any kind of armor protection or water-tight compartments or bulkheads, they are more suited for use as outpost ships on the skirmish line, or for the capturing of trading vessels. Their employment as war ships is entirely out of the question.

The German navy, as described in the preceding chapters, does not appear insignificant by any means. It does not suffice, however, for the task alloted, namely, the defence of the German coast and its harbors, or for the protection of imperial subjects and their interests in foreign countries. The annual expenditure on behalf of the navy, amounts to 82,000,000 marks, while the total value of the foreign commerce, and the ships engaged in the latter, represents a sum of 4,600,000,000 marks. The foregoing statement ought to show clearly that the increase of expenditure recently granted by the Imperial Diet does not stand in any proportion to the value of the ships and lives to be protected. According to a law passed by the Imperial Diet on March 28th, 1898, the strength of the German navy — torpedo boats, training-ships, ships for special

H. M. Second-Class Protected Cruisers "Princess Wilhelm" and "Irene" at Dover.

use, and gunboats excluded — is to be raised to 17 ships of the line, ready for immediate service; 8 coast-defence battleships; 9 large cruisers; 26 small cruisers; all to be put in commission at once. To the naval reserves are to be added 2 ships of the line, 3 large cruisers, and 2 small cruisers. Subtracted from this number are 12 ships of the line, 8 coast-defence battleships, 10 large cruisers, and 23 small cruisers, which are already in commission or in course of construction. The real increase amounts to 7 ships of the line, 2 large cruisers, and 5 small cruisers. The first-, second-, and third-class battleships are rated as ships of the line; the fourth-class battleships are designated as coast-defence battleships; the armored cruisers, and first- and second-class protected cruisers are called large cruisers; while all the third- and fourth-class protected cruisers and the despatch-boats are classed as small cruisers. In five years, that is in the year 1904, the navy will be raised to the above strength. The force of the navy's *personnel* is likewise to be raised to 1,598 officers and 25,039 men, the marine infantry and marine artillery excluded.

These important increases of the German navy are necessary in order to provide proper protection to the German commercial interests abroad, and to secure to the German Empire an adequate position amongst seafaring nations. The foresight which the government displays in the development of Germany's power at sea, the love and zeal manifested by those serving in the navy, the general interest which is shown by the public at large in the welfare and growth of all German enterprises abroad, are augurs of an enhanced efficiency of the German navy. Its duty is to hold aloft and protect the German flag abroad, and, allied with the army, to defend German coasts and her foreign possessions when they are endangered. Its powerful position on land and sea, commanding universal respect, is in itself a protection of Germany against any attack or encroachment. In case of war, however, the German navy will undoubtedly endeavor to win an honorable place alongside the army in the annals of the heroic deeds achieved by the German nation.*

* The statistics, which this part of the book, " Germany's Navy," contain, are mostly taken from the work, " Germany's Sea-Power," by Wislicenus.

CLASSIFICATION OF THE NAVY

Commander-in-Chief, His Majesty, the Emperor and King, William II.

NAVAL CABINET AT BERLIN

IMPERIAL NAVAL ADMINISTRATION, BERLIN

1. Central department.
2. General marine department: *a*, military section; *b*, section pertaining to pensions and legal affairs; *c*, section treating on the affairs of the government of Kiau-Chou.
3. Technical department, consisting of the former marine department and the bureau of construction.
4. Department of Administration proper.
5. Bureau of Ordnance.
6. Bureau treating on the *personnel* of the navy.
7. Nautical department.
8. Medical department.
9. Justiciary department.
10. Intelligence bureau.

General naval inspection department, Berlin. Staff of the admiralty, transacting the business of the admiralty and treating on naval and political matters.

Command of the Baltic naval station, Kiel: 1st division of marine artillery, Friedrichsort; 1st torpedo division, Kiel; 1st battalion of marines, Kiel. 1st naval inspection, Kiel: 1st seamen division (1st and 2nd detachments), Kiel; 1st dock-yard division, Kiel.

Command of the North Sea naval station, Wilhelmshaven: 2nd, 3rd, and 4th divisions of marine artillery, Wilhelmshaven, Lehe, and Geestemünde; 2nd torpedo division, Wilhelmshaven. 2nd naval inspection, Wilhelmshaven: 2nd seamen division, Wilhelmshaven; 2nd dock-yard division, Wilhelmshaven.

Bureau of inspection of the torpedo service, Kiel, including the command of the department for torpedo tests at Kiel and the torpedo laboratory at Friedrichsort.

Bureau of inspection of the marine infantry, Kiel: 1st battalion of marines at Kiel, 2nd battalion at Wilhelmshaven.

Bureau of inspection of the marine artillery, Wilhelmshaven, including the naval-telegraph school at Lehe and the commission of naval tests at Kiel.

Department of the marine depot inspection, Wilhelmshaven, including four ordnance and mine depots at Friedrichsort, Wilhelmshaven, Geestemünde, and Cuxhaven.

Inspection department of the navy's educational institutes, Kiel: Naval academy, Kiel; naval school, Kiel; school for deck officers, Kiel; ship-boy division, Friedrichsort; government of Kiau-Chou; 2nd battalion of marines at Tsintau.

Inspectorates of the German littoral: 1st, East- and West-Prussia, Neufahrwasser; 2nd, Pomerania and Mecklenburg, Stettin; 3rd, Lübeck and eastern coast of Schleswig-Holstein, Kiel; 4th, western coast of Schleswig-Holstein, Husum; 5th, the district of the Elbe and Weser, Bremerhaven; 6th, Jahde, the East-Frisian coast and Heligoland, Wilhelmshaven.

Technical institutes: The navy-yards of Kiel, Wilhelmshaven, and Dantzic; commission for ship tests, Kiel; naval observatory, Hamburg.

Bureaus intrusted with the clothing of the navy, Kiel and Wilhelmshaven.

WAR SHIPS AND WAR VESSELS

FIRST TYPE — BATTLESHIPS

First-class sea-going battleships: *Kaiser Friedrich III.*, '96, *Kaiser Wilhelm II.*, '98, each of 11,081 t., 13,000 h.p., 655 men; *Kaiser Wilhelm der Grosse*, '99, of 12,000 t. (in course of construction); *Kurfürst Friedrich Wilhelm*, '91, *Brandenburg*, '91, *Weissenburg*, '91, *Wörth*, '92, each of 10,033 t., 9,000 h.p., 556 men.

Second-class sea-going battleships: *König Wilhelm*, '68, of 9,757 t., 8,000 h.p., 732 men; *Kaiser*, '74, *Deutschland*, '74, each of 7,676 t., 8,000 h.p., 644 men.

Third-class sea-going battleships: *Preussen*, '73, *Friedrich der Grosse*, '74, each of 6,770 t., 5,400 h.p., 544 men; *Sachsen*, '77, *Württemberg*, '78, each of 7,400 t., 5,600 h.p., 389 men; *Bayern*, '78, of 7,400 t., 6,000 h.p., 389 men; *Baden*, '80, of 7,400 t., 6,000 h.p., 389 men; *Oldenburg*, '84, of 5,200 t., 3,900 h.p., 389 men.

Fourth-class battleships: *Siegfried*, '89, of 3,495 t., 4,800 h.p., 271 men; *Beowulf*, '90, *Frithjof*, '91, *Hildebrand*, '92, *Heimdall*, '92, *Hagen*, '93, *Odin*, '94, each of 3,495 t., 4,800 h.p., 276 men; *Aegir*, '95, of 3,530 t., 4,800 h.p., 276 men.

SECOND TYPE — ARMORED GUNBOATS

Wespe, '76, *Viper*, '76, *Biene*, '76, *Mücke*, '77, *Skorpion*, '77, *Basilisk*, '78, *Camäleon*, '78, *Krokodil*, '79, *Salamander*, '80, *Natter*, '80, *Hummel*, '81, each of 1,109 t., 700 h.p., 88 men; *Brummer*, '83, and *Bremse*, '84, each of 866 t., 1,500 h.p., 78 men.

THIRD TYPE — ARMORED CRUISERS

Fürst Bismarck, '98, of 10,650 t., 13,500 h.p., 565 men.

FOURTH TYPE — PROTECTED CRUISERS

First-class protected cruisers: None.

Second-class protected cruisers: *Kaiserin Augusta*, '92, of 6,052 t., 12,000 h.p., 418 men; *Irene*, '88, of 4,400 t., 8,000 h.p., 365 men; *Princess Wilhelm*, '87, of 4,400 t., 8,000 h.p., 365 men; *Freya*, '98, *Hertha*, '98, each of 5,628 t., 10,000 h.p., 439 men; *Viktoria Luise*, *Hansa*, *Vineta*, and two more, of 5,628 t., 10,000 h.p., 439 men (in course of construction).

Third-class protected cruisers: *Gefion*, '93, of 4,109 t., 9,000 h.p., 302 men; *Arcona*, '85, *Alexandrine*, '85, each of 2,373 t., 2,400 h.p., 269 men; *Gazelle*, of 2,645 t., 6,000 h.p.; *Olga*, '80, *Marie*, '81, *Sophie*, '82, each of 2,169 t., 2,100 h.p., 269 men.

Fourth-class protected cruisers: *Seeadler* '92, *Condor*, '92, *Cormoran*, '92, *Geier*, '94, each of 1,640 t., 2,800 h.p., 269 men; *Schwalbe*, '87, *Sperber*, '89, each of 1,120 t., 1,500 h.p., 116 men; *Bussard*, '90, *Falke*, '91, each of 1,580 t., 2,800 h.p., 160 men; and one boat in course of construction.

FIFTH TYPE — GUNBOATS

Iltis, of 895 t., 1,300 h.p., 130 men; *Habicht*, '79, of 848 t., 600 h.p., 129 men; *Jaguar*, of 895 t., 4,300 h.p.; and *Wolf*, '78, of 489 t., 340 h.p., 85 men.

SIXTH TYPE — DESPATCH-BOATS

Kaiseradler, '76, of 1,700 t., 3,000 h.p., 150 men; *Greif*, '86, of 2,000 t., 5,400 h.p., 155 men; *Blitz*, '82, *Pfeil*, '82, each of 1,382 t., 2,700 h.p., 134 men; *Wacht*, '88, *Jagd*, '88, each of 1,250 t., 4,000 h.p., 140 men; *Zieten*, '76, of 975 t., 2,350 h.p., 115 men; *Meteor*, '90, of 946 t., 4,500 h.p., 115 men; *Komet*, '92, of 946 t., 5,000 h.p., 115 men; *Hela*, '93, 2,003 t., 6,000 h.p., 168 men; and one boat in course of construction.

SEVENTH TYPE — TRAINING SHIPS

Mars, '79, 3,333 t., 2,000 h.p., 697 men; *Charlotte*,

'85, 3,222 t., 3,000 h.p., 455 men; *Stosch*, '77, *Stein*, '79, each of 2,856 t., 2,500 h.p., 446 men; *Moltke*, '77, *Gneisenau*, '77, each of 2,856 t., 2,000 h.p., 461 men; *Blücher*, of 2,856 t., 2,500 h.p., 460 men; *Nixe*, '85, 1,760 t., 700 h.p., 384 men; *Carola*, '80, of 2,169 t., 2,100 h.p., 269 men; *Rhein*, '67, of 498 t., 200 h.p., 80 men; *Ulan*, '76, 377 t., 800 h.p., 41 men; *Grille*, '57, of 350 t., 700 h.p., 74 men; *Hay*, '81, of 203 t., 160 h.p., 40 men; *Otter*, '77, 129 t., 140 h.p., 43 men.

EIGHTH TYPE — TORPEDO BOATS

Eleven torpedo-boat destroyers or torpedo-division boats, '87–'95, of 300–380 t., 2,000–4,000 h.p., 15–40 men.

First class: 46 torpedo boats, '90–'98, of 110–150 t., 1,500–2,500 h.p., 15–20 men.

Second class: 74 torpedo boats, '82–'90, of 50–100 t., 500–1,000 h.p., about 15 men.

NINTH TYPE — SHIPS FOR SPECIAL USE

Hohenzollern, '92, of 4,178 t., 9,000 h.p., 307 men; *Arminius*, '64, of 1,583 t., 1,200 h.p., 130 men; *Kronprinz*, '67, of 5,568 t., 4,800 h.p., 540 men; *Friedrich Karl*, '67, of 6,007 t., 3,500 h.p., 540 men; *Luise*, '72, of 1,719 t., 2,100 h.p., 238 men; *Möve*, '79, of 848 t., 600 h.p., 132 men; *Albatross*, '71, of 716 t., 600 h.p., 99 men; *Nautilus*, '71, of 716 t., 600 h.p., 99 men; *Pelikan*, '91, of 2,360 t., 3,000 h.p., 183 men; *Kraft* and *Norder*, of 800 t., 1,200 h.p.; *Aeolus*, of 50 h.p.; *Boreas*, of 380 t., 900 h.p.; *Notus*, of 600 h.p.; *Zephyr*, of 250 h.p.; *Friedrichsort*, of 67 t., 75 h.p.; *Swine*, of 50 h.p.; *Rival*, of 190 t., 250 h.p.; *Motlar*, of 130 t., 320 h.p.

TENTH TYPE — AUXILIARY CRUISERS

Fast steamers of the Hamburg mail-boat line: *Fürst Bismarck*, 8,874 t., 20½ knots; *Palatia*, 7,118 t., 20 knots; *Patria*, 7,187 t., 20 knots; and *Augusta Viktoria*, 7,671 t., 19½ knots.

Fast steamers of the North-German Lloyd: *Lahn*, 5,351 t., 19½ knots; *Saale*, 5,267 t., 17½ knots; *Trave*, 5,262 t., 17½ knots; *Aller*, 5,217 t., 17½ knots; *Ems*, 4,912 t., 17½ knots; *Werra*, 4,900 t., 17½ knots.